IMAGES
of America

AROUND BILTMORE VILLAGE

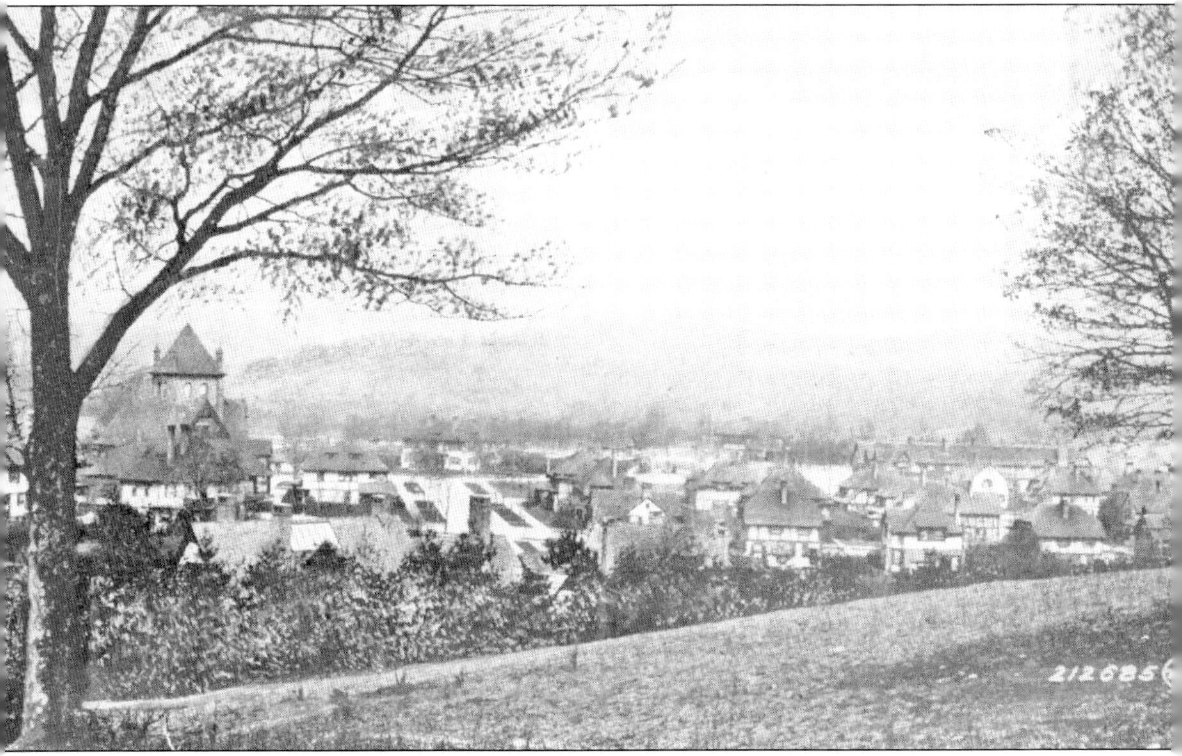

Bird's-Eye View of Biltmore, North Carolina. This postcard of Biltmore Village, appearing peaceful and civilized, illustrates the masterful layout by landscape architect Frederick Law Olmsted, enhanced by the distinctive designs of architects Richard Morris Hunt and Richard Sharp Smith. George Vanderbilt first called his estate Bilton Forest and the village Bilton, but the postal service did not approve it because of the similarity to Bolton and Boilston, North Carolina. (Hal Branch.)

On the Cover: Before the Wedding, April 1924. In the days before the wedding of Cornelia Stuyvesant Vanderbilt to the Honorable John Francis Amherst Cecil, Biltmore Village bustled with activity as family members, friends, and guests from around the world arrived. Guests stayed at the Grove Park and Kenilworth Inns, Biltmore Forest Country Club, and at Biltmore House. In this photograph, Edith Vanderbilt, front left, and Cornelia, back left, are enjoying the company of unidentified guests near the Biltmore-Oteen Bank on Lodge Street as preparations are being made for the much-anticipated event. (Biltmore Estate archives.)

IMAGES
of America

AROUND BILTMORE VILLAGE

Bill Alexander

ARCADIA
PUBLISHING

ISBN 978-0-7385-6853-9

Published by Arcadia Publishing
Charleston, South Carolina

Printed in the United States of America

Library of Congress Catalog Card Number: 2008935095

For all general information contact Arcadia Publishing at:
Telephone 843-853-2070
Fax 843-853-0044
E-mail sales@arcadiapublishing.com
For customer service and orders:
Toll-Free 1-888-313-2665

Visit us on the Internet at www.arcadiapublishing.com

*To Mary Hyde and all the volunteers
of the Biltmore Village Historic Museum,
whose enthusiasm and passion to discover and record the rich history of
Biltmore Village and their tireless efforts to develop a museum
to commemorate, preserve, and share its heritage
has been an inspiration to all.*

Contents

Acknowledgments		6
Introduction		7
1.	Before Biltmore	9
2.	A Millionaire's Village	27
3.	Work, Play, Worship	49
4.	Where Life Is Worthwhile	71
5.	The Changing Face of Biltmore	89
6.	Biltmore Forest	113

ACKNOWLEDGMENTS

When I took on this project, I realized very quickly how dependent I would be on so many people in so many places. To all who helped in any way, big or small, even if it was just a word of encouragement, I sincerely thank you. With the fear of omitting someone, I offer my heartfelt appreciation and thanks to the following individuals (presented in no particular order) for allowing use of photographs and for sharing other memorabilia, information, or stories: Hal Branch, my friend and high school classmate; John S. (Jack) Stevens, a friend and great local historian; my niece Trinity Briggs; Tommy and Catherine Arakas; Dave and Eleanor Stephens Johnson; Richard (Dick) Gray; Mitch Leonard; Bill Rusher, Sue Ovel, and April Sprinkle (Davene Boynton Rusher's family albums); and Susan J. Blake (Estate of Agnes [Bell] Barber Blake).

I want to personally thank the following individuals and institutions for their assistance and permission to use archival images and written material: Zoe Rhine and Betsy Murray, North Carolina Collection, Pack Memorial Public Library; Helen Weikle and Sally Klipp, Special Collections, D. H. Ramsey Library, University of North Carolina at Asheville; Alix Reiskind, visual resources librarian, Frances Loeb Library, Harvard Graduate School of Design; Michele Clark, Frederick Law Olmsted National Historic Site; Allison Dennis, Town of Biltmore Forest; and Mary Hyde, Biltmore Village Historic Museum.

I owe a debt of gratitude to my fellow associates and colleagues in Biltmore Estate's Museum Services Department, without whom I could not have completed this book. It has made my project easier just knowing I have the support and technical assistance of such a great group of people. My special thanks go to Trina Apple for assistance with scanning and organizing images early in the project; Marjorie Roof for her many hours of scanning and organizing images; Jill Hawkins for her many hours of scanning, assisting with research, fact checking, and moral support; Leslie Klingner and Lori Garst for tracking down pieces of information or images and checking facts as needed; and Ellen Rickman and Darren Poupore for their support.

Last but not least, I want to thank my wife, Jackie, for her extraordinary patience and understanding, and for giving me time and space at home to get this project done. She is happy to have our dining room table back for the use it was intended. I want to thank my publisher, Maggie Bullwinkel, at Arcadia Publishing, who has gently prodded but graciously waited for my completed draft.

Except where otherwise noted, the images used in this book are from the Biltmore Estate archives.

INTRODUCTION

Around Biltmore Village offers a glimpse into the early history of a place that has attracted both year-round residents and seasonal visitors for generations. The crossroads settlement of Best or Asheville Junction, which boasted the area's first railroad station, was largely purchased by George W. Vanderbilt in the late 19th century and was transformed into an idyllic village that served not only to provide a fitting entrance to his Biltmore Estate, but also to function as an independent and self-sustaining community. From its beginning, Biltmore Village was written about and described in newspapers and magazines as a "model village" and as "A Millionaire's Village: An Ideal Village in the Hills of North Carolina, Designed as a Whole and Built to Order." Whatever epithet was used to describe it, Biltmore Village was and is a uniquely designed place—unique because it was originally built and owned by a single individual, but also because it was designed and built as one of the earliest examples of a planned mixed-use community where people would live and work and have all the necessary amenities, including stores, post office, school, and church, close at hand. Renowned landscape architect and park maker Frederick Law Olmsted and École des Beaux-Arts–trained architect Richard Morris Hunt, both near the end of their careers, worked with Vanderbilt to develop a vision and detailed layout for the village in conjunction with their masterful designs of Biltmore Estate's buildings and grounds. While the village would serve some of Biltmore Estate's needs and that of its employees, it was never intended to be a worker's village, as is sometimes erroneously thought. Olmsted meshed his own ideas with those of Vanderbilt that resulted in three basic goals for the village: to provide easy access to the estate from the train station through an aesthetically pleasing entrance; to create a source of income through rentals of residences and businesses; and to develop a framework for establishing and carrying out philanthropic programs in the community.

Even though it is generally thought that the plan for Biltmore Village was the collaborative efforts of Hunt and Olmsted, existing drawings and documents specifying the layout of the streets and tree plantings, arrangements of the business and social centers, residential areas, and alignment with the estate entrance and public thoroughfares were clearly executed by Olmsted. The extent of Hunt's overall involvement in the planning of Biltmore Village is not clear, and due in part to his death early in the construction phase of the project, it is difficult to get a complete understanding of his intentions other than his designs for the church and several anchor buildings. As a whole, Olmsted disagreed with Hunt's plan for buildings in the village and complained to his partners that Hunt's ideas were not consistent or reconcilable with his own design that he felt had been implicitly approved by Vanderbilt. Olmsted disliked Hunt's view of creating a village styled after French models and as such unsuitable for American habits. Olmsted expressed the opinion that Hunt should be required to revise his plans, which were quite elaborate. Nevertheless, the completed village reflected the ideas of both artists and those of George Vanderbilt, along with the numerous building designs of Hunt's supervising architect, Richard Sharp Smith, and the later grading and planting plans of the Olmsted Brothers after their father's failing health forced his retirement from the firm.

It is difficult to discuss Biltmore Village out of the context of its immediate surroundings and the influences the village had on the local community or how events and affairs impacted the village over time. It is also both interesting and helpful to review some of the early history of the area to gain an understanding of the setting and conditions of the locale George Vanderbilt decided to leave his mark on. The first chapter, "Before Biltmore," gives an insight into some of that early history and paints some images of life as it existed through a century of settlement before Biltmore Village came into being. The story of the design and construction of the village is illustrated through archival photographs from a variety of sources in chapter two, "A Millionaire's Village," and in the third chapter, "Work, Play, Worship," sketches of life in the village are explored through selected images of some of the people associated with the village, its businesses, and social aspects. The fourth chapter, "Where Life is Worthwhile," presents a sampling of peripheral areas from Kenilworth Inn to Victoria and gives a glimpse of some of the local community immediately around Biltmore in the early part of the 20th century. Chapter five, "Changing Face of Biltmore," spans time through four devastating floods, two world wars, the sale of Biltmore Village, and other events that have changed and shaped the village and surrounding area over several decades. Lastly in chapter six, "Biltmore Forest," a thumbnail sketch of another equally unique and intriguing development south of Biltmore is given through archival images and text.

The format of this book is intended to present only a glimpse into the captivating history of Biltmore Village and surrounding areas through photographs and captions rather than a comprehensive detailed account. In some cases, it represents many little stories that are connected in one way or another, and for every one printed here, there are a thousand more waiting to be told. Due to limitations of space for text and images, it was decided to focus mainly on the early history through the 1940s. Even so, many images and pages of information had to be omitted due to lack of space. From the 1950s and 1960s forward, a period of rapid development and change began to occur in and around Biltmore, and the stories of that era could easily fill another volume. It is hoped that this book resonates with those who have memories or attachments to Biltmore and those who are discovering it for the first time. May it inspire the reader to dig a little deeper into the rich and fascinating story of the special place that is within and around Biltmore Village.

One

Before Biltmore

Long before George W. Vanderbilt began purchasing land in 1888 to create his vast country estate with a model village that he would call Biltmore, the area centered around the confluence of the Swannanoa and French Broad Rivers already had a long and storied past. Archaeological evidence reveals that prehistoric people frequented or even inhabited the region as early as 9,000 to 10,000 years ago. The junction of the rivers became the crossroads of ancient Native American trails connecting the mountain wilderness with the piedmont and coastal areas of Virginia and the Carolinas to the east and south, the rich river valleys of Tennessee and Ohio to the west and north, and other points of the compass in between. Around 2,000 or more years ago, largely nomadic groups began to establish semipermanent hamlets or villages along the fertile bottoms of the Swannanoa and French Broad Rivers. The early Spanish explorers to the region, beginning with Hernando De Soto's expedition in 1540 and Juan Pardo's in 1566–1568, largely utilized the long-established network of trails to find their way into and through the mountain terrain. A century later, in 1673, the British explorers James Needham and Gabriel Arthur from Virginia penetrated the Blue Ridge country on their way to Cherokee towns. In September 1776, Gen. Griffith Rutherford, with some 2,400 militiamen organized at Davidson's Fort (Old Fort), followed the native trail through the gap in the Blue Ridge and down the Swannanoa. The expedition, on its way to destroy the Cherokee towns to the west and ease the threat to the settlers east of the mountains, crossed the War Ford on the French Broad River two miles upstream from the junction of the Swannanoa. At the end of the Revolutionary War, the signing of the Treaty of Paris in September 1783 opened the way for the first settlers into the mountains, many of whom came down the Swannanoa River to what is now Biltmore and points beyond.

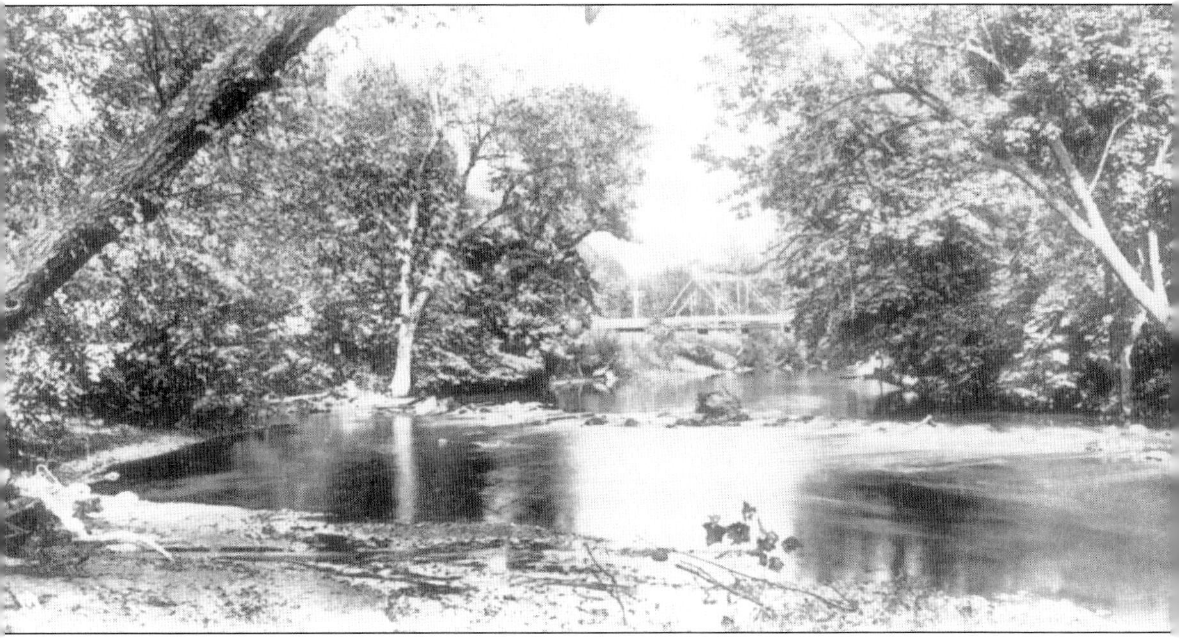

SWANNANOA RIVER. This early postcard portrays the beauty and charm of the Swannanoa below the Biltmore Bridge near where Buncombe County was organized in 1792. Samuel Davidson, who attempted the first settlement west of the Blue Ridge Mountains in 1784 in the Swannanoa Valley near Christian Creek, was killed by the Cherokee. A few months later in 1785, some of Davidson's relatives formed a settlement at the mouth of Bee Tree Creek, a tributary of the Swannanoa a few miles upstream from Biltmore. Col. William Davidson and Daniel Smith soon established farms farther west near the confluence of the Swannanoa with the French Broad River. Buncombe County was formally organized at nearby Gum Spring on Davidson's farm on April 16, 1792. Capt. Thomas Foster, son of William Forster, one of the county's founders, built the first bridge across the Swannanoa River in 1796. (Bill Alexander.)

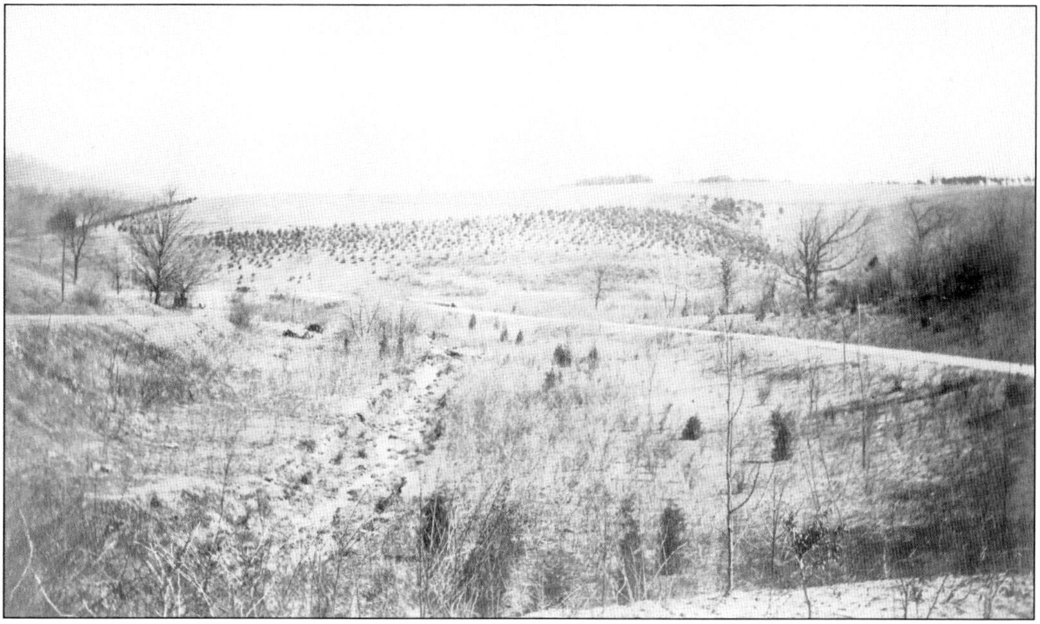

EARLY ROADS. One of the first roads built when Buncombe County was organized in April 1792 originated at Col. William Davidson's ford on the Swannanoa River and became known as Long Shoals Road. Crossing the French Broad River to the south at the Long Shoals, it connected with the Boylston Road being constructed at the same time. In the above 1896 view, the rutted wagon tracks of the road, abandoned after George Vanderbilt acquired the surrounding land to create Biltmore Estate, are still visible on the hillside to the left and in the distance beyond the tree grove near the junction of the new Approach and Service Roads to Biltmore House. In 1795, the first road from South Carolina to Asheville, later part of the Buncombe Turnpike, came down the distant ridge. Below, a pair of mules pulling a covered wagon pauses to rest in 1899 along the adjacent electric street railway line near the old Newton Academy cemetery on South Main Street. (Below, donated by Howard C. Weeks.)

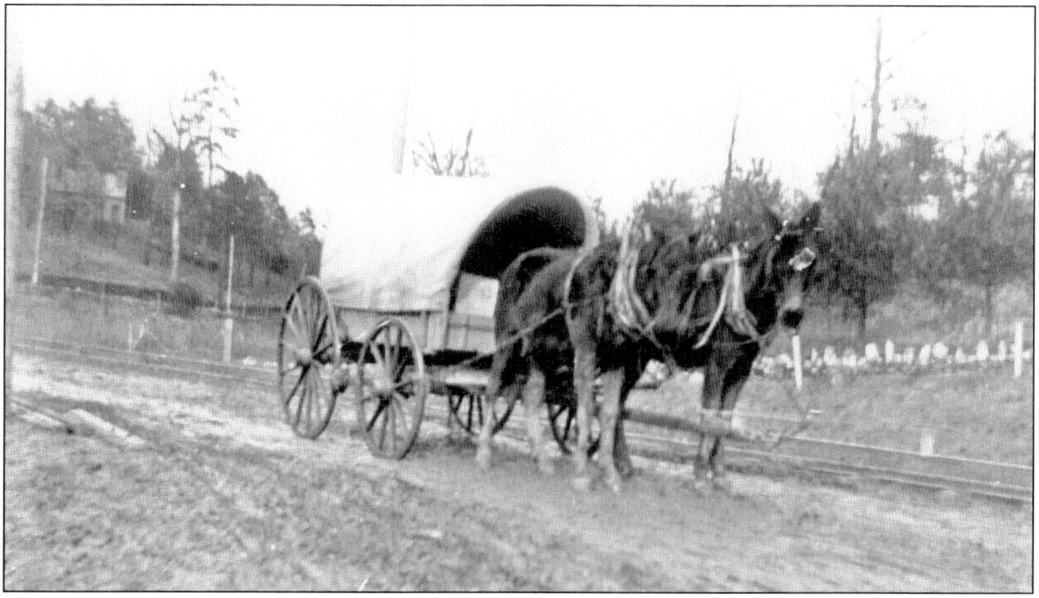

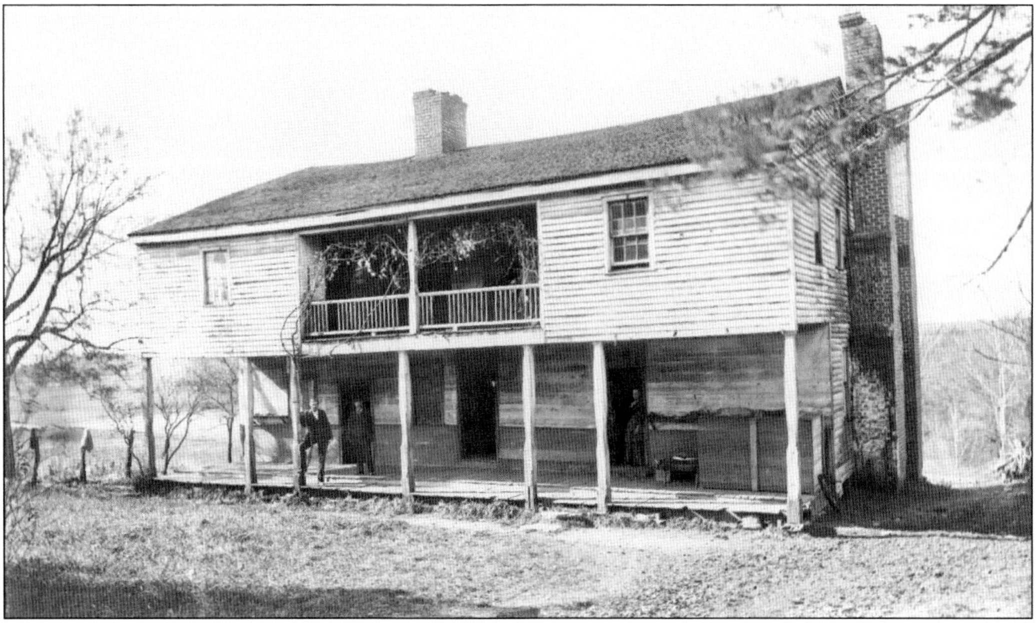

PATTON HOUSE, C. 1890. Col. John Patton, born on April 4, 1765, was one of Buncombe County's first settlers. Appointed to preside over the first court when the county was organized in April 1792, he was elected to the important office of county surveyor. Patton later bought land that had been part of the former Col. William Davidson farm on the south bank of the Swannanoa River and built his house near Davidson's ford. John and his wife, Ann Mallory Patton, raised a large family in their house, where he resided until his death in 1831. Situated at the junction of historic Long Shoals Road and the Buncombe Turnpike, the Patton house was famous for many years as a stopping place for travelers and drovers. Sometime after the Civil War, the house fell into ruins and was known locally as the "Haunted House" for the strange noises heard within. It was temporarily repaired and served as a boardinghouse for workers during construction of Biltmore Estate before being razed in 1895.

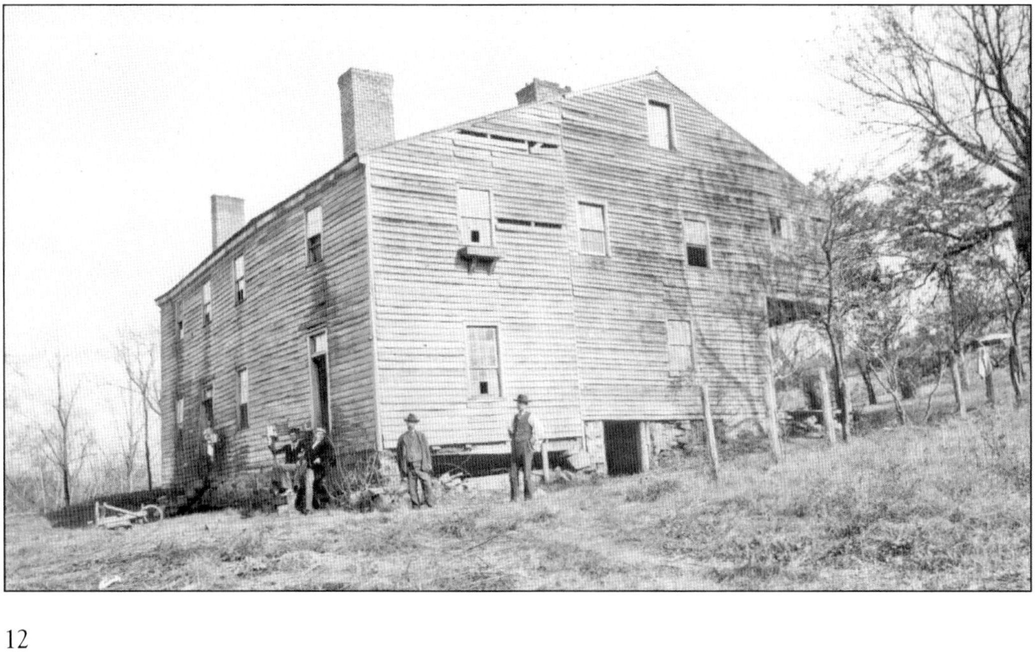

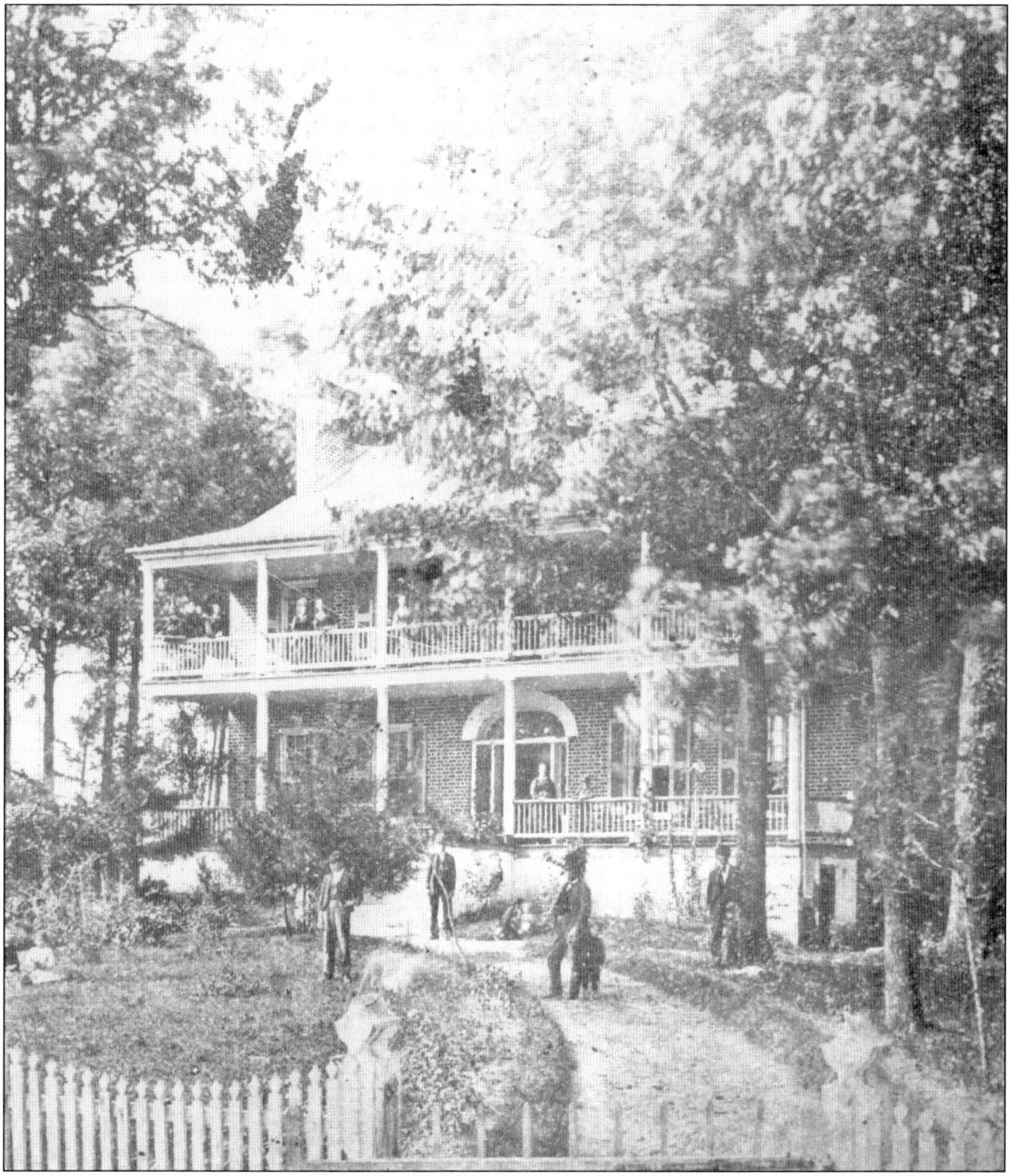

SMITH-McDOWELL HOUSE, c. 1875. Situated on a portion of a land grant issued to Col. Daniel Smith after the Revolutionary War, this *c.* 1840 antebellum mansion was built by Smith's son, James McConnell Smith, born on June 14, 1787, who is said to have been the first white child born west of the Blue Ridge in North Carolina. At one time owning more than 30,000 acres across Buncombe County, he was one of the wealthiest landowners in the county during the early part of the 19th century. In addition to building and operating a toll bridge over the French Broad River, James owned and operated a tannery, a mercantile business, and the Buck Hotel in downtown Asheville. After his death, Smith's daughter, Sarah Lucinda, and her husband, William Wallace McDowell, raised nine children and lived in the house until 1880. (Smith-McDowell Museum.)

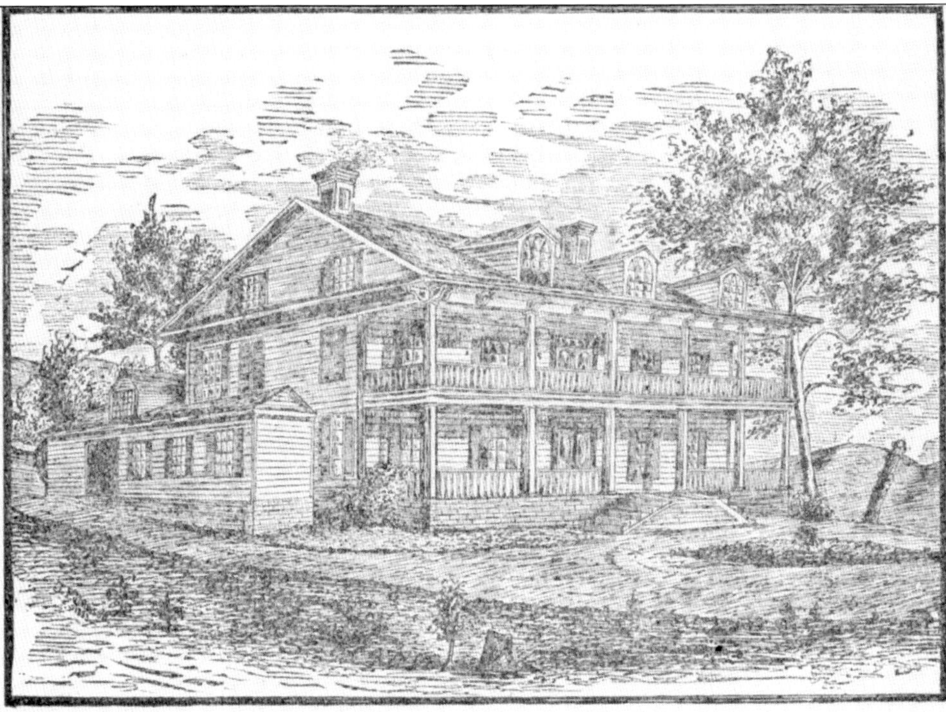

ANTLER HALL, ON FRENCH-BROAD RIVER, NEAR ASHEVILLE,
RESIDENCE OF G. B. TENNENT.

ANTLER HALL, 1884. This picture in the 1883–1884 Asheville City Directory and Gazetteer of Buncombe County was labeled as "Antler Hall, on French-Broad River, Near Asheville, Residence of G. B. Tennent," and advertised "summer boarding 2 1/2 miles west [of Best]." Antler Hall was used to house assistants of forester Carl A. Schenck and dairy employees and their families for several decades following the establishment of Biltmore Estate. (North Carolina Collection, Pack Memorial Library.)

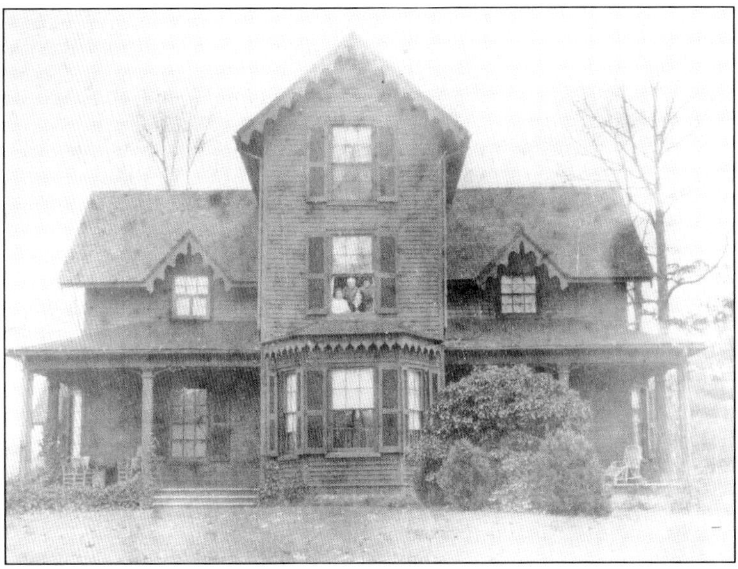

WEST HOUSE, c. 1895. George W. West was listed as a principal farmer owning 550 acres two miles west of Best (or Asheville Junction) in the 1883–1884 Gazetteer of Buncombe County. The West farm and associated house and farm buildings were purchased by George Vanderbilt to create Biltmore Estate. The West house became the primary residence of the estate's forester, Carl A. Schenck, from 1895 to 1909.

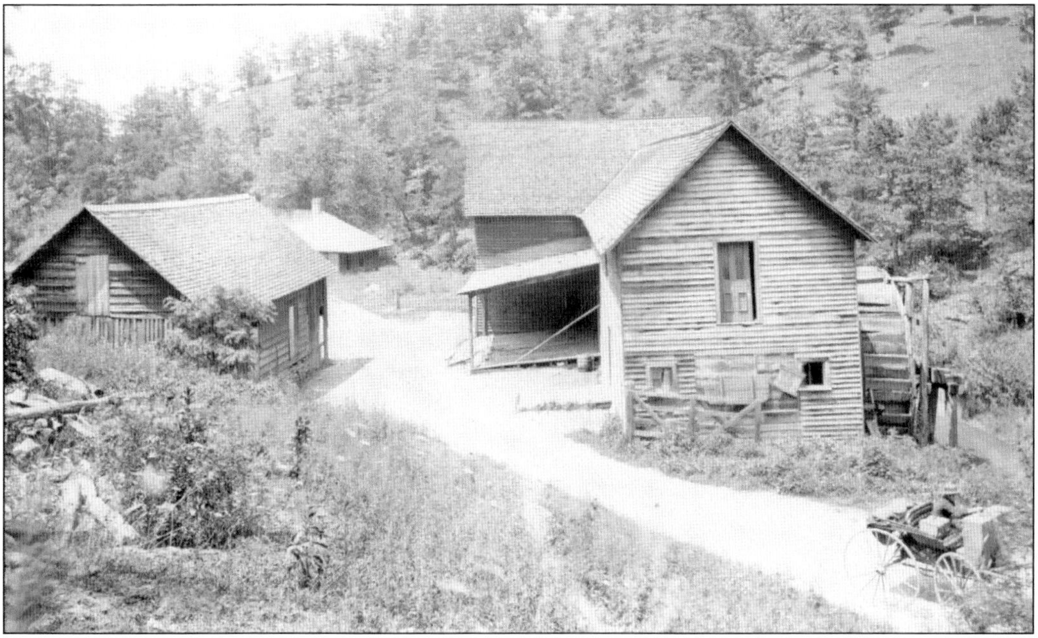

ALEXANDER MILL ON FOUR-MILE BRANCH, C. 1888. B. J. (Benjamin Julius) Alexander was listed in the 1883–1884 Gazetteer of Buncombe County as a principal farmer with 307 acres three miles southwest of Best and operating both grist and sawmills. George Vanderbilt purchased his land, which included a derelict bridge across the French Broad River, in 1889, as well as an adjoining 400-acre farm owned by W. J. Alexander, who also operated both grist and sawmills on Busbee or Six-Mile Branch.

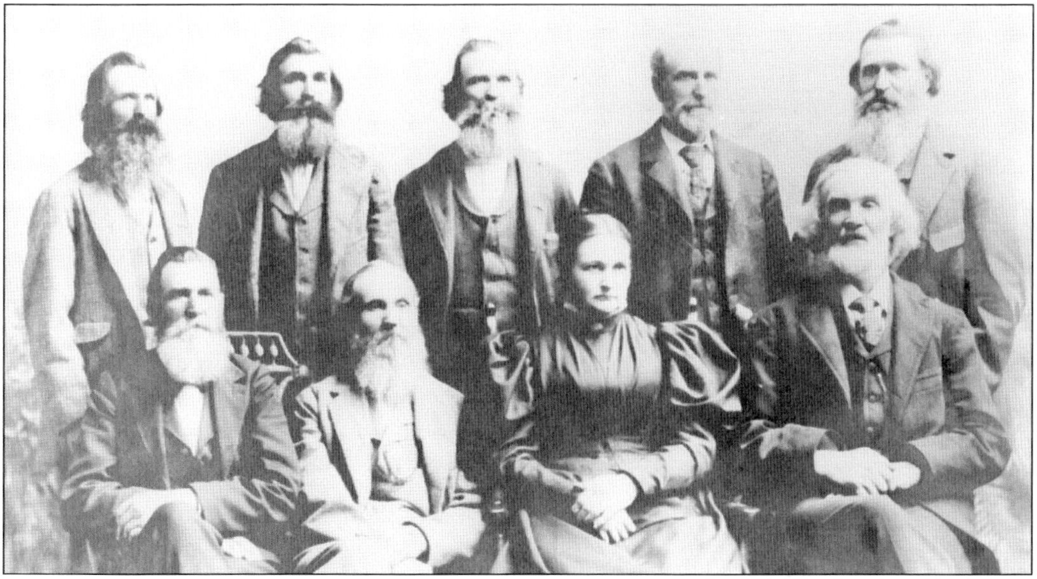

STEVENS BROTHERS, C. 1890. The eight men, all brothers, in this portrait of Henry Stevens's children, had the distinction of being the largest number from one family in Buncombe County who served in the Civil War and all returned home alive. The Stevens farm was located at Buena Vista on the west side of the Buncombe Turnpike (Hendersonville Road) just south of Asheville Junction or Best. (John S. Stevens.)

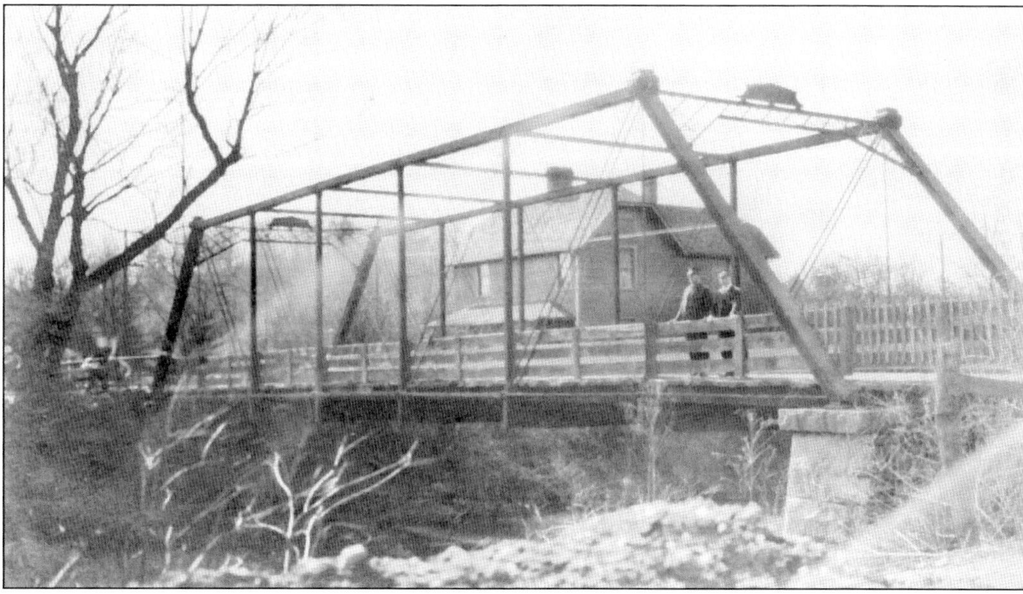

SWANNANOA BRIDGE, C. 1900. Many residents referred to their settlement along the river as Swannanoa Bridge long before the railroad came in 1880. Farms, houses, and businesses had been established on both sides of the Swannanoa River since the 1780s. The house pictured in this photograph was the residence of Capt. James C. Lipe, who perished in the flood of 1916. (Biltmore Village Historic Museum.)

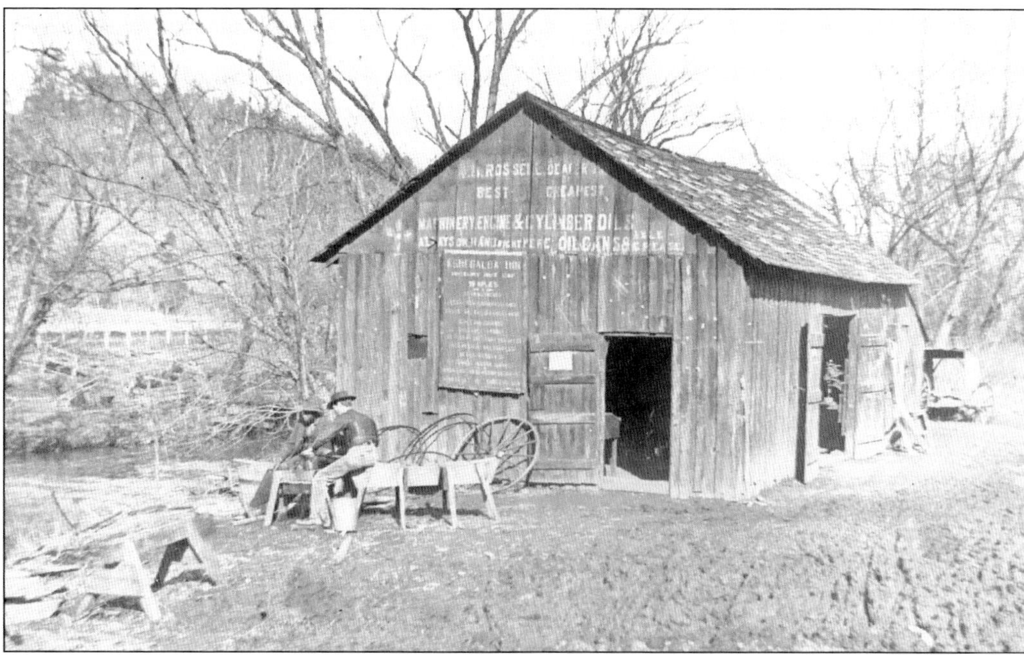

H. B. ROSSELL, DEALER. Located adjacent to the Swannanoa River, Rossell was a manufacturer of bolted and unbolted meal, grits, hominy, feed, and so on. An advertisement on Rossell's shop promoted Esmerelda Inn near Hickory Nut Gap as being 19 miles away. Vanderbilt purchased two tracts of land from Rossell in early 1893. (Louis Weeks's photograph donated by Howard C. Weeks.)

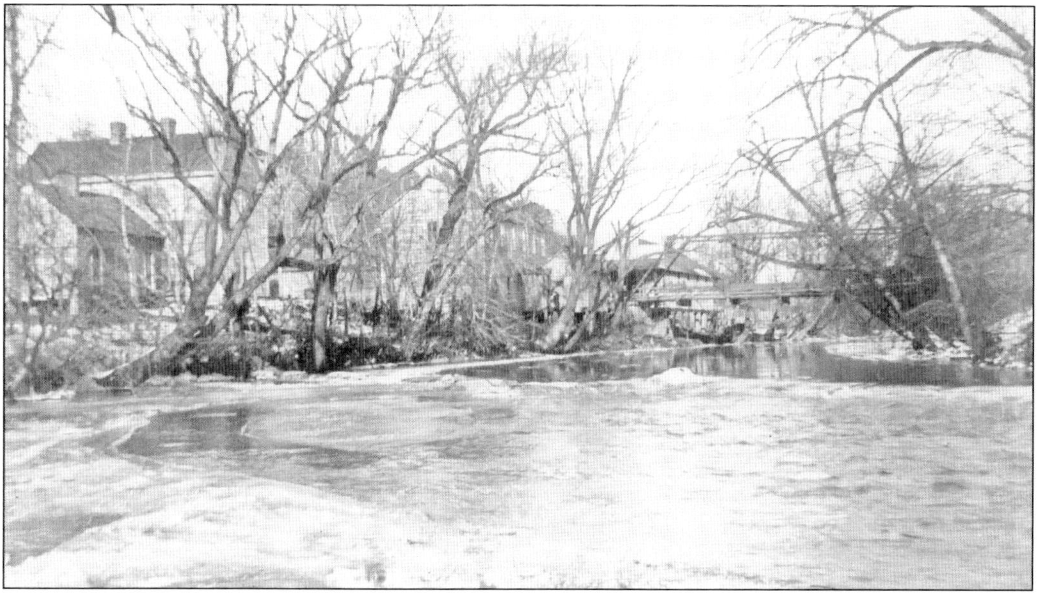

BUILDINGS ON NORTH SIDE OF SWANNANOA RIVER, 1899. Sanborn Company maps for 1896 and 1901 show a cluster of commercial buildings and dwellings near the iron bridge. Businesses included three general stores, a stable, a blacksmith, a grocer, a meat market, a drugstore, a shoe market, a tailor, a barber, a restaurant, a confectionery, and lunch establishments. (Louis Weeks's photograph donated by Howard C. Weeks.)

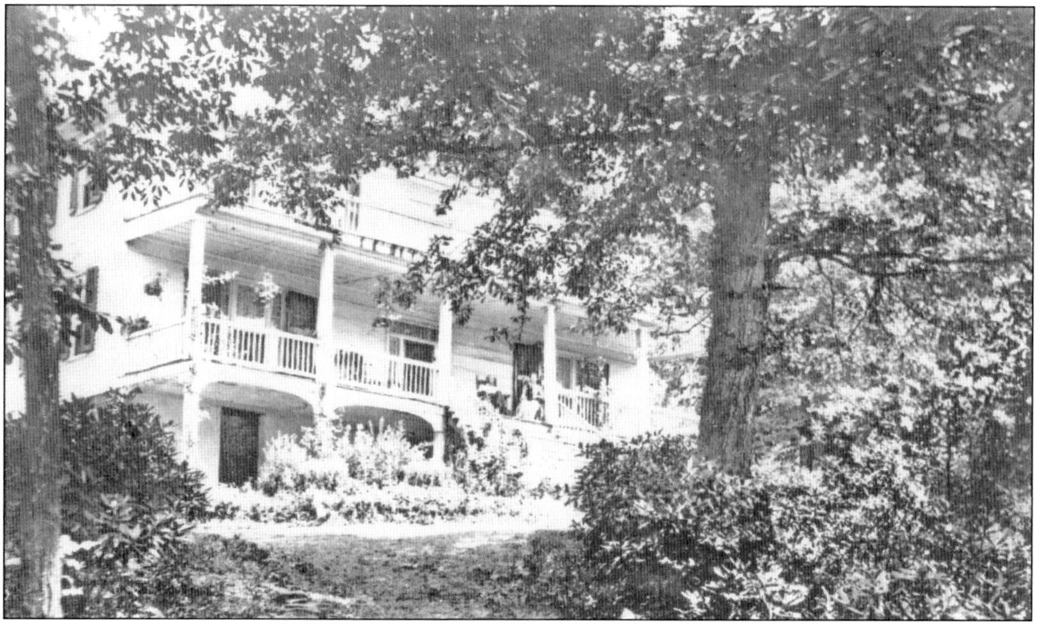

AZALEA, BILTMORE. Located along the Swannanoa River upstream from the Biltmore bridge, the Trescott-Cheesborough House, as it was sometimes known, was built around 1848 for a man from Charleston, South Carolina, named Trescott. William Patton, whose farm later became a part of the Kenilworth community, named it Azalea in the 1850s. The house was owned afterwards by John Cheesborough and his descendants. (North Carolina Collection, Pack Memorial Public Library.)

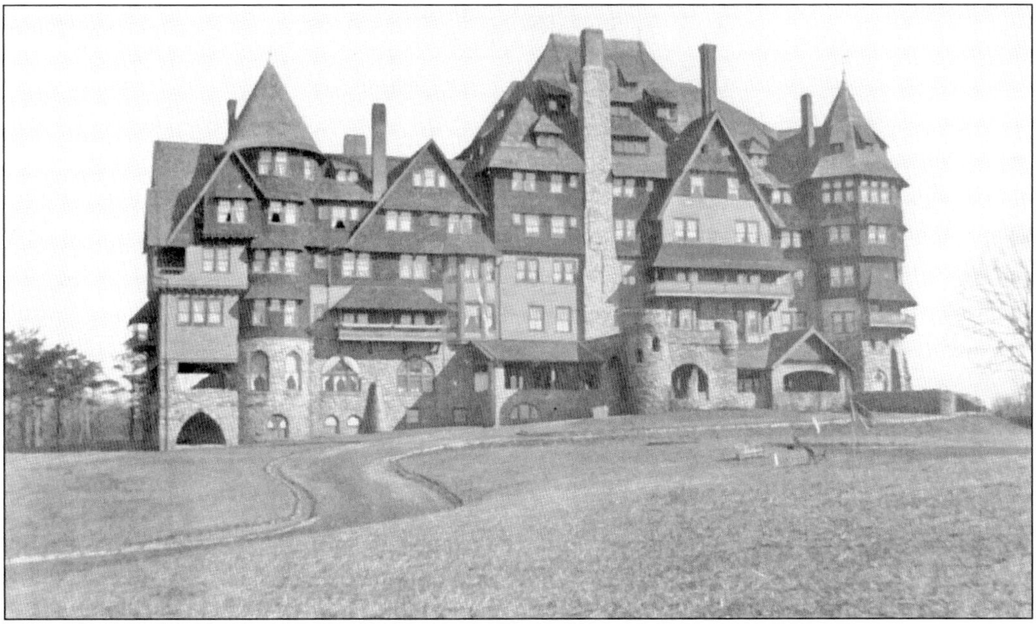

KENILWORTH INN, 1899. Kenilworth Inn was prominently situated on a hill above the Swannanoa River and had been chartered by the legislature in 1891 contingent on the maintenance of the turnpike between the city of Asheville and Biltmore by the inn, not the county. Developed in 1891 by Joseph M. Gazzam and other investors, including George Vanderbilt, Kenilworth Inn met with financial problems almost from the beginning that were attributed to poor management by its many proprietors. (Louis Weeks's photograph donated by Howard C. Weeks.)

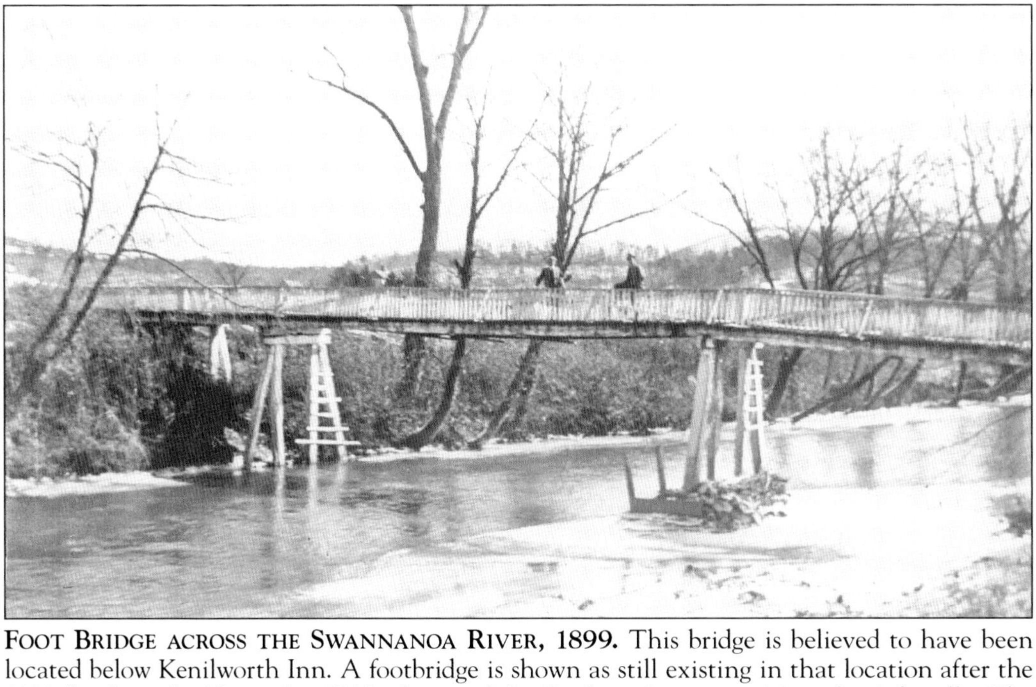

FOOT BRIDGE ACROSS THE SWANNANOA RIVER, 1899. This bridge is believed to have been located below Kenilworth Inn. A footbridge is shown as still existing in that location after the 1916 flood on the November 1917 edition of the Sanborn Insurance Maps for Asheville. The men on the bridge are unidentified. (Louis Weeks's photograph donated by Howard C. Weeks.)

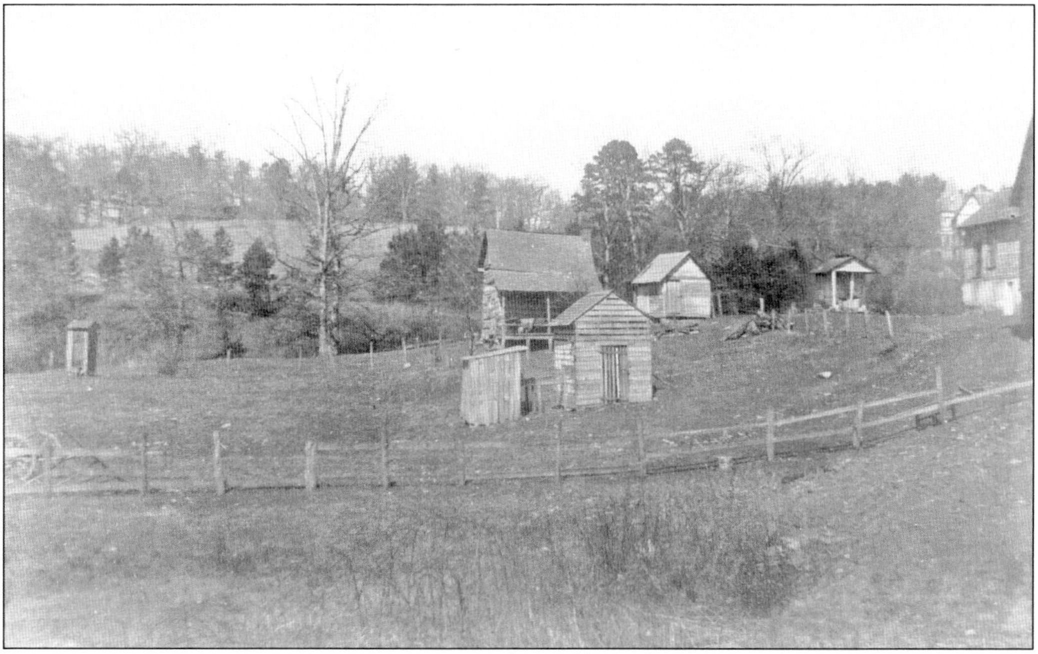

UNIDENTIFIED FARM AND FAMILY, 1899. This hillside farm was located just north of the Swannanoa River and adjacent to Biltmore Road (South Main Street). While Asheville was a progressive town with one of the country's first electric street railway systems, which ran by this farm, the surrounding region was still largely rural and sparsely settled. Hewn-log houses and barns were common sights throughout the area. The steeply gabled roof of the Queen Anne–style house, dubbed Swannanoa Hill when it was built by prominent banker William Breese, is visible on the hill above on the right side of the photograph. (Both, Louis Weeks's photographs donated by Howard C. Weeks.)

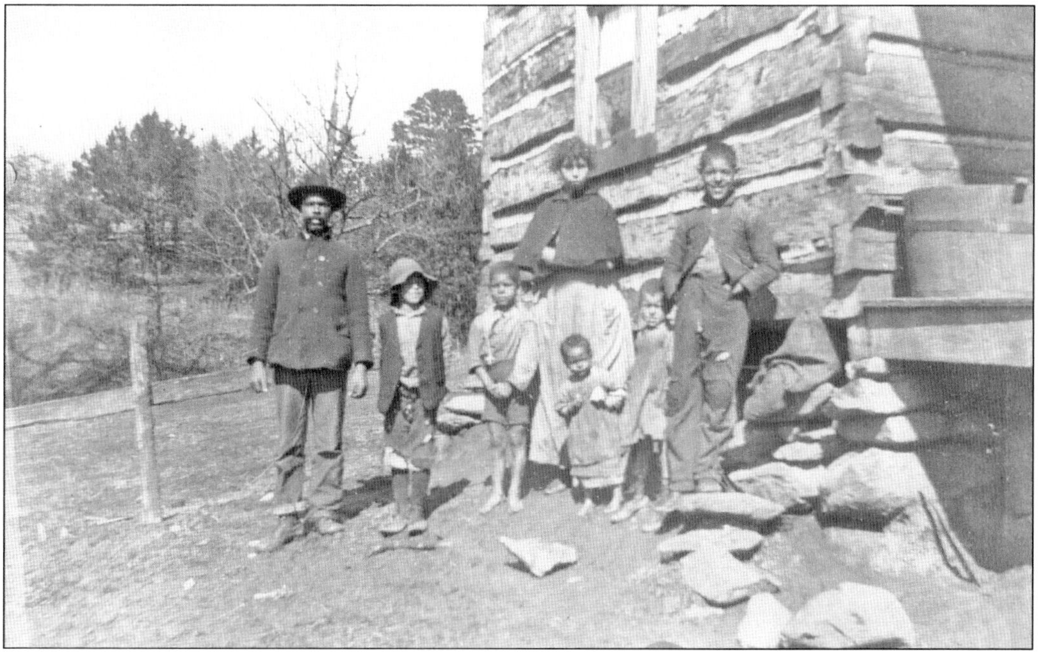

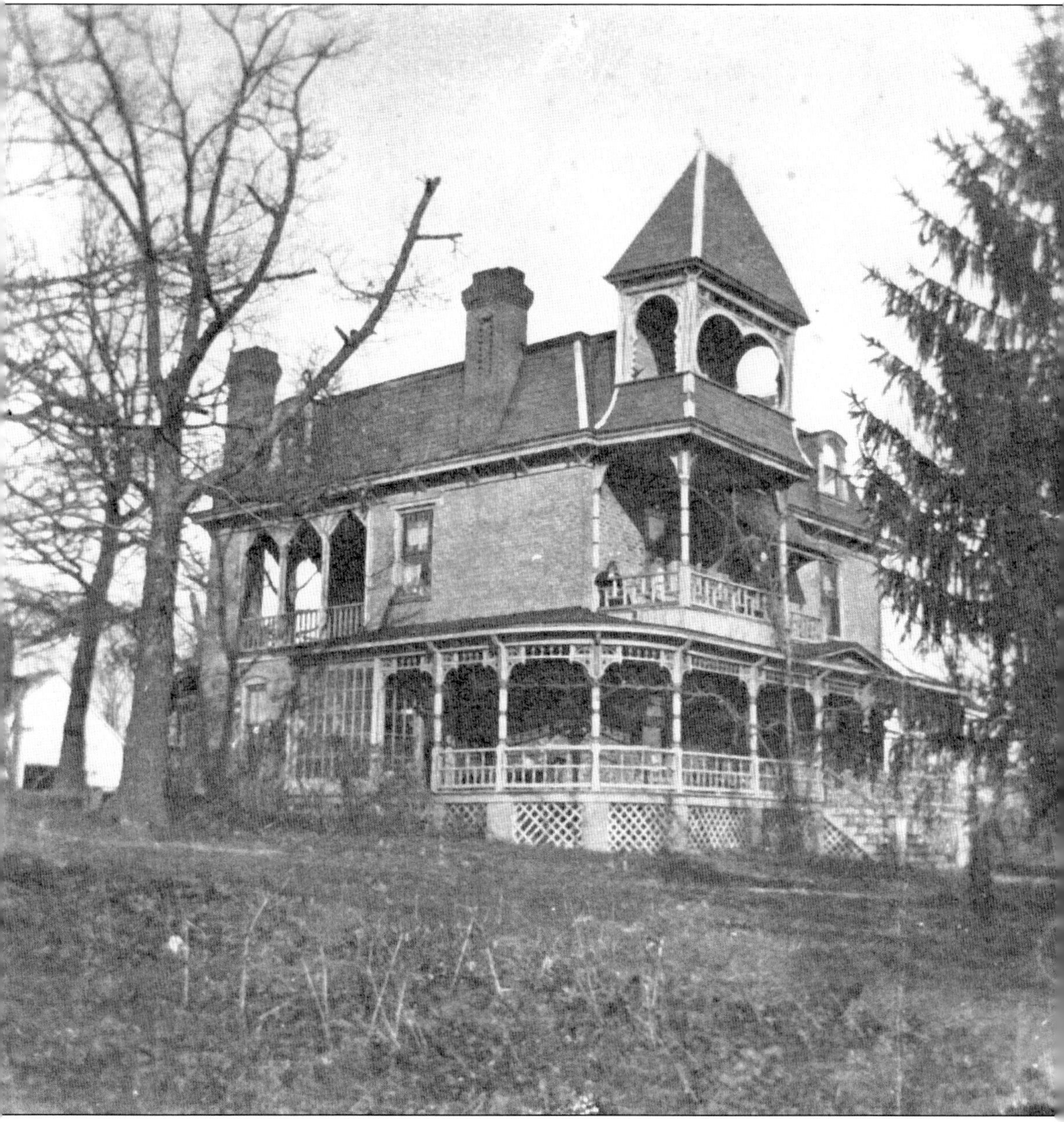

WALKER PLACE, 1900. This charming Victorian house with covered porches on two levels and an artistically designed lookout tower on the third was located along Hendersonville Road in the area that came to be known as South Biltmore. Across the street from the residence of C. L. Boynton, chief plant collector for the Biltmore Nursery and Herbarium, the house was used as a rental by Biltmore Estate during the years that Biltmore Village was being developed. George Vanderbilt purchased numerous parcels of land, mostly on the west side of Hendersonville Road between the villages of Best and Buena Vista. (Davene Boynton Rusher.)

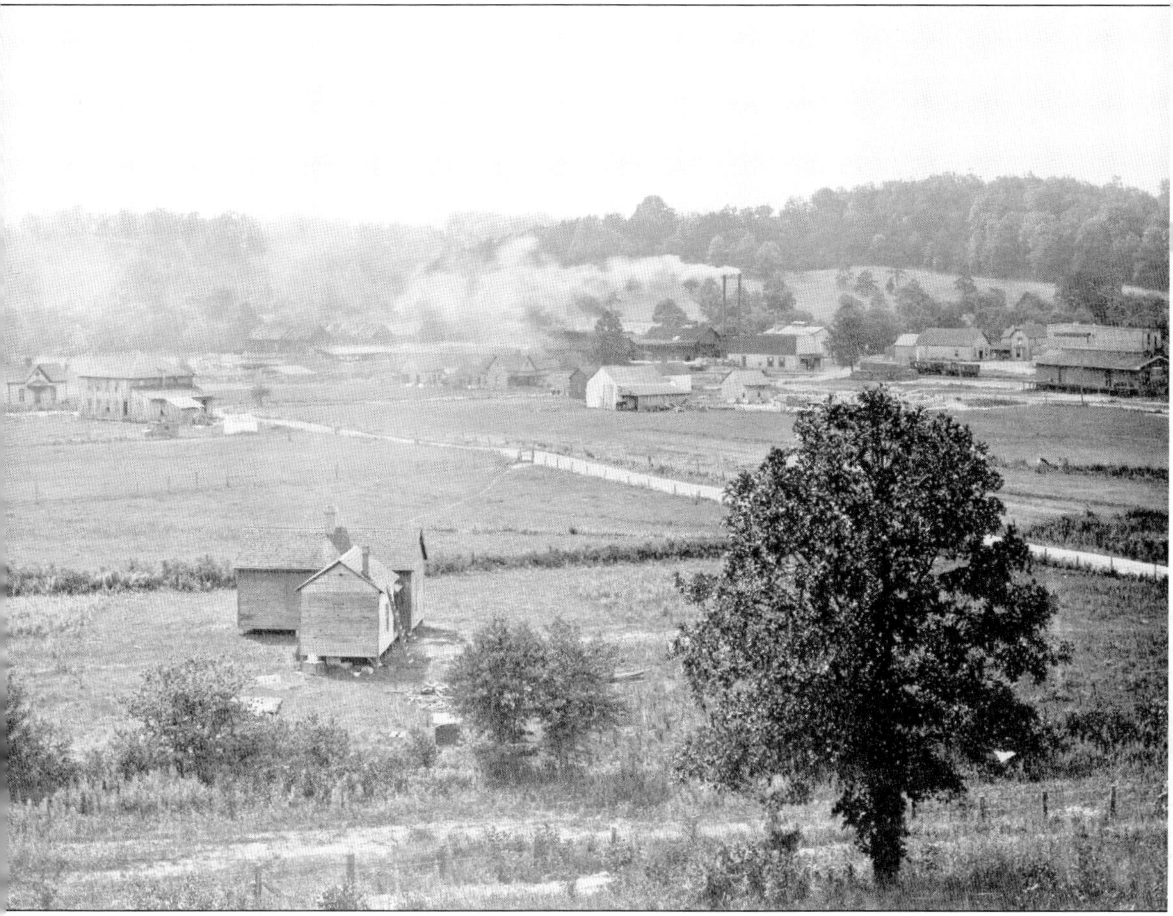

BEST OR ASHEVILLE JUNCTION, JULY 7, 1894. The village took its name from William Best, one of the principals of the Western North Carolina Railroad Company, which had succeeded in bringing rail service to the region in 1880. The Asheville City Directory of 1883–1884 included the Gazetteer of Buncombe County, which described this settlement: "Called Asheville Junction by the Railroad Company and Swannanoa Bridge by nearly everybody else, but Best by the Post-Office Department. A station on the Western North Carolina Railroad, at the proposed junction of the Spartanburg and Asheville Railroad, 2 miles south of Asheville court house. Is the shipping point for a considerable region to the south, southeast and southwest. Extensive improvements in the shape of new buildings and the filling up of Blowgun Gulch, long a dangerous pitfall for the inebriated pilgrim have lately been originated." George Vanderbilt purchased several tracts of land, which comprised the village of Best, from Samuel H. Reed and others beginning in 1888.

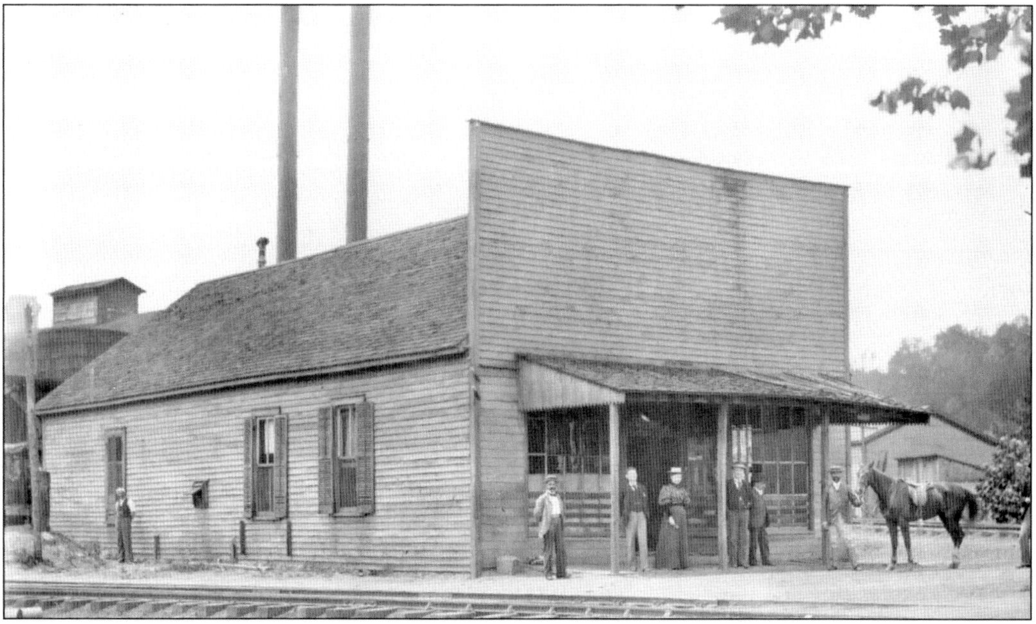

BILTMORE BRICK WORKS OFFICE, C. 1891. This wood-frame building stood between Eagle Mills (gristmill and grocery) and the former ice factory on the west side of the road to Asheville. Other nearby businesses included two additional groceries, a general store, a meat market, a bakery, a cobbler, a blacksmith shop, and a doctor's office. The building served as offices for the brick works and Biltmore Estate, and the post office during the early construction period.

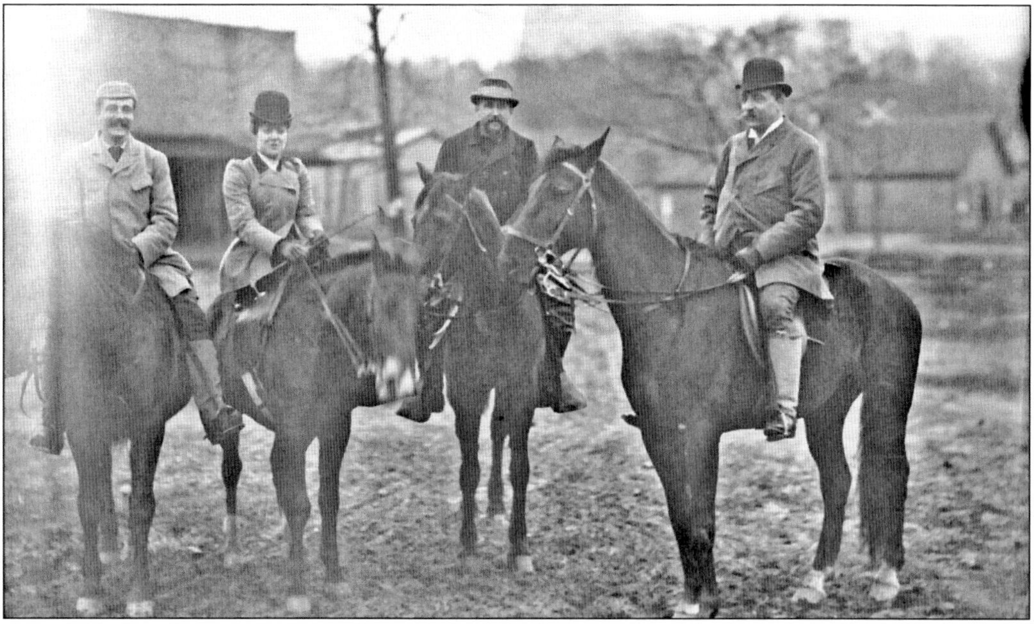

EXPLORING THE TOWN, C. 1892. From left to right are Gifford Pinchot, newly hired by George Vanderbilt as chief forester; Vanderbilt's niece Adele Sloan; purchasing agent and agricultural advisor Edward Burnett; and Vanderbilt's friend Walter Rathbone Bacon. Various buildings that made up the business district of Best or Asheville Junction can be seen clustered along the road to Asheville near the railroad tracks.

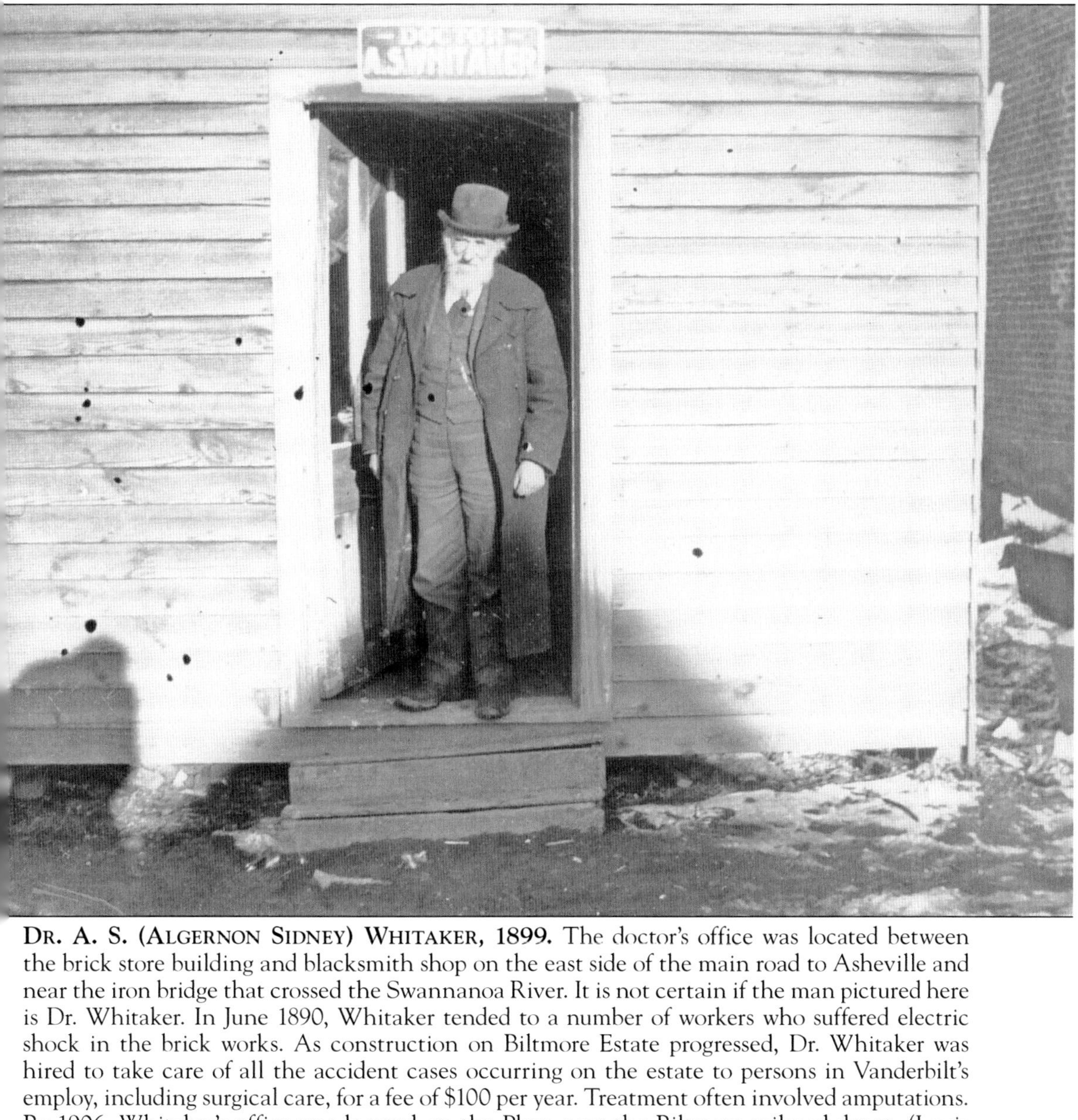

DR. A. S. (ALGERNON SIDNEY) WHITAKER, 1899. The doctor's office was located between the brick store building and blacksmith shop on the east side of the main road to Asheville and near the iron bridge that crossed the Swannanoa River. It is not certain if the man pictured here is Dr. Whitaker. In June 1890, Whitaker tended to a number of workers who suffered electric shock in the brick works. As construction on Biltmore Estate progressed, Dr. Whitaker was hired to take care of all the accident cases occurring on the estate to persons in Vanderbilt's employ, including surgical care, for a fee of $100 per year. Treatment often involved amputations. By 1906, Whitaker's office was located on the Plaza near the Biltmore railroad depot. (Louis Weeks's photographs donated by Howard C. Weeks.)

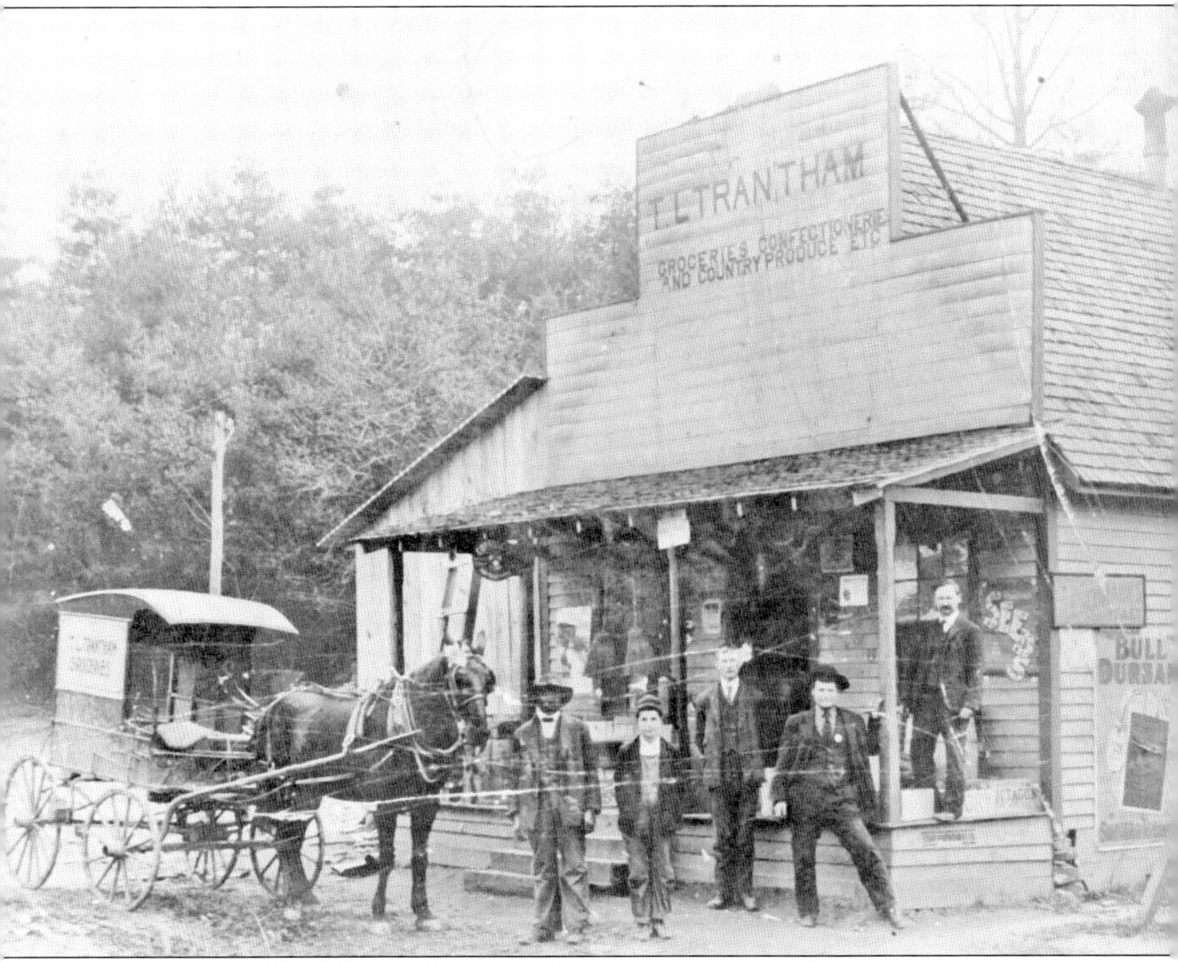

TRANTHAM GROCERY STORE, 1908. Thomas L. "Tom" Trantham, one of the area's pioneer businessmen, started in the grocery business around 1891. The Asheville City Directory of 1899–1900 lists T. L. Trantham, grocer, as being on Victoria Street in the town of Victoria and on Brook Street at the corner of Reed Street in 1908. The 1917 directory lists Tranthams' Café as well as T. L. Trantham, grocer, on Brook Street. The back of the photograph identifies the men from left to right as Bob White, store delivery boy; George McQuinn; "Perison" or Person McMinn, store clerk; Sheriff George Marshall Sr., and store owner Tom Trantham. Robert L. (Bob) White is holding the reins of a horse identified as Buncombe, hitched to the store delivery wagon. (North Carolina Collection, Pack Memorial Public Library.)

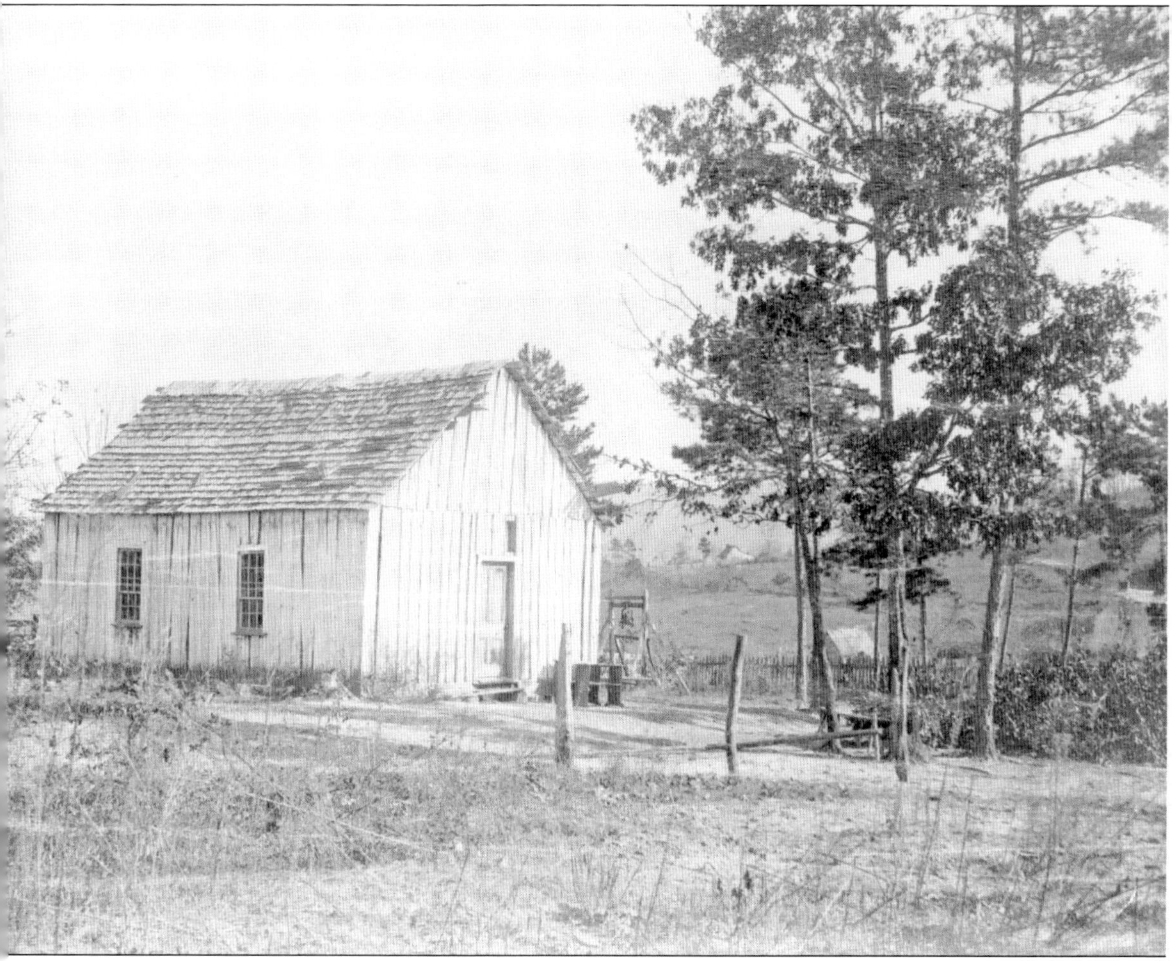

SHILOH A.M.E. CHURCH, C. 1889. Established in 1874, this one-room African Methodist Episcopal church was located one and a half miles south of Best. George Vanderbilt purchased the church and the acre it stood on in September 1889 for $1,000 and the promise to build a new, larger, and nicer church for the congregation and to move their deceased to the new church cemetery. The new church, dedicated in May 1890, was not only larger and nicer, but was also furnished with stained-glass windows, pews, and a bell, all provided by Vanderbilt. A letter of gratitude was written to Charles McNamee, the estate superintendent, by the pastor on behalf of the trustees and congregation. It expressed "our heartfelt thanks for the New Shiloh Church which you have given us for our former Shiloh which we sold to you. . . . We pray that you and Mr. Vanderbilt may live long to do good in our community."

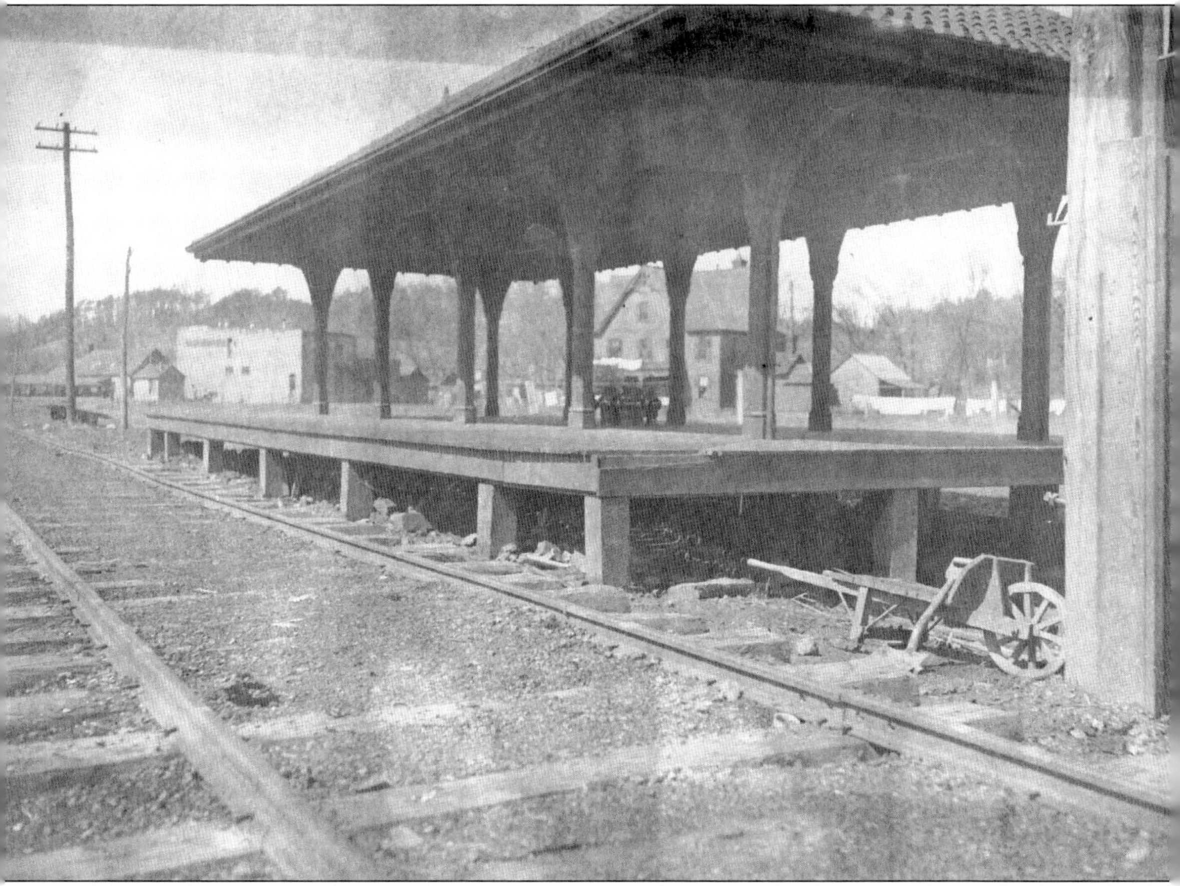

STATION INN NEAR RAILROAD DEPOT, C. 1890. George Vanderbilt purchased a number of properties that made up the village of Best, including the Station Inn, visible through the railroad freight platform. In the fall of 1890, estate superintendent Charles McNamee placed orders for dishes, glasses, flatware, a number of towels, counterpanes, blankets, and other bedding items to furnish "the little hotel here." The Station Inn, although acquired by Vanderbilt to board workmen from the estate, was leased to E. H. Nies for operation in late November of that year. McNamee wrote to Nies in February 1891 telling him to improve the food quality at the Biltmore Inn and informing him to be prepared for the arrival of Robert Douglas, a nurseryman and tree consultant from Illinois; Vanderbilt's landscape architect Frederick Law Olmsted and assistant Warren H. Manning; and Edward Burnett, an agricultural advisor from Massachusetts.

Two

A Millionaire's Village

When landscape architect Frederick Law Olmsted was developing his comprehensive master plan for Biltmore Estate, the treatment of the entrance to the estate and Approach Road to the chateau was of the highest priority in Olmsted's mind. He wished to create a pleasing and lasting impression of the estate for George Vanderbilt and his guests beginning at the entrance. He suggested to Vanderbilt, "I think that a village at the Junction and a group of villas on the neighboring hills very desirable to be had in view." Olmsted's extensive experience in planning parks and other public spaces, communities, and subdivisions had prepared him well for laying the framework of a model village reminiscent of similar ones in Europe but unique and adaptive to the local setting and conditions and one that would suit his client's objectives, which were threefold. The first was to provide easy access to the estate from the train station through an aesthetically pleasing entrance. The second was to create a source of income through rentals of residences and businesses that would help to support and sustain it. The third was to develop a community setting as a place for establishing and carrying out philanthropic programs. Olmsted felt that the village could be designed to accomplish these objectives but thought it important that the public would perceive it as a viable and livable community rather than just a millionaire's display of his power and wealth. Olmsted summarized his ideas to Vanderbilt: "An entrance to the approach of Biltmore Estate will open from the village, but it is not advised that the main characteristic expression of the village as a whole should be that simply of a dependency of the private estate. . . . Rather the effect should be that the village is obviously occupied by a community, the members of which are engaged, independently of the owner of the estate, in various kinds of businesses, the pursuit of which requires that they should be in intimate intercourse, commercially, and otherwise, with people at a distance from the village." Vanderbilt trusted the wisdom of Olmsted, and the village plans and construction progressed rapidly to fulfill the collective vision of landscape architect and client.

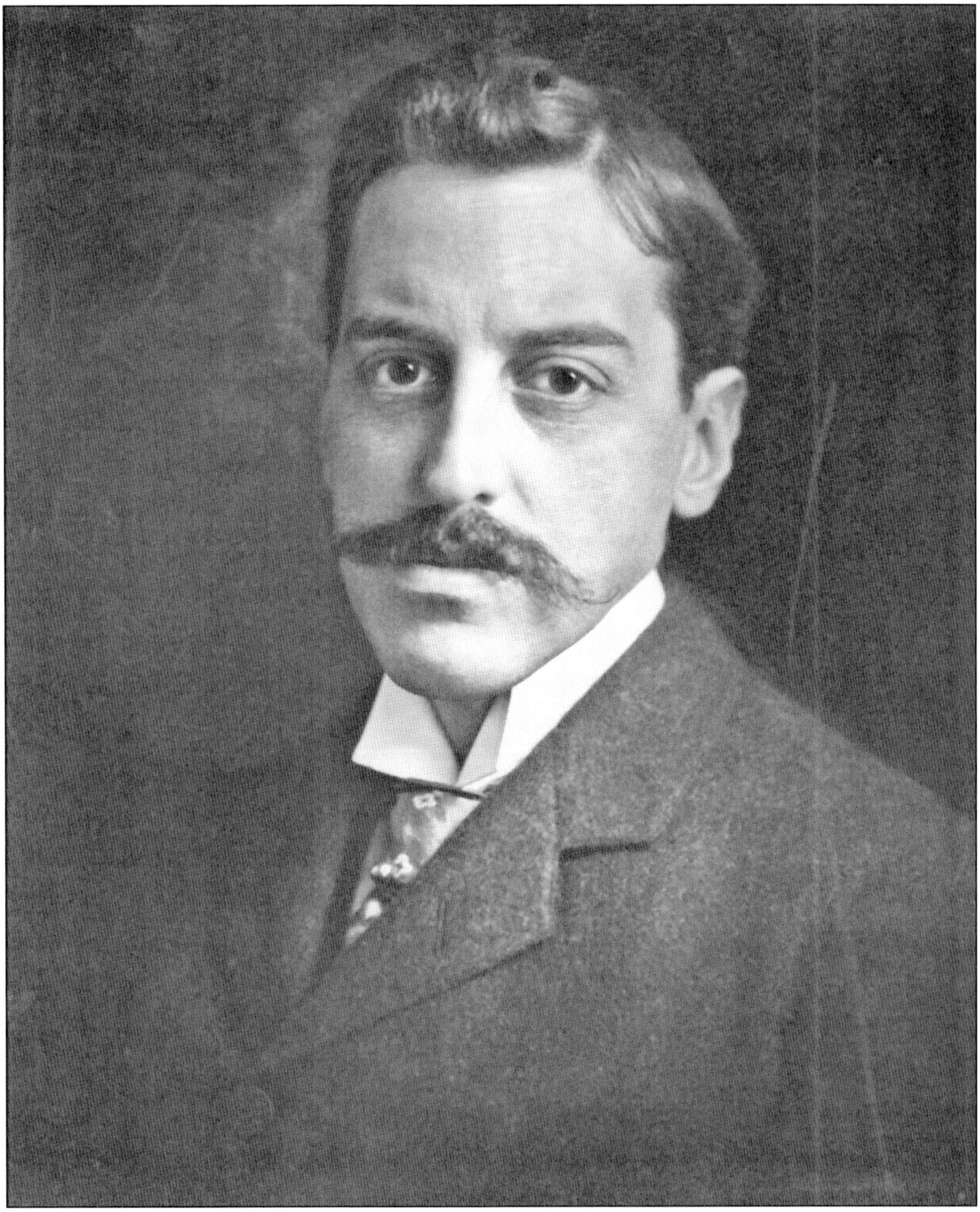

GEORGE WASHINGTON VANDERBILT, 1914. George Vanderbilt came to Asheville in 1888 with his mother to recreate in the healthful climate of Asheville. Vanderbilt, with time on his hands, enjoyed the distant views of the Blue Ridge Mountains, the invigorating air, and exploring the countryside south of Asheville near the Swannanoa and French Broad Rivers, and he decided to purchase land to build a house. One of the early tracts he acquired included the village of Best, a crossroads settlement near the Swannanoa River. At the time, he had not envisioned that he would ultimately remove the scattered houses and buildings clustered around the railroad tracks along the banks of the river to make way for a model village of orderly streets with rental cottages, businesses, a church, and a school.

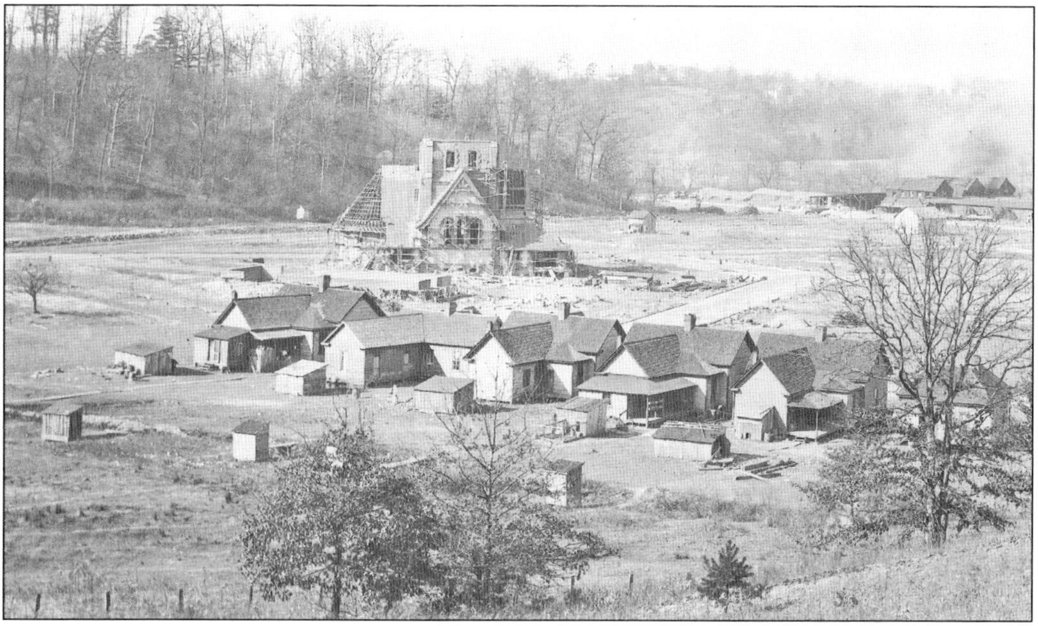

ALL SOULS CHURCH UNDER CONSTRUCTION, WINTER OF 1895–1896. The transformation of the village of Best to Biltmore was well underway by 1895. The primary streets had been laid out, and construction of several of the key buildings, including the church, was making good progress. The houses in the foreground were moved to this location to temporarily house workers during construction. Sixty log rollers were brought to the site to assist with their removal in January 1899.

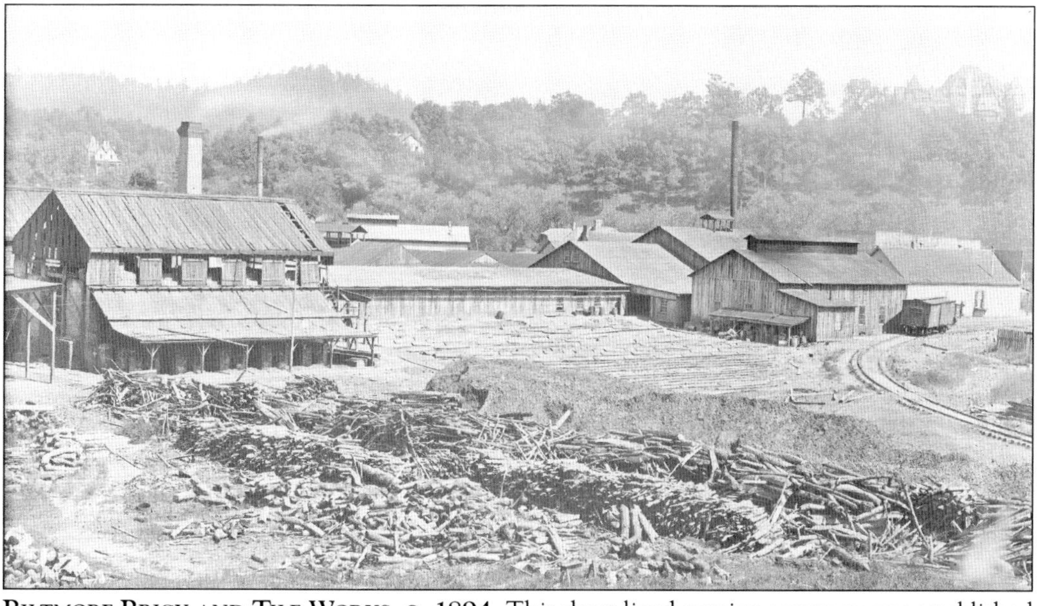

BILTMORE BRICK AND TILE WORKS, C. 1894. This short-lived captive company was established to manufacture the vast quantities of brick, roofing tiles, and other clay products needed for the construction of the estate and village. A narrow-gauge tram transported clay from the estate to the brick works. The track was laid by October 2, 1891, and the small locomotive arrived, making its first trip to the clay bank in six minutes.

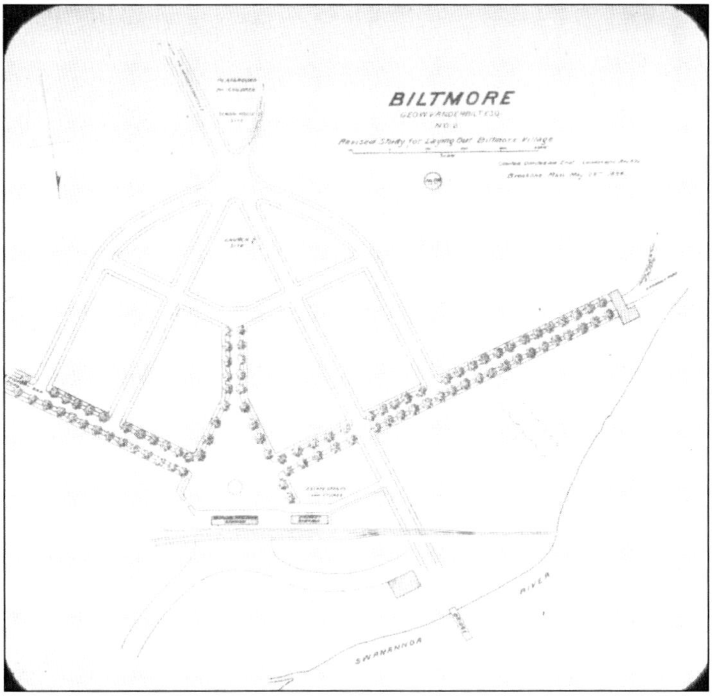

REVISED STUDY FOR LAYING OUT BILTMORE VILLAGE, MAY 28, 1894. Frederick Law Olmsted's symmetrical layout of the village streets bisected by the public thoroughfare of the Biltmore-Hendersonville Road at right angles with the tree-lined Lodge Street reflected his belief that the village should be more than a grand entrance to Biltmore Estate. It would be a community in its own right. (Frances Loeb Library, Harvard Graduate School of Design.)

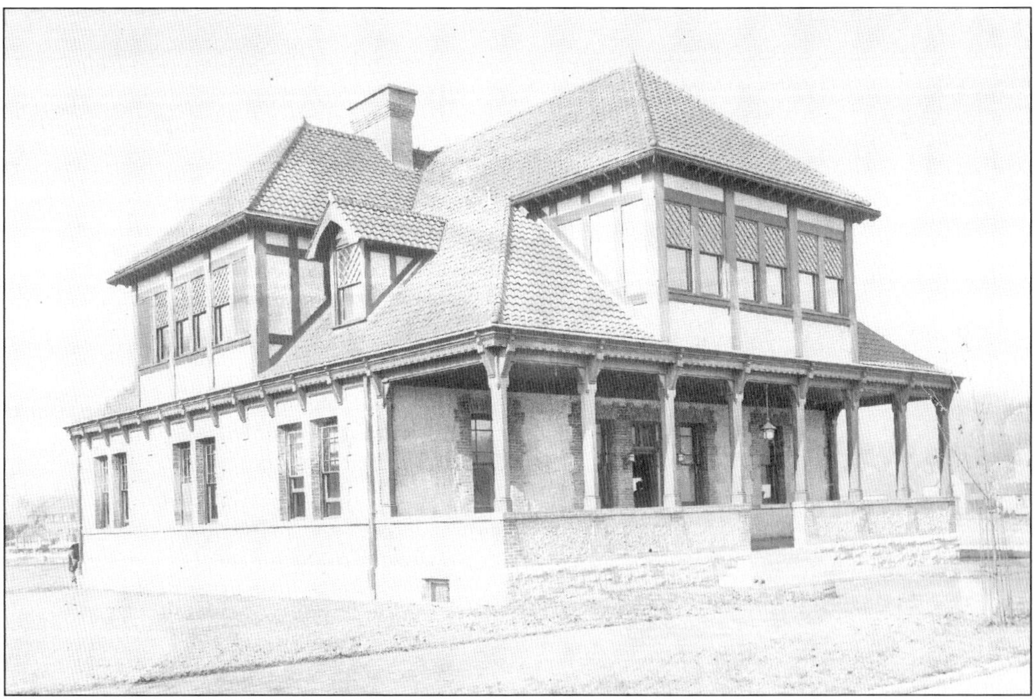

BILTMORE OFFICE BUILDING, 1895. Designed by Richard Morris Hunt, the estate office was one of the first structures to be completed in the village and was done in record time. The foundation were excavated in April 1894, and estate superintendent Charles McNamee awarded the masonry contract for his new office building in July. By late September, the office building was nearly complete, and plans were being made to tear down the old office.

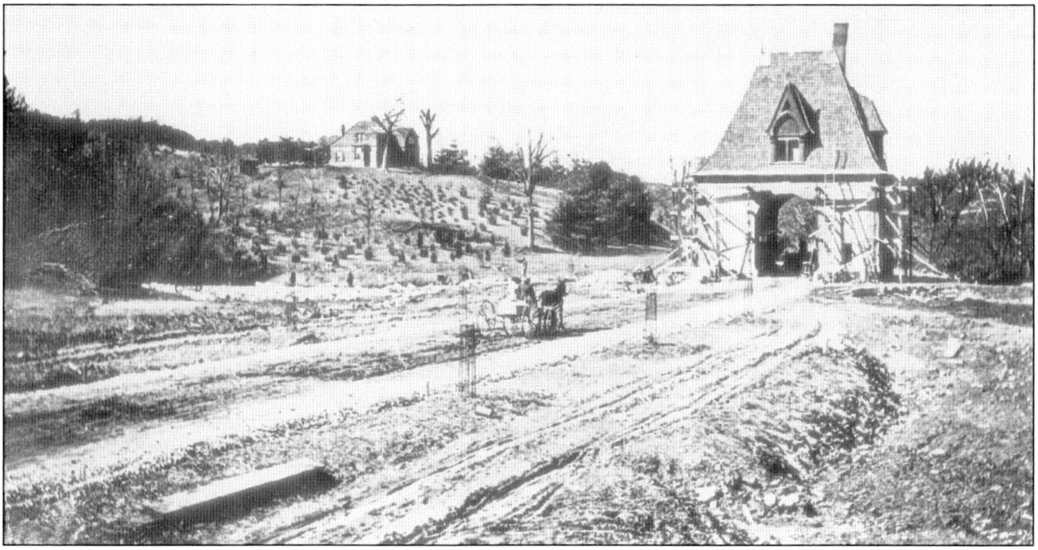

LODGE GATE UNDER CONSTRUCTION, C. 1895. The main entrance to Biltmore Estate was constructed at the end of Lodge Street, which connected it to the central plaza of the village, where the train station, estate office, shops, and post office were located. The preexisting house on the knoll above the gatehouse was renovated and served initially as the residence of Edward Harding, assistant to estate superintendent Charles McNamee. (Frances Loeb Library, Harvard Graduate School of Design.)

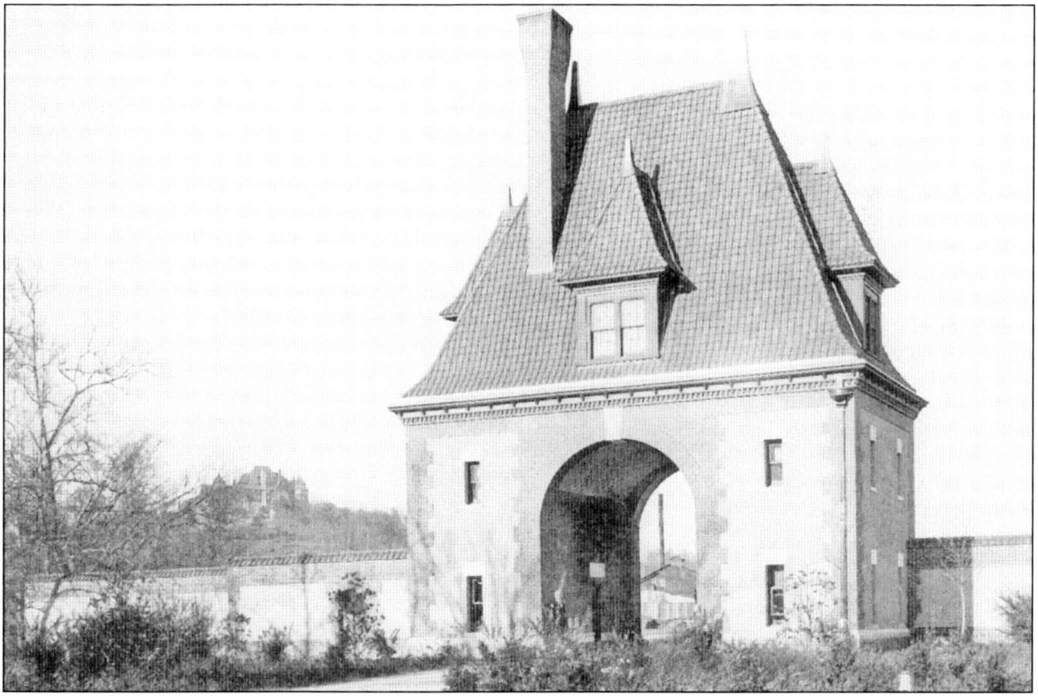

LODGE GATE, C. 1896. Known also as the Gate Lodge, this imposing structure served as a residence for the gatekeeper as well as a secure entrance to the estate. The Olmsted firm requested that a high wall be erected on the north side to enclose a "back yard for the occupant of the Lodge." Kenilworth Inn and the Brick Works are visible beyond.

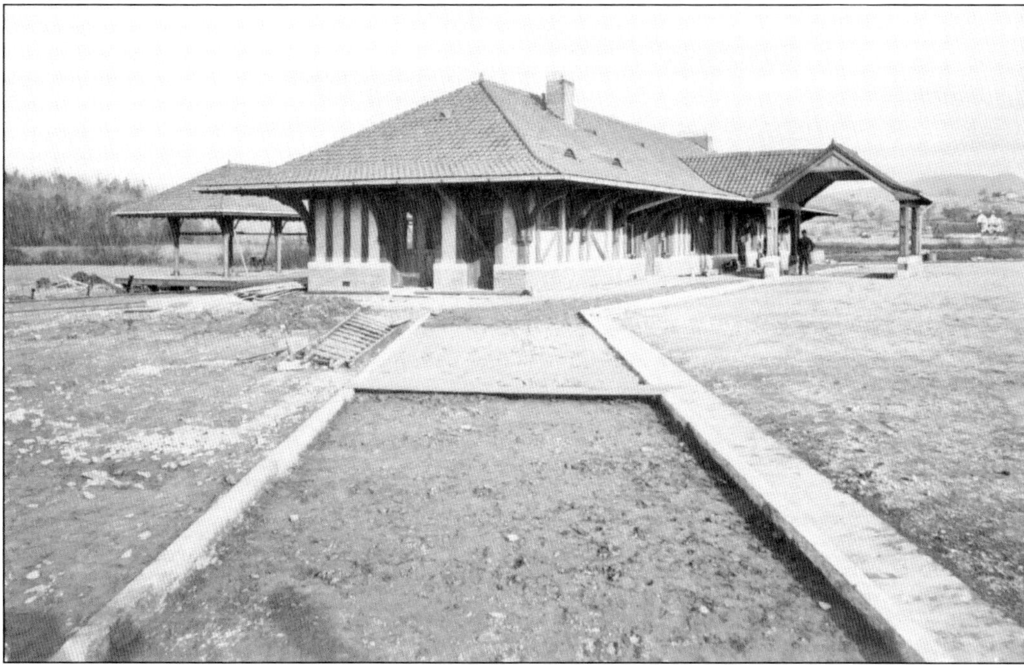

BILTMORE PASSENGER STATION, C. 1895. By October 1894, George Vanderbilt had an agreement with the Southern Railroad Company to shift the railroad tracks at Biltmore so that a new station could be built to replace the existing one. Designed by Richard Morris Hunt, the new station is shown here near completion. The covered platform behind and across the tracks served for unloading freight until the new freight depot was constructed in 1900.

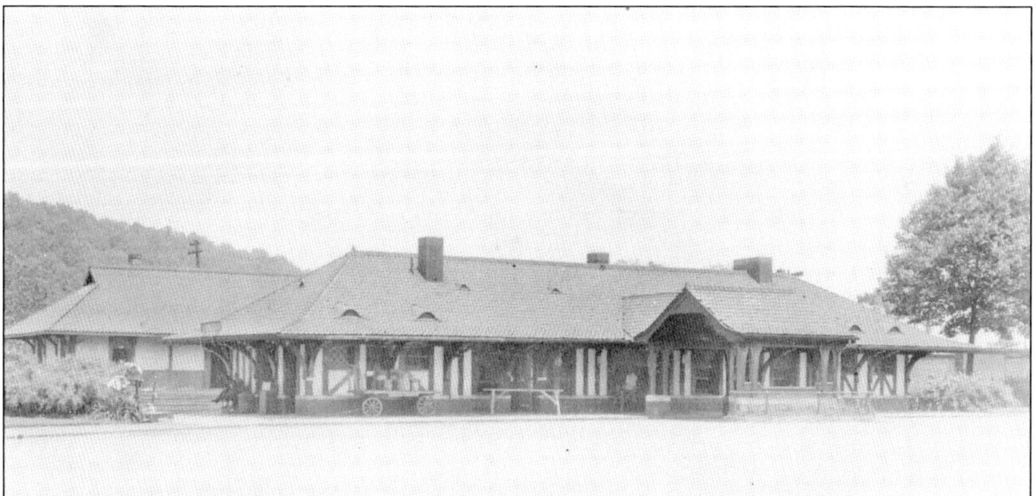

BILTMORE PASSENGER AND FREIGHT STATIONS, C. 1920. Vanderbilt's initial decision in July 1895 was to renovate the existing freight station and not build a new one. In May 1900, Chauncey Beadle wrote to the Southern Railroad Company to discuss the location of a new freight depot. The Olmsted firm sent plans for grading and landscaping around the freight station in February 1901. (William A. Barnhill Collection, Pack Memorial Public Library.)

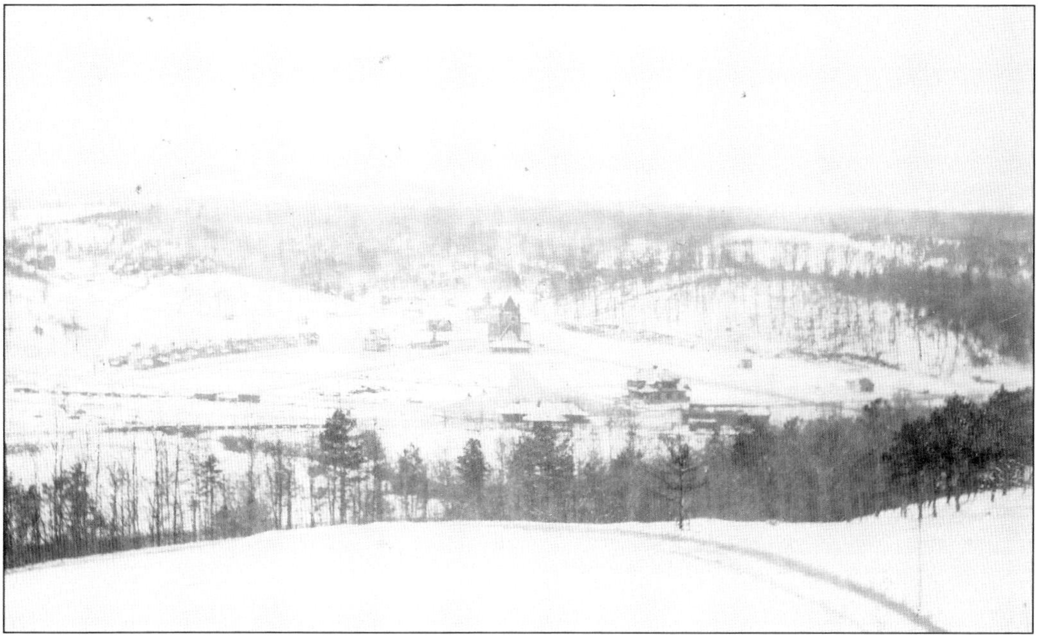

Biltmore Village from Kenilworth Inn, March 20, 1896. This wintry view of the village shows three of the primary anchor buildings designed by Richard Morris Hunt—All Souls Church, the Biltmore Estate Office, and the passenger station—strategically located within the symmetrical grid of streets. The temporary residences for workers are lined up in a row along All Souls Crescent, and the Rectory and the foundations of the Parish Hall are to the left of the church.

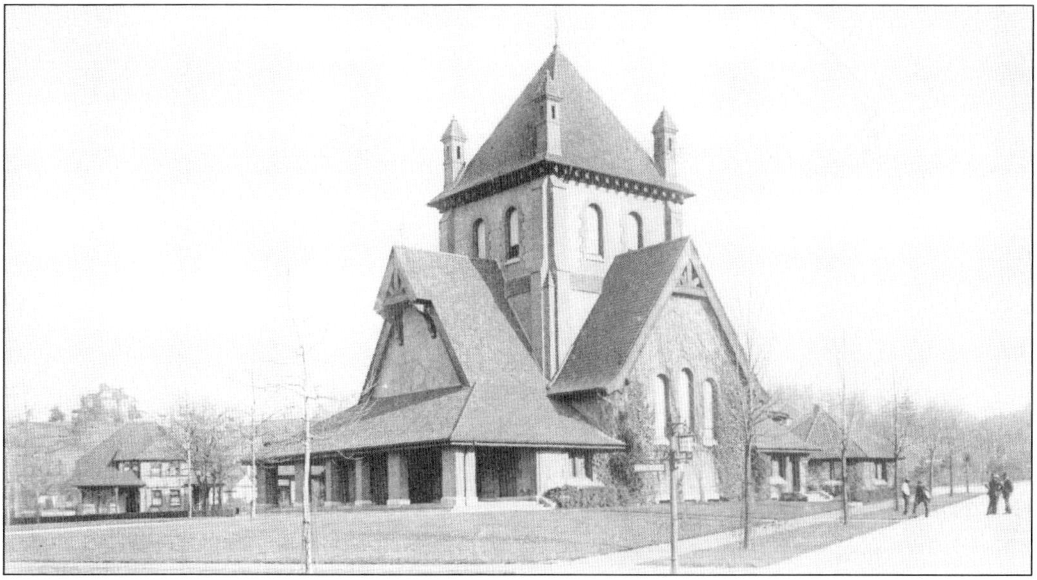

Postcard of All Souls Church and Rectory, c. 1900. In *Early Days: All Souls' Church and Biltmore Village* (1933), Marie Louise Boyer wrote, "The architectural style is early pointed or Gothic of the period of the transition from the Norman to Romanesque. This is shown by the pointed arches and the buttresses of the Gothic and the circular topped windows of the Norman." (Hal Branch.)

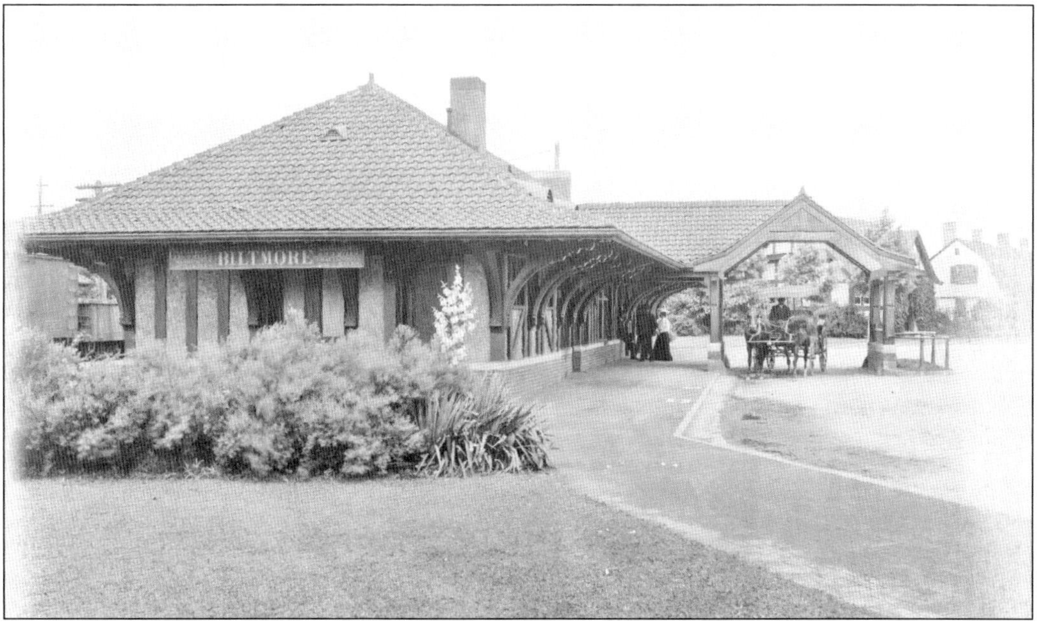

BILTMORE PASSENGER STATION, C. 1905. The station building and roads and walks to it were finished by April 1896, and the Olmsted firm sent instructions for completing the planting of the grounds and specified: "This area will be covered with loam and an edging of low bushes planted in the part nearest the station. . . . Four or five trees will be planted for shade near the edge of these grounds."

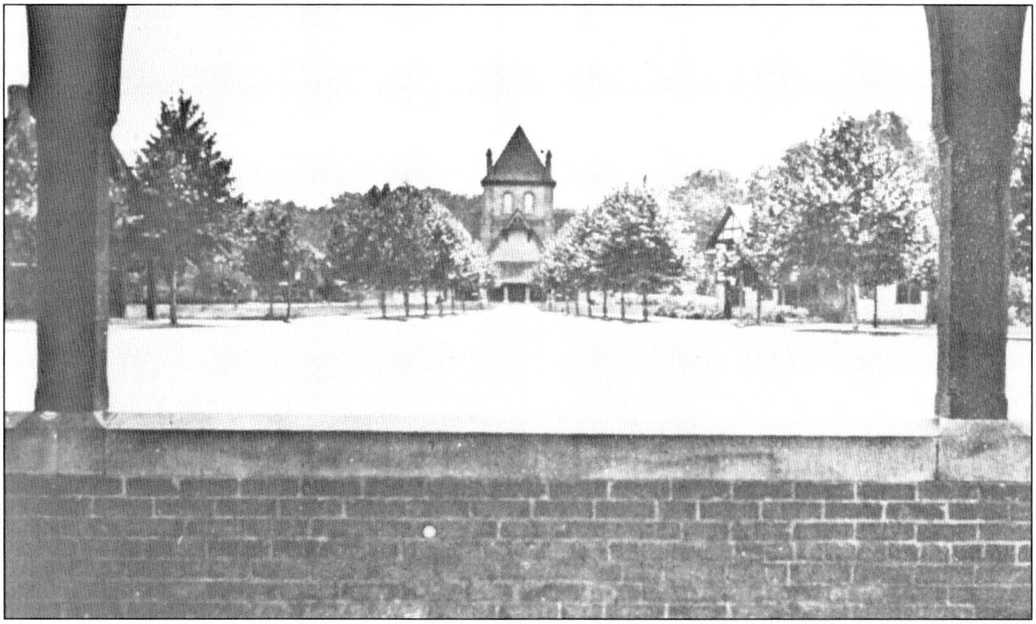

VIEW OF ALL SOULS CHURCH FROM PASSENGER STATION, C. 1905. Frederick Law Olmsted advised George Vanderbilt that it would be desirable that the village should have a social center "further removed from the noise of trains and the bustle of traffic," the position of which would be manifested by a church tower that "shall be apparent to strangers on stepping out from the station." (Frances Loeb Library, Harvard Graduate School of Design.)

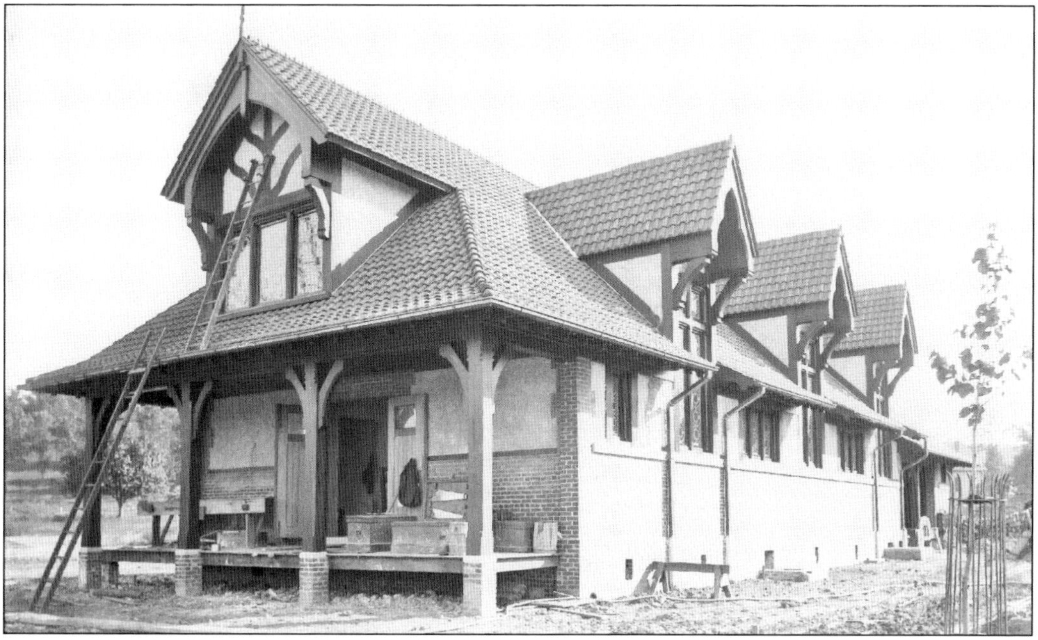

SUNDAY SCHOOL OR PARISH HALL UNDER CONSTRUCTION, C. 1895. The Parish Hall utilized similar architectural elements as the church but had its own distinctive design. Originally constructed as a freestanding building, the one-and-one-half-story structure featured a hipped roof with wide eaves, prominent dormers, a timbered trefoil trim, and a high, brick foundation wall.

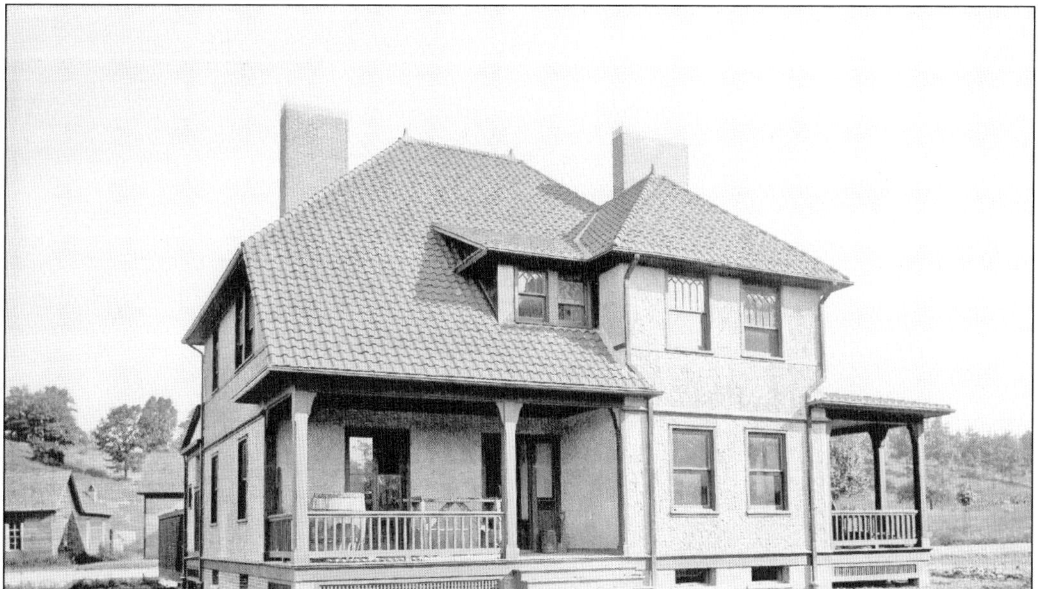

RECTORY, 1895. Asked by George Vanderbilt to rush construction, Richard Sharp Smith designed the Rectory, the first cottage to be built in the village. Situated near the Parish Hall, it became the residence of Dr. Rodney Swope, the first rector of All Souls Church. In 1899, a new, larger rectory was built for Dr. Swope on the southeast side of All Souls Crescent, and the old rectory became the schoolteacher's house.

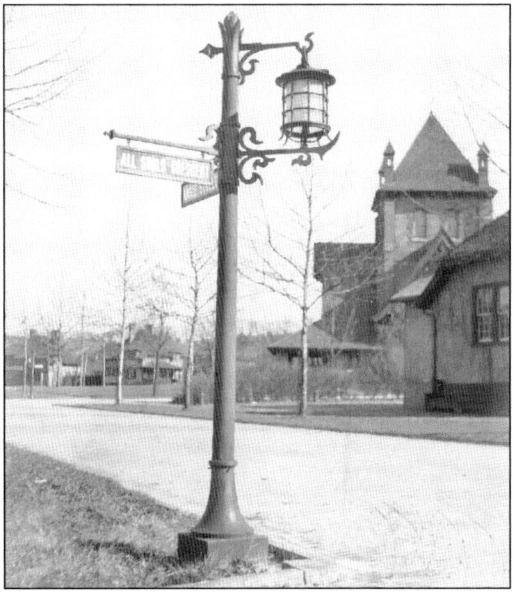

ALL SOULS CHURCH AND PARISH DAY SCHOOL, 1905. The Parish Day School opened in October 1898 with two teachers and 29 students. The school building in the right foreground was constructed in 1900. The Biltmore Village lampposts were designed especially for George Vanderbilt by Richard M. Hunt and were made to his special order by a Northern foundry. (North Carolina Collection, Pack Memorial Public Library.)

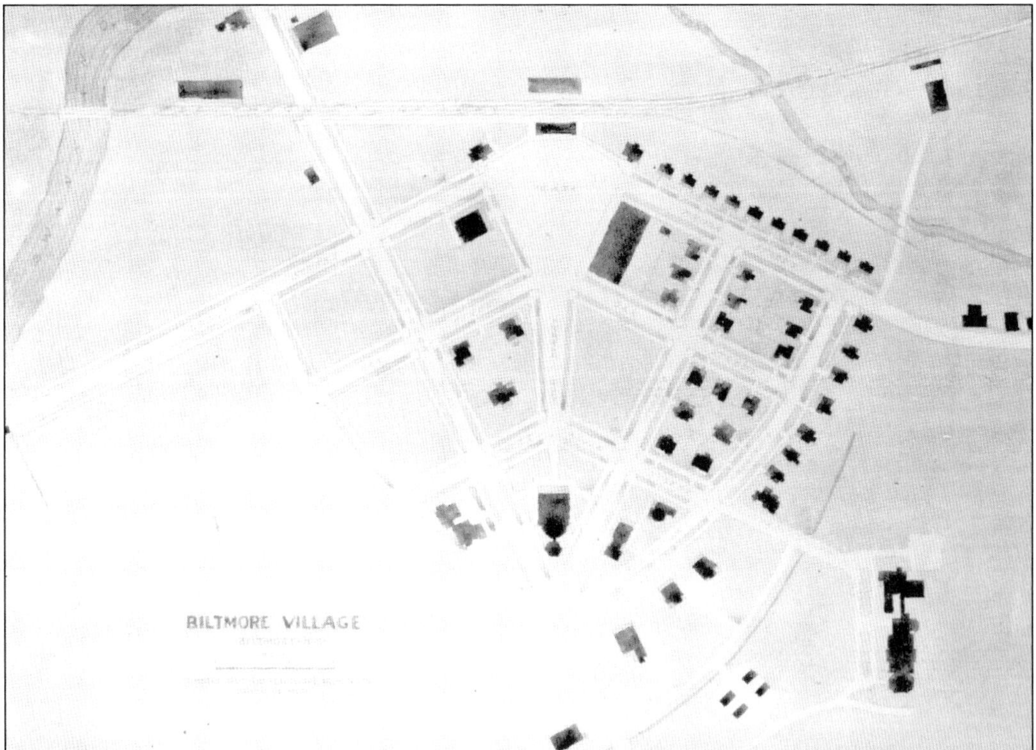

BILTMORE VILLAGE STREET PLAN SHOWING BUILDINGS, C. 1902. A four-page summary of buildings under construction in June 1900 included: the hospital and dispensary, 22 houses in the village, a freight depot, the day school building, the post office building, a store building on the east side of the square, two houses next to the Rectory, and three buildings south of the estate office, as well as numerous structures on the main estate. (National Park Service, Frederick Law Olmsted National Historic Site.)

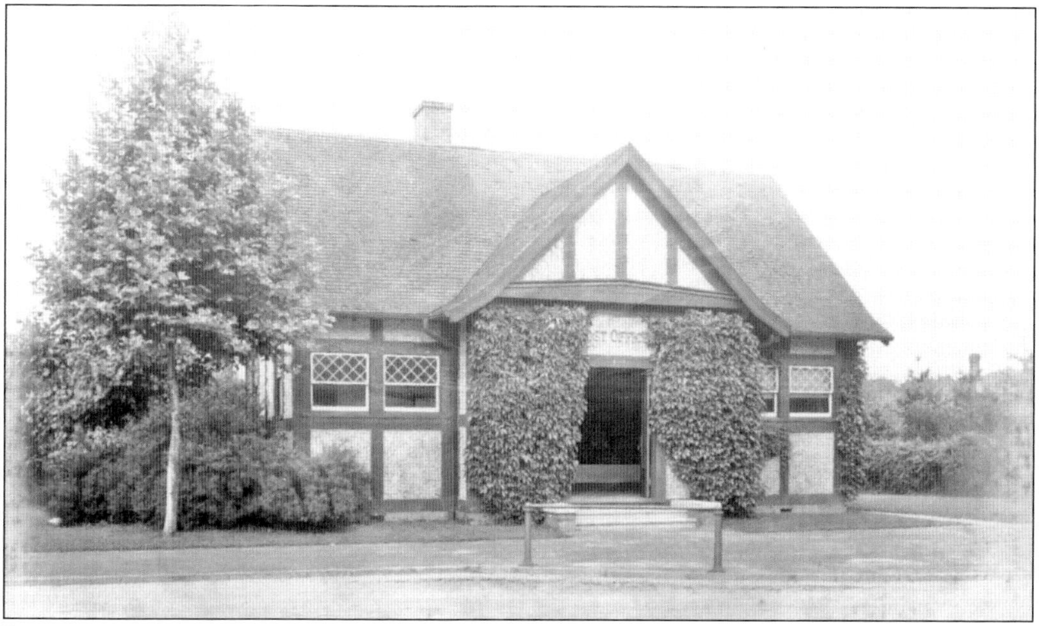

BILTMORE POST OFFICE, C. 1905. The post office was located in one of the old store buildings adjacent to the railroad tracks when George Vanderbilt purchased the village of Best. In March 1893, a petition to move the post office to the town of Victoria was not approved. This new post office, designed by Richard Sharp Smith and built in 1900, was located just east of the railroad station on Brook Street.

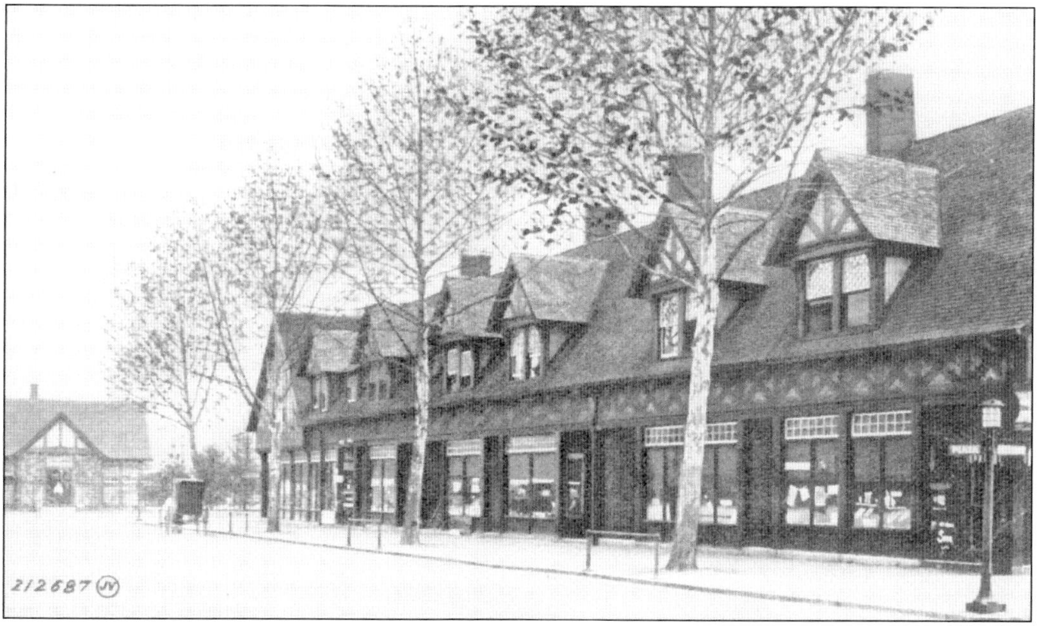

PLAZA BLOCK AND POST OFFICE, C. 1910. The Plaza Store Building with second-floor apartments was completed in late 1900 and filled the entire block on the east side of the Plaza, forming the core of Frederick Law Olmsted's proposed "business centre." Plaza tenants included a general merchandise store, dry goods, a grocery, a meat market, a produce market, hardware and paints, a café, a drugstore, and Biltmore Estate Industries. (Hal Branch.)

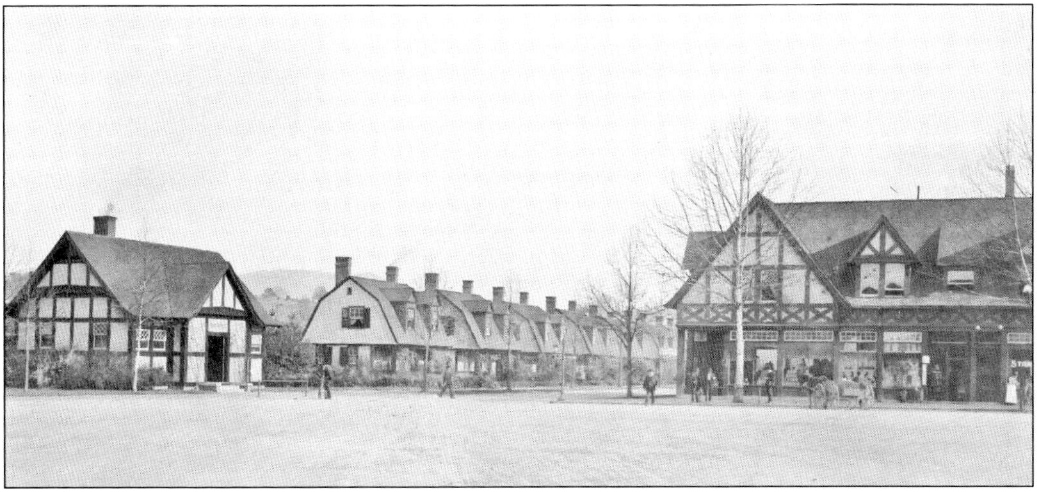

BILTMORE PLAZA AND BROOK STREET, C. 1906. Frederick Law Olmsted expressed his vision for the village to George Vanderbilt in a letter in December 1893: "Rather the effect should be that the village is obviously occupied by a community, the members of which are engaged, independently of the owner of the estate, in various kinds of business." (W. B. McEwen and Caroline Nichols McEwen Collection, D. H. Ramsey Library, Special Collections, University of North Carolina at Asheville.)

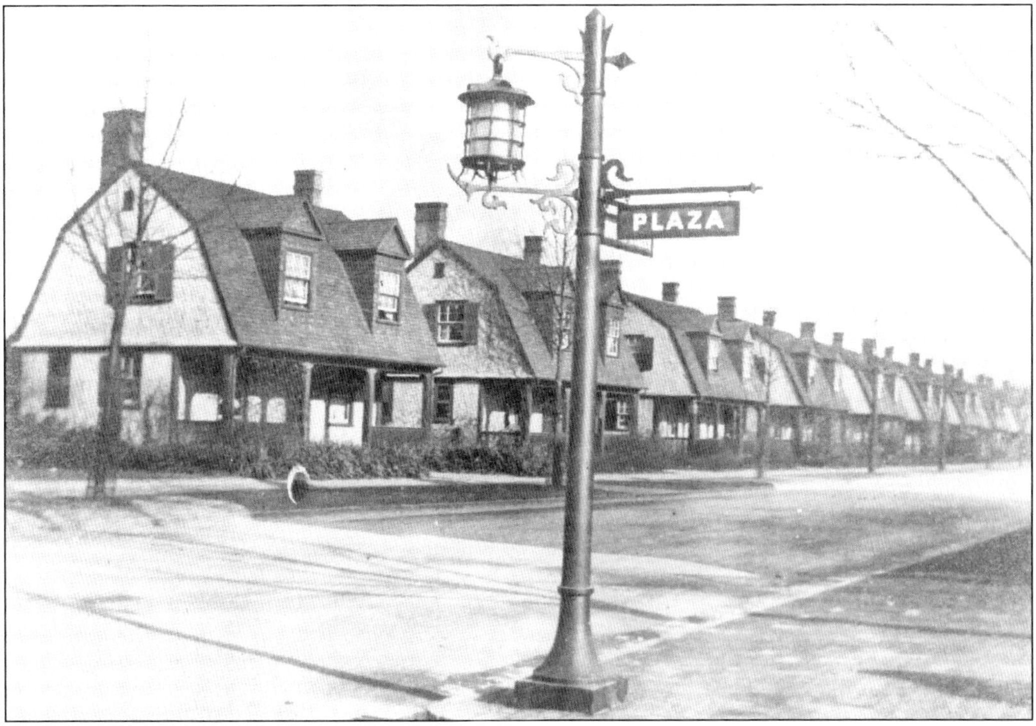

BROOK STREET COTTAGES, 1909. Richard Sharp Smith designed a row of 10 nearly identical cottages with gambrel roofs and twin dormers on Brook Street east of the Plaza. These cottages had the lowest rental rates due to their location between the busy thoroughfare leading east and the railroad tracks immediately behind them. (North Carolina Collection, Pack Memorial Public Library.)

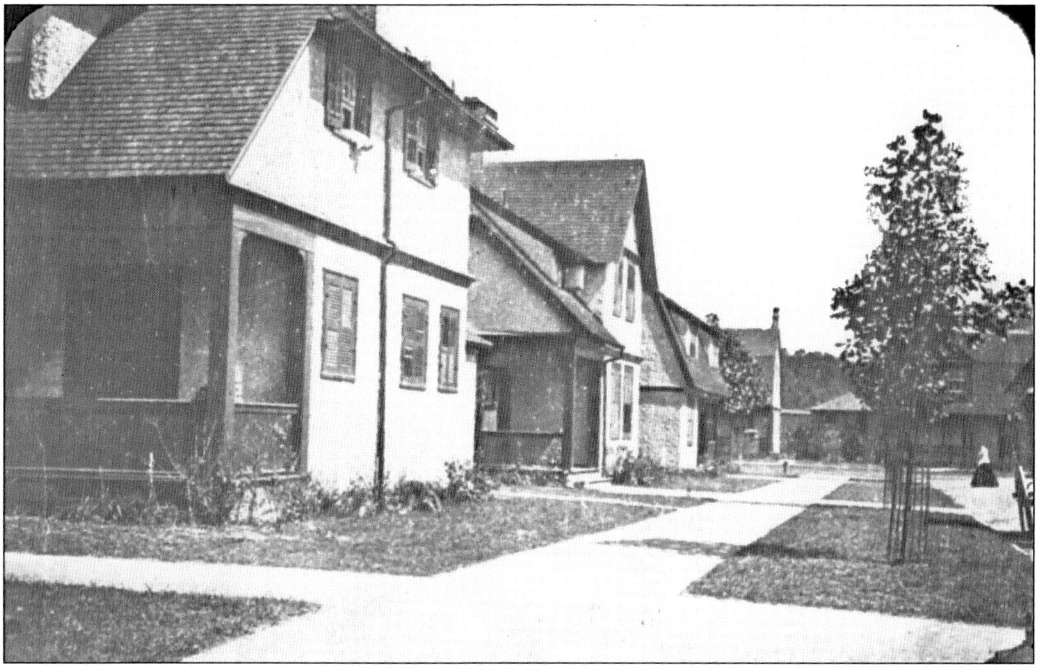

COTTAGES ON ALL SOULS CRESCENT BETWEEN OAK AND BROOK STREETS, C. 1900. The village cottages designed by Richard Sharp Smith were typically one-and-a-half or two-story structures featuring roughcast mortar or pebble dash exteriors, brick foundations and chimneys, variable roof styles from gambrel to hip roofs, multiple gables and dormers, half-timbered accents, and recessed porches. (Frances Loeb Library, Harvard Graduate School of Design.)

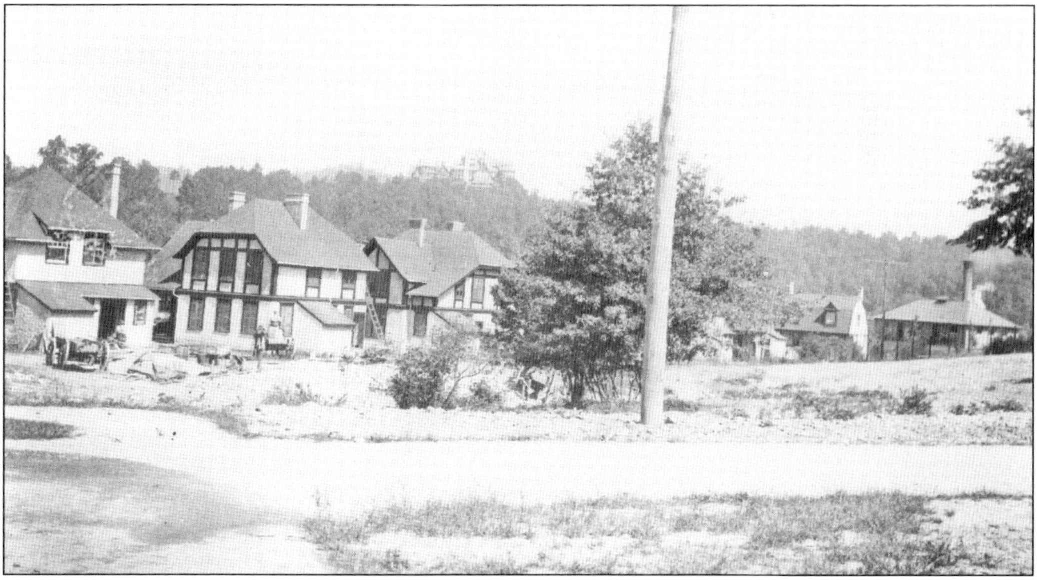

REAR VIEW OF COTTAGES NEARING COMPLETION, C. 1900. The three large cottages are on the east side of All Souls Crescent, and the one to the right with the gambrel roof is across the intersection on Brook Street. The building in the background on the right is believed to be the Biltmore powerhouse, constructed in 1898, which supplied electricity to the village. (National Park Service, Frederick Law Olmsted National Historic Site.)

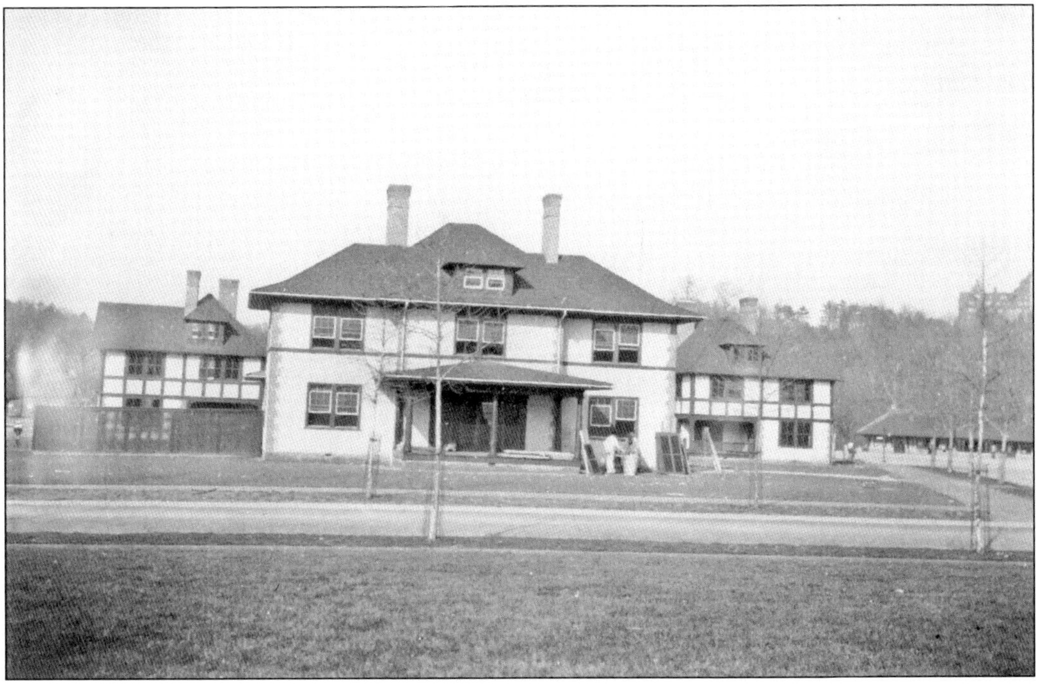

COTTAGE AT 4 SHORT STREET, C. 1900. This view, looking across Angle Street, includes the three large cottages constructed in the block bounded by Biltmore Road and Oak, Short, and Angle Streets. The passenger station is visible across the Plaza, and Kenilworth Inn is on the hill beyond. (National Park Service, Frederick Law Olmsted National Historic Site.)

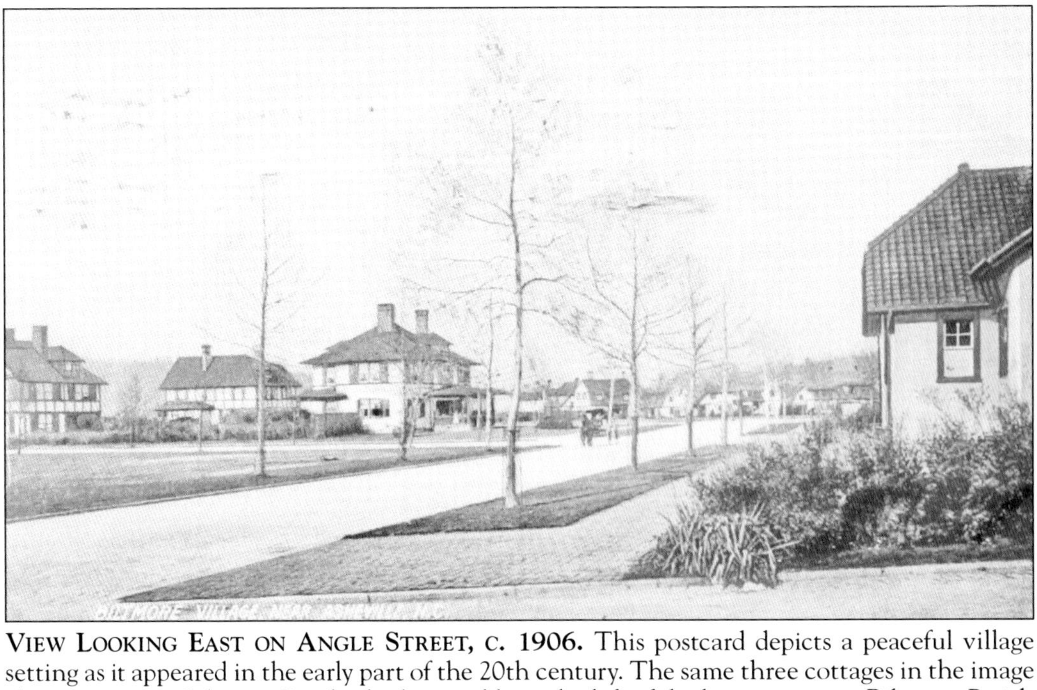

VIEW LOOKING EAST ON ANGLE STREET, C. 1906. This postcard depicts a peaceful village setting as it appeared in the early part of the 20th century. The same three cottages in the image above are across Biltmore Road, which is visible to the left of the horse carriage. Biltmore Parish School is in the right foreground. (Hal Branch.)

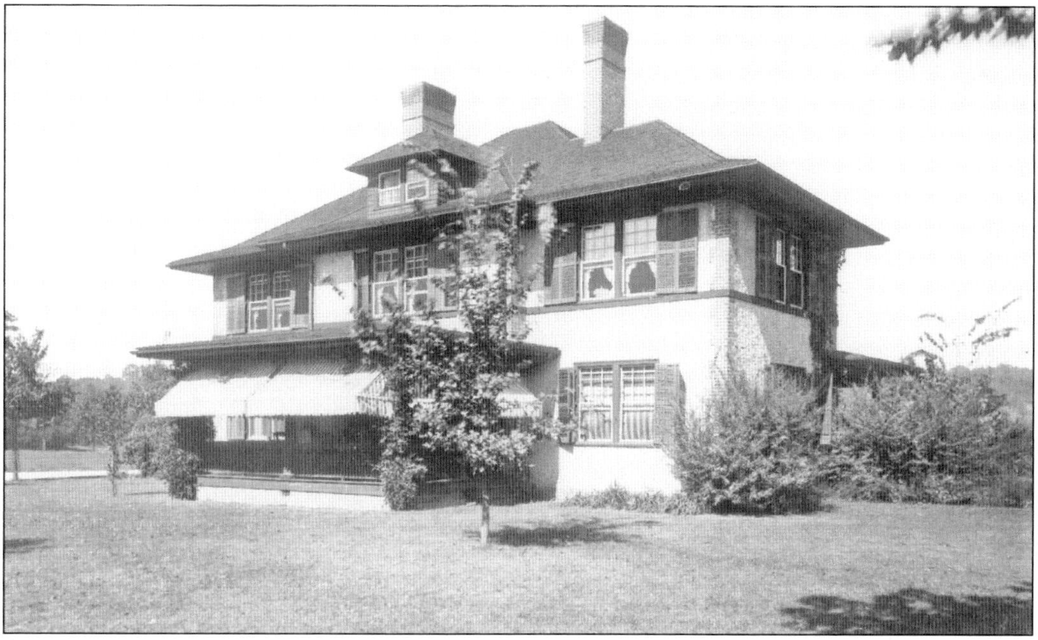

COTTAGE AT 4 SHORT STREET, C. 1906. The cottage seen on the previous page is shown adorned with landscaped grounds, window shutters, and canvas awning on the covered porch exposed to the southwest. The undeveloped block between Biltmore Road and All Souls Crescent and the village green beyond are seen to the left of the photograph. (National Park Service, Frederick Law Olmsted National Historic Site.)

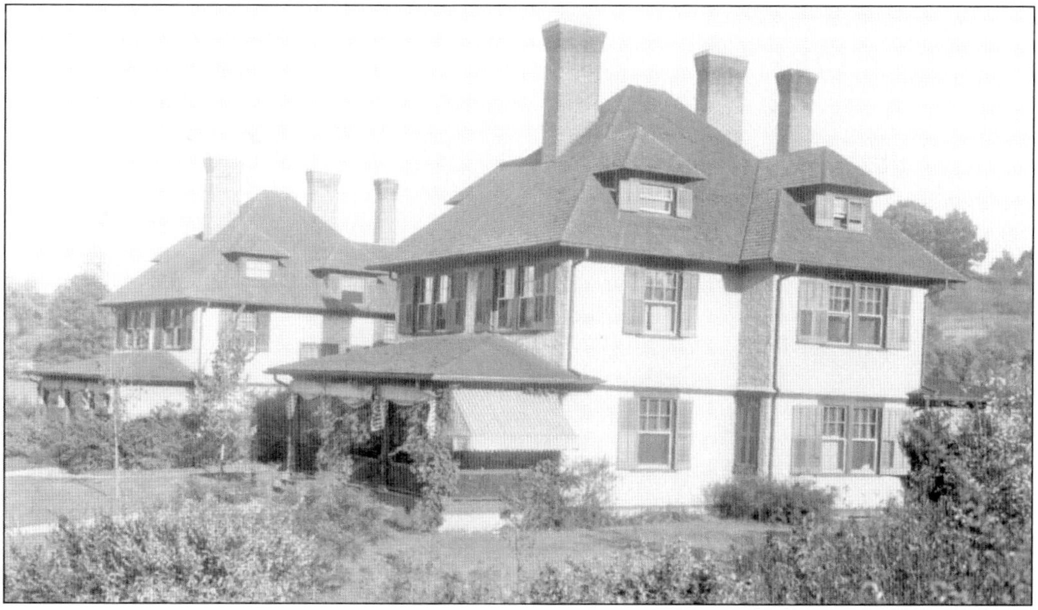

COTTAGES ON ALL SOULS CRESCENT, C. 1906. These two substantial cottages with hip roofs, which were constructed in 1900, are believed to have been located on the southeast side of All Souls Crescent and east of the new Rectory. Reed Hill is seen beyond to the right. The cottages block the view of Clarence Barker Memorial Hospital. (National Park Service, Frederick Law Olmsted National Historic Site.)

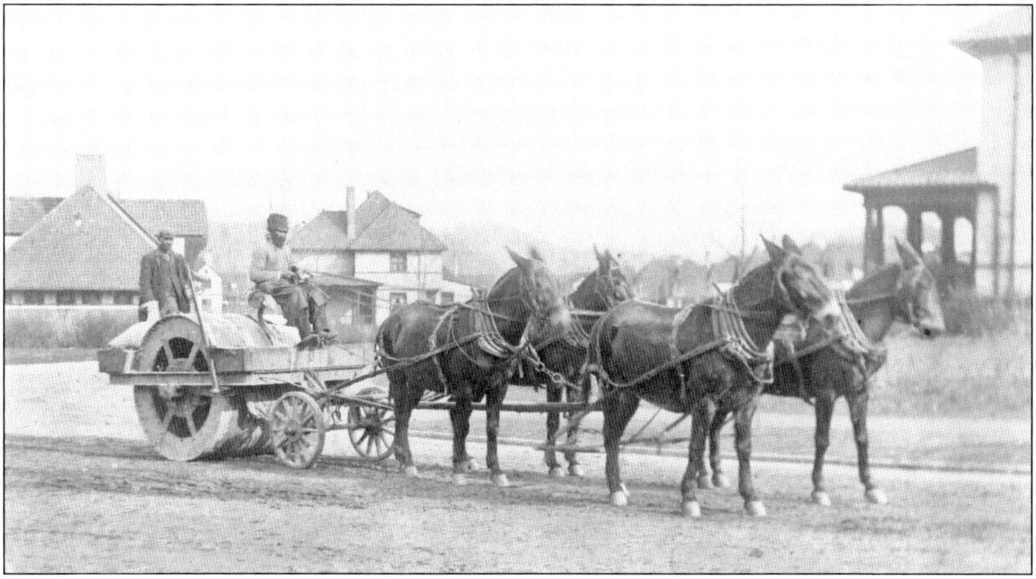

ROLLING THE MACADAM, C. 1905. Frederick Law Olmsted introduced expertly engineered macadam roads into the region on Biltmore Estate, Biltmore Village, and nearby public roads, including parts of Biltmore, Hendersonville, Swannanoa, and Victoria Roads, for which George Vanderbilt bore the majority of the expense. The crushed stone aggregate, applied as the surface over a deep bed of coarse stone, was maintained by watering and compacting with rollers, as seen here. (Biltmore Village Historic Museum.)

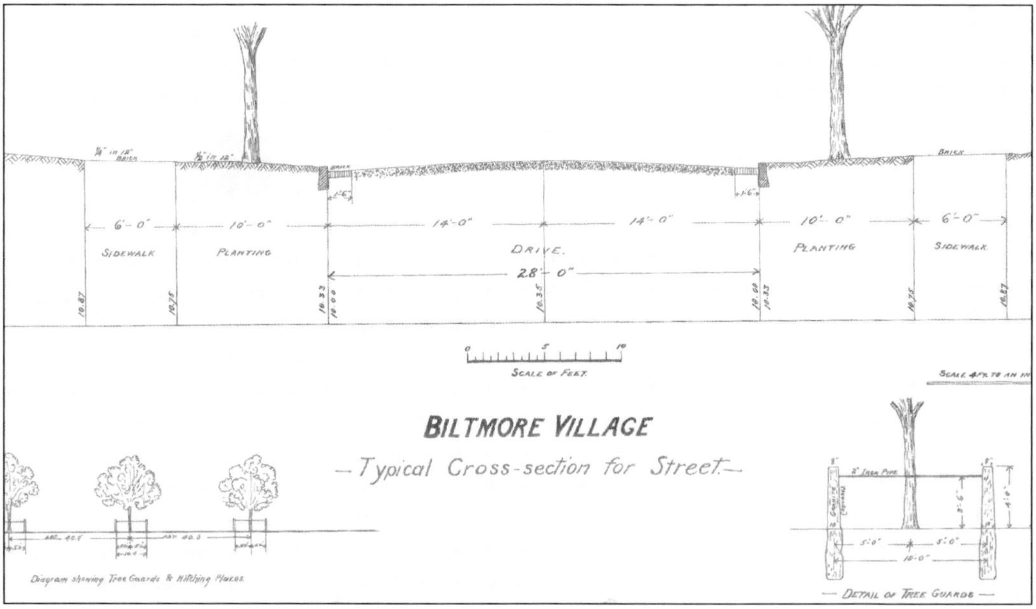

TYPICAL CROSS-SECTION FOR STREET. This drawing from the Olmsted firm provides the details and dimensions for the streets, tree planting spaces, sidewalks, tree guards, and hitching places for the village. Construction of the 28-foot-wide streets, crowned for proper drainage and lined with curbstones with drain inlets, brought state-of-the-art street engineering technology into the region. Ten-foot-wide tree planting trenches to insure adequate soil and space for root development set standards that are often not followed today.

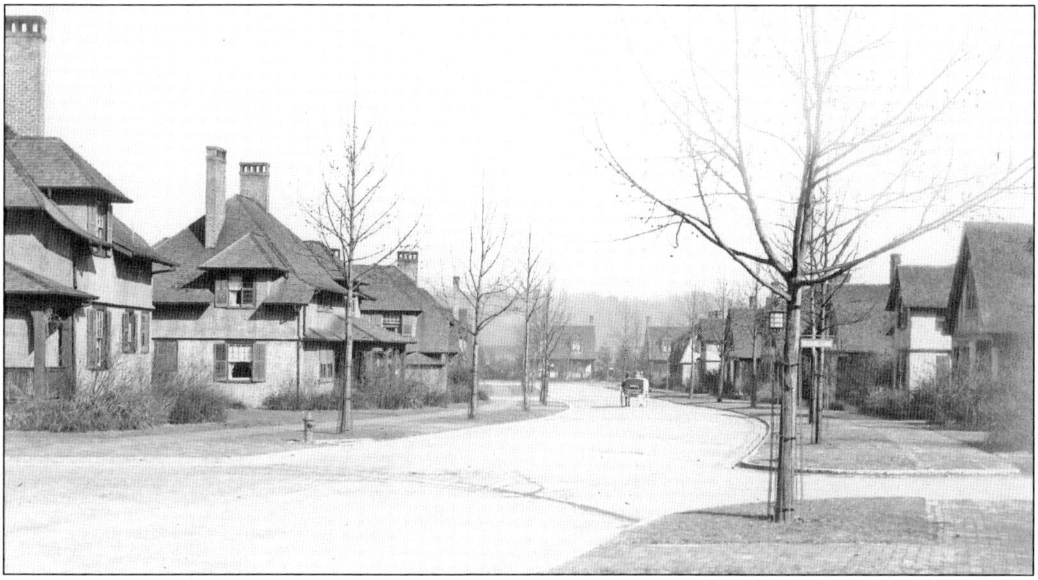

Cottages on All Souls Crescent, 1906. The skills and expertise of the architects and designers that George Vanderbilt brought together to create Biltmore Village are evident in this scene. Wide, tree-lined streets, brick sidewalks, and artistically designed landscaping complemented the vernacular architecture of the residential cottages surrounding the convenient business and social districts of the village. Amenities included indoor plumbing, steam heat, and electricity and telephone service supplied by underground conduits.

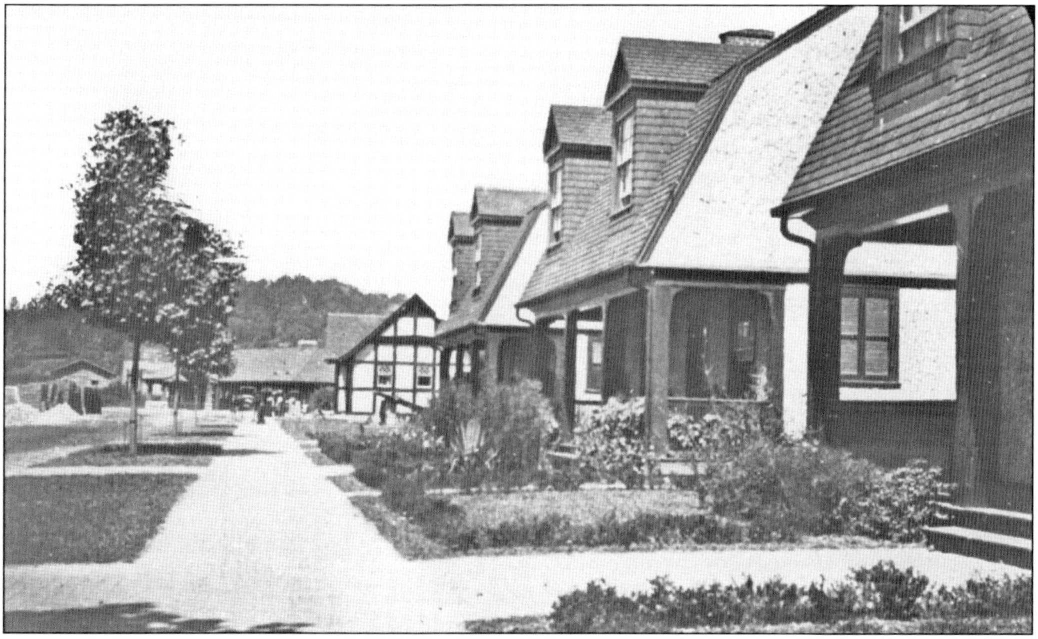

Landscaped Cottages on Brook Street, c. 1905. In this view looking west, three of the 10 identical cottages, the post office, and the new passenger station can be seen. The old train station on the left was temporarily used as a warehouse. The Olmsted Brothers' list of plants for the village lots contained nearly 300 varieties of trees, shrubs, roses, ornamental vines, and hardy, perennial flowers. (Frances Loeb Library, Harvard Graduate School of Design.)

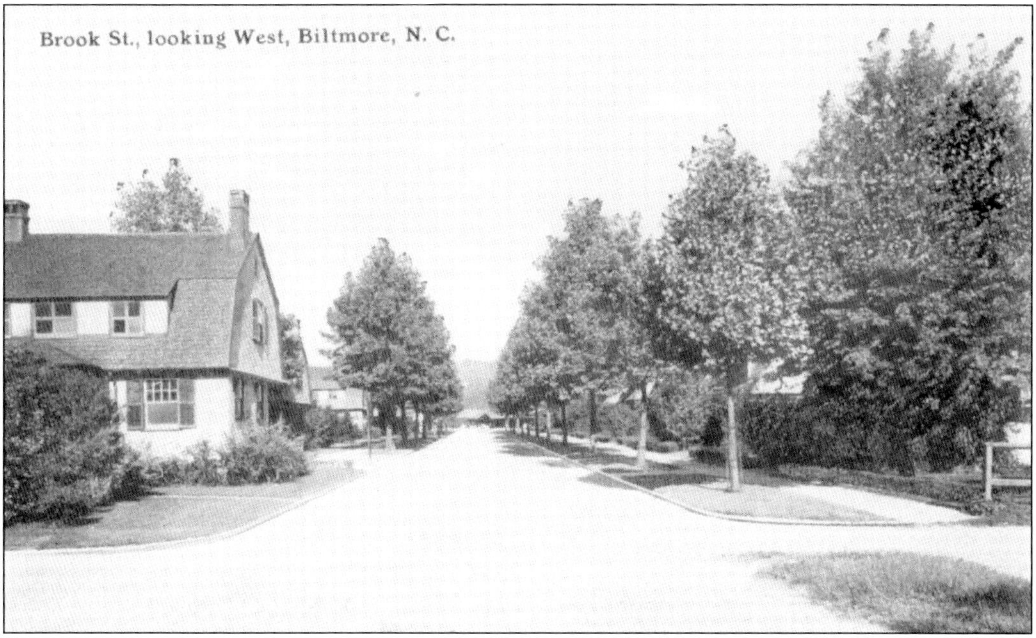

BROOK STREET, LOOKING WEST, C. 1906. This postcard view was taken from the intersection of Reed Street on the left and the road to the right, which led to the powerhouse on the north side of Sweeten Creek in the Y of the railroad tracks. The rows of tulip poplars continued past the Plaza and passenger station on Lodge Street to the Biltmore Estate Lodge Gate. (Hal Branch.)

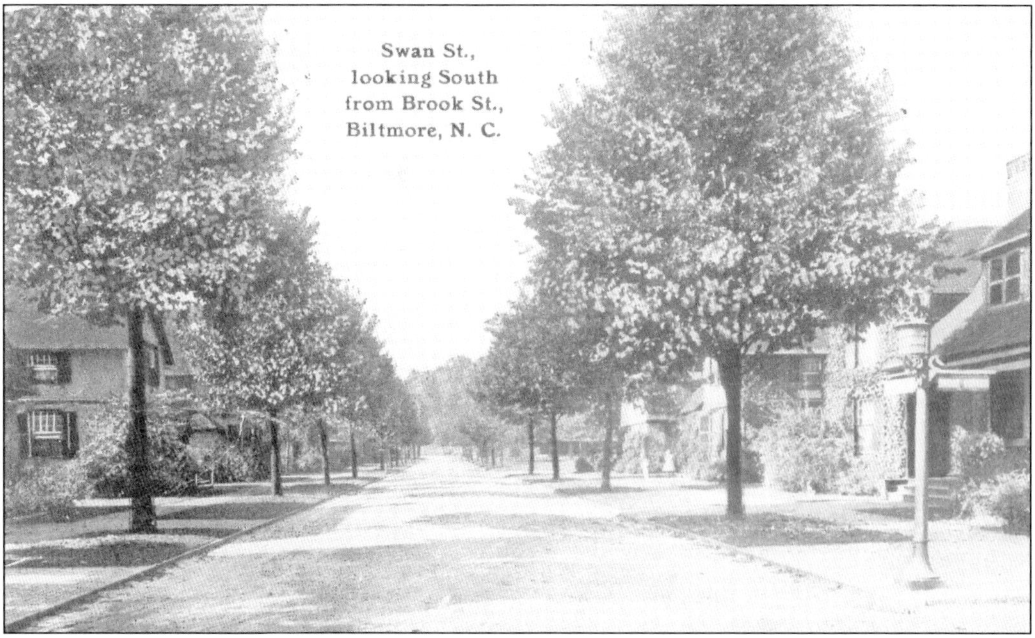

SWAN STREET, LOOKING SOUTH FROM BROOK STREET, C. 1915. In this postcard, the orderly plantings of linden trees lining the street characterized the village landscape envisioned by landscape architect Frederick Law Olmsted. Trees, he felt, were the "permanent furniture of the city." In April 1895, landscape department foreman James Gall reported needing 260 tree guards for Biltmore Village. (Hal Branch.)

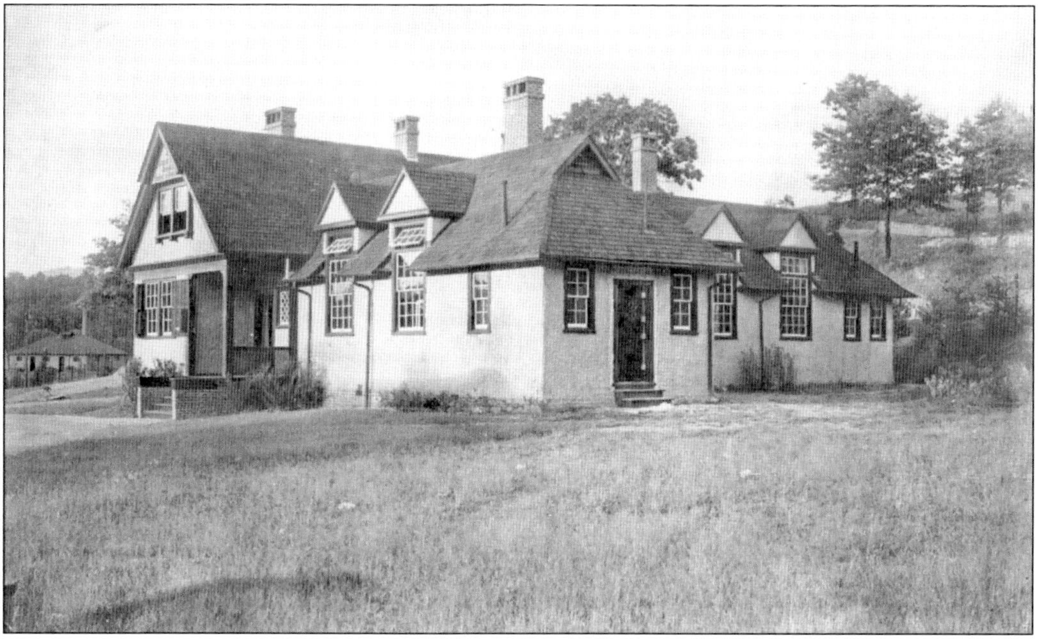

Clarence Barker Memorial Hospital, c. 1901. The 1901 All Souls yearbook stated, "The Hospital and Dispensary was erected and furnished by Mrs. Adele Elma Barker Schmidt and Mrs. Virginia Purdey as a memorial to their brother the late Clarence Barker, Mr. George Vanderbilt giving the institution the sum of twenty thousand dollars as a partial endowment." Vanderbilt also donated the land to his cousins for the hospital. (North Carolina Collection, Pack Memorial Public Library.)

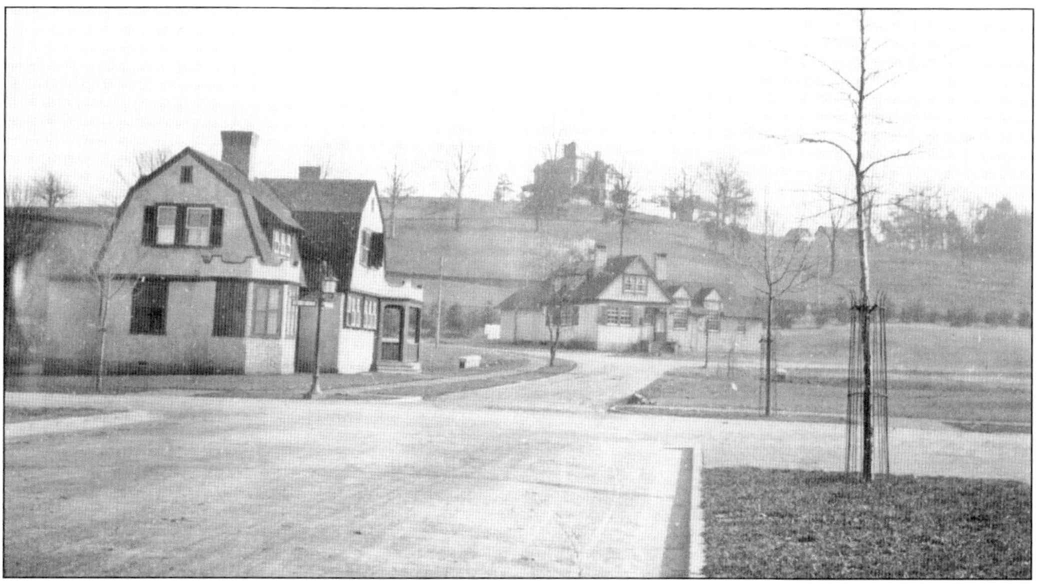

View of Cottage and Clarence Barker Memorial Hospital, c. 1900. Designed by Richard Sharp Smith, the hospital, with accommodations for 10 patients, was opened on September 4, 1900. The governing board was the rector and vestry of All Souls Church, with Dr. S. Westray Battle as the medical director. Samuel H. Reed's house, prominently situated on the hill, was built in 1892. (National Park Service, Frederick Law Olmsted National Historic Site.)

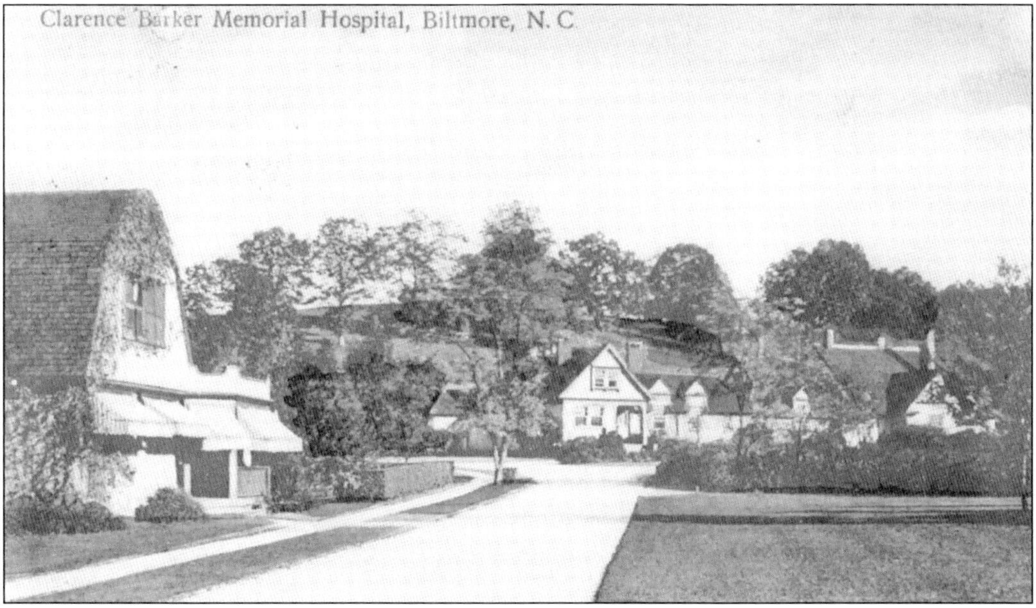

CLARENCE BARKER MEMORIAL HOSPITAL, C. 1902. By the summer of 1902, plans were being made for constructing a new wing. Architect William Henry Lord, hired to complete the unfinished work on the hospital, designed the addition. This postcard shows the expanded hospital. The cottage on the left was most likely the one known as the "Doctor's House," where the first resident physician, Dr. L. J. Holmes, lived. (Hal Branch.)

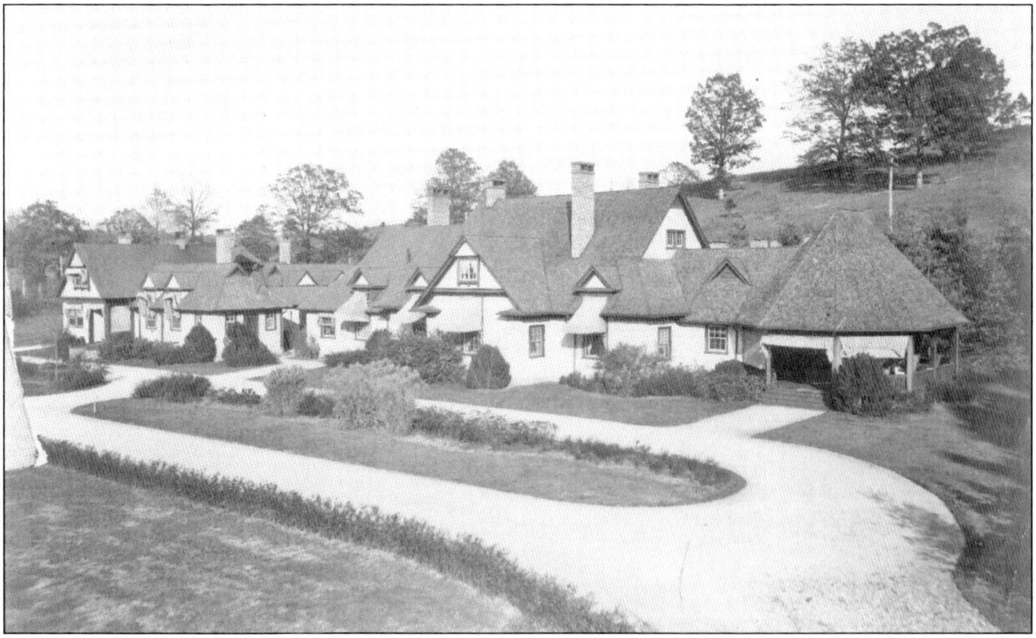

CLARENCE BARKER MEMORIAL HOSPITAL, C. 1906. The completed hospital with its new wing included additional beds and an operating room. On April 28, 1905, George Vanderbilt held a hospital benefit concert at Biltmore House. Chauncey Beadle ordered 1,500 programs for the concert. The program included director Emil Paur, soloist Madame Gadski, and the Pittsburg Orchestra. (National Park Service, Frederick Law Olmsted National Historic Site.)

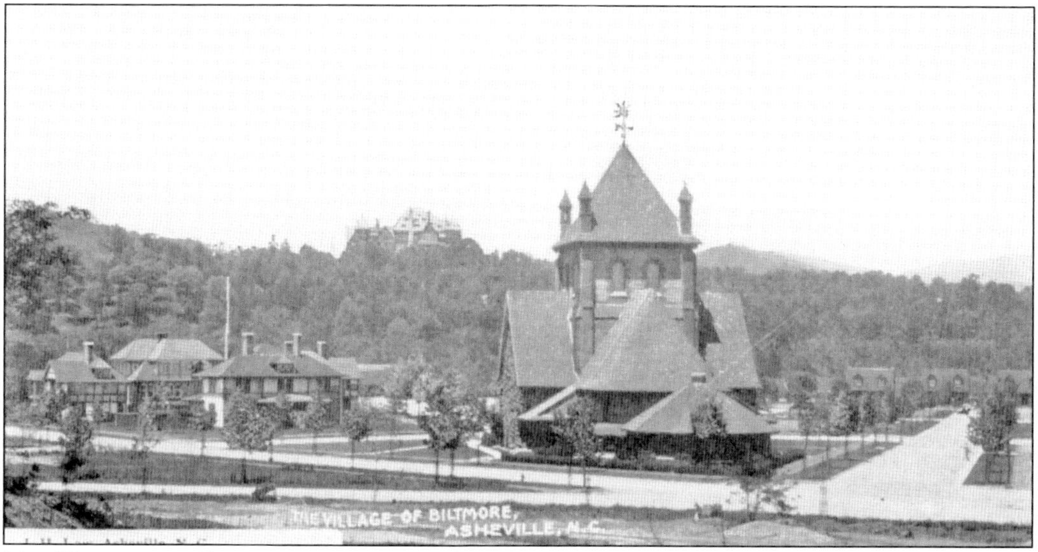

The Village of Biltmore, c. 1906. The village was largely complete and fully occupied by 1906. Forty-one houses provided steady rental income. Vanderbilt's and Olmsted's early goals for Biltmore Village had been met—that it not only be merely a dependency of a private estate, but also a community in its own right, complete with thriving businesses and convenient shipping, a school, a hospital, and a church with numerous philanthropic missions. (North Carolina Collection, Pack Memorial Public Library.)

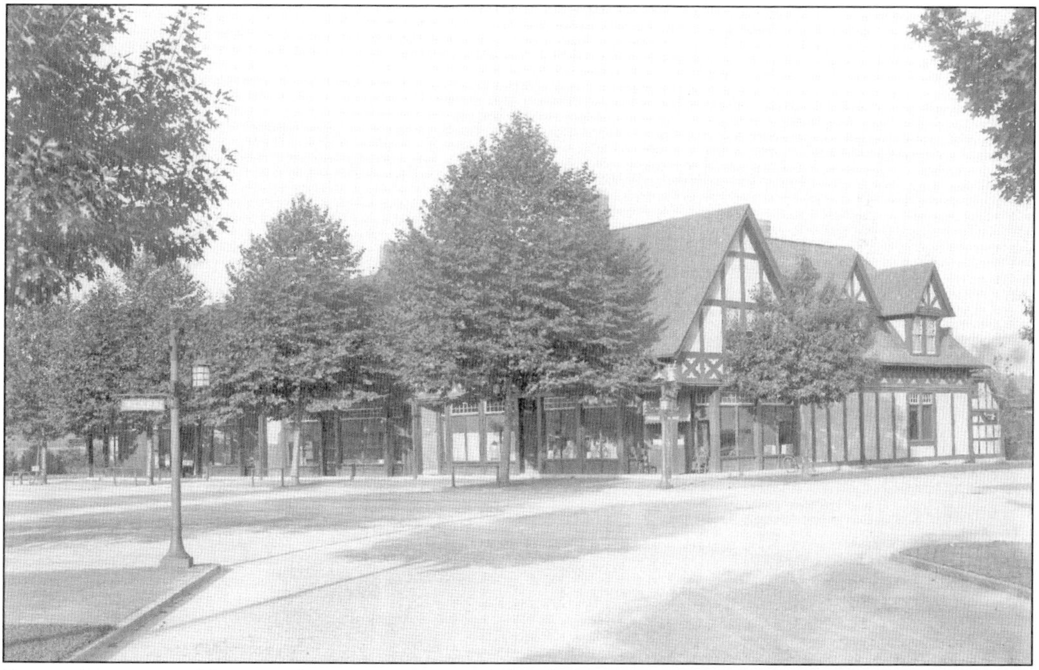

Plaza Block of Retail Stores, c. 1910. The Biltmore Drug Store occupied 10 Plaza at the corner of Oak Street from the time the building was opened for business. The 1912 City Directory listed other occupants: A. D. Stoner, general merchandise; the Star Meat Market; and Biltmore Estate Industries. Thomas McDonald, a barber, and Dr. A. S. Whitaker shared the building west of the passenger depot. (North Carolina Collection, Pack Memorial Public Library.)

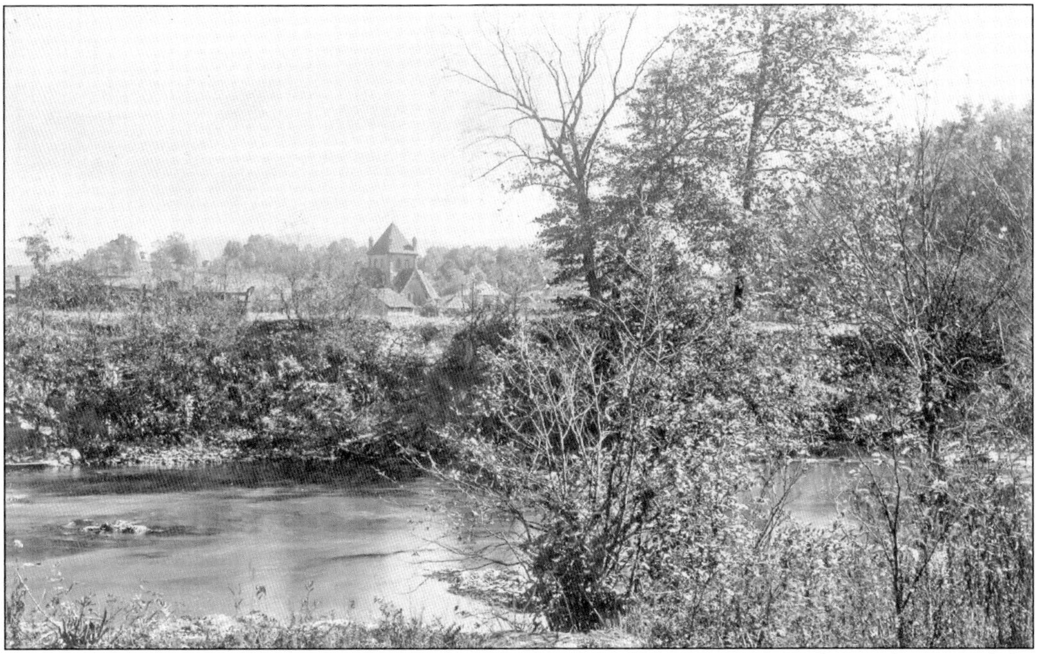

VIEW OF BILTMORE VILLAGE ACROSS THE SWANNANOA RIVER, C. 1900. This early view of the village was taken by John H. Tarbell as it appeared from near the Biltmore Road coming from Asheville. It portrays the village as a peaceful, idyllic setting with the commanding presence of All Souls Episcopal Church radiating a sense of community and welcoming all visitors. (North Carolina Collection, Pack Memorial Public Library.)

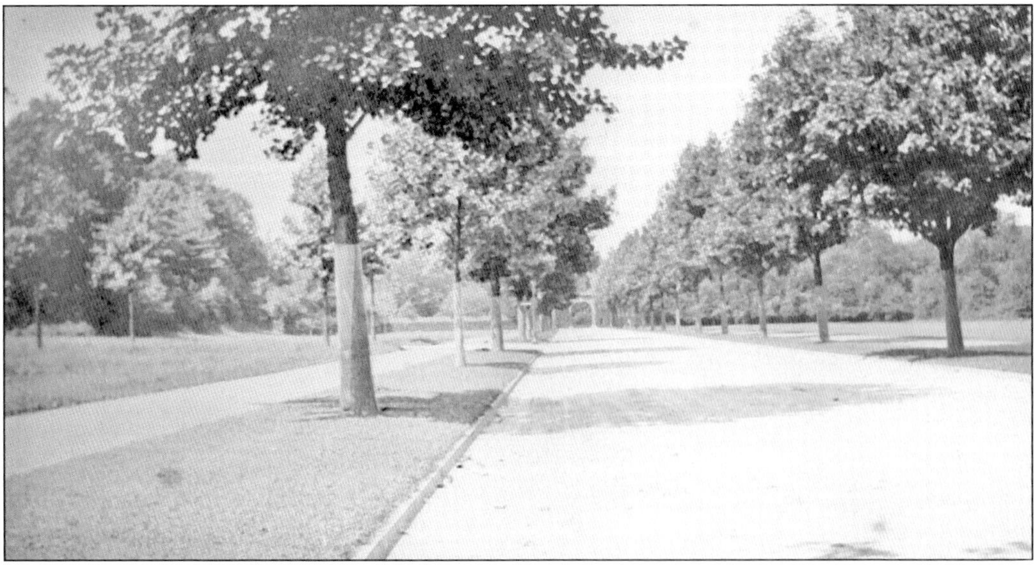

LODGE STREET, LOOKING WEST, C. 1910. The wide avenue lined with tulip poplars draws visitors from Biltmore Village into an intriguing world of picturesque and pastoral landscapes beyond the gatehouse of Biltmore Estate. The village, although functioning as a separate and independent community, became a fitting portal of entry to America's grandest country estate. (W. B. McEwen and Caroline Nichols McEwen Collection, D. H. Ramsey Library, Special Collections, University of North Carolina at Asheville.)

Three

Work, Play, Worship

In the article "Vanderbilt of the Mountain" in the September 1909 issue of *Ladies World Magazine*, author Day Allen Willey wrote, "Leave it and go down where three hundred people of this little domain are spending their lives out of his sight, out of his hearing. There is Biltmore Village. Strolling along its highways it is easy to think you are in England, with the hawthorns at the corners of the 'roads' and 'lanes' instead of streets and avenues, the very English design of church, with its chimes and service, which is really Anglican rather than Episcopal, the cottages of rural Britain with even their roses and vines. In Biltmore Village are the shops where the Vanderbilt colony trade, the post-office and the offices of the Vanderbilt estate. In the houses dwell these folk, the trades-people and some Northerners who come here to enjoy the winter climate. Biltmore Village has no saloon, no newspaper." As early as 1895, months before Biltmore House opened and with only a few cottages constructed, George Vanderbilt was anxious to attract reputable tenants of strong character, good health, and financial stability. He advertised nationally as well as locally, hoping that the reputation of Asheville and the surrounding mountain resorts would attract prospective residents, either year-round or seasonal. Advertisements generated interest from more than 20 states and promoted "Attractive homes for rent, furnished and unfurnished houses in Biltmore Village . . . new houses with all modern conveniences, beautiful surroundings, pure water, and artistic kept grounds." Frederick Law Olmsted Jr. wrote to his father on February 12, 1895, "Mr. V. wants to make a presentable show with his village as soon as possible. He wants to make it agreeable to live in as soon as possible." A few employees of the estate resided in the village at various times. The Plaza Store Building was completed in 1900 with merchant or shop spaces at street level and second-floor apartments, making it attractive to prospective entrepreneurs. Residents included railroad employees, a barber, a druggist, a postman, a grocer, a butcher, and other shopkeepers. The hospital employed a doctor and nurses, and the Parish School employed teachers. All Souls Church, with its various outreach programs, educational classes, and clubs, formed the heart of the village social center, making it a vibrant place to live, work, play, and worship.

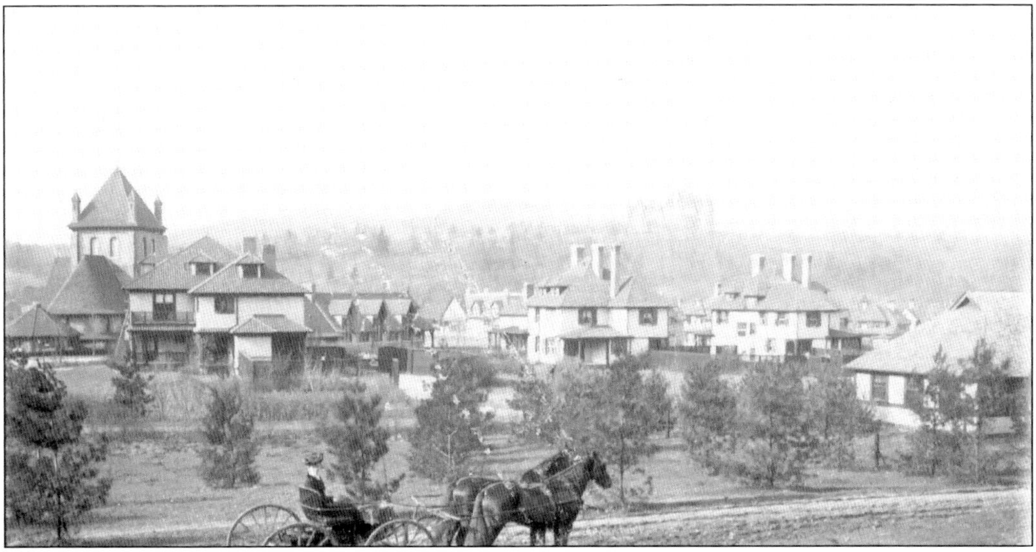

BILTMORE VILLAGE, 1903. Viewed from a hill on the south side of the village, All Souls Church stands out as the focal point of the community, both architecturally and socially. Clarence Barker Memorial Hospital is seen in the right foreground. Kenilworth Inn, constructed in 1890–1891, dominates a hill above the Swannanoa River on the north side of the village. (North Carolina Collection, Pack Memorial Public Library.)

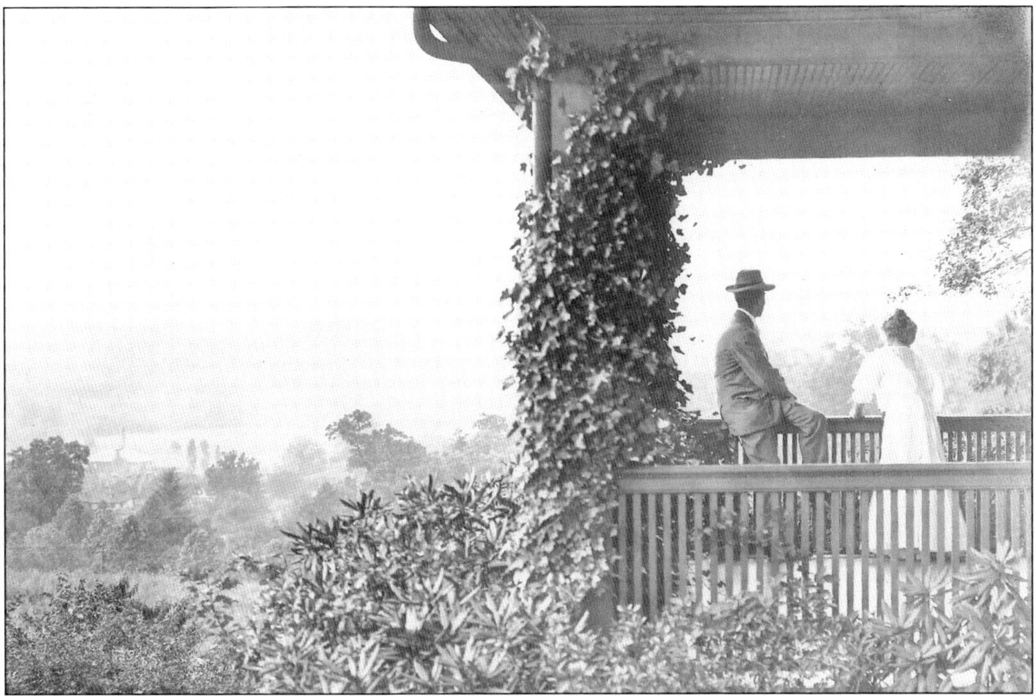

VIEW FROM EASTCOTE, 1906. Chauncey D. Beadle and his wife, Margaretta, resided at Eastcote, his home on Brandon Hill overlooking Biltmore Village. Hired in 1890 as the estate's nurseryman, Beadle supervised the landscaping of the village planned by the Olmsted firm. He assumed the role of estate superintendent after Charles McNamee left in 1904 and managed the business affairs of the estate and village until his retirement in 1945. (Donated by Jeanette Angel.)

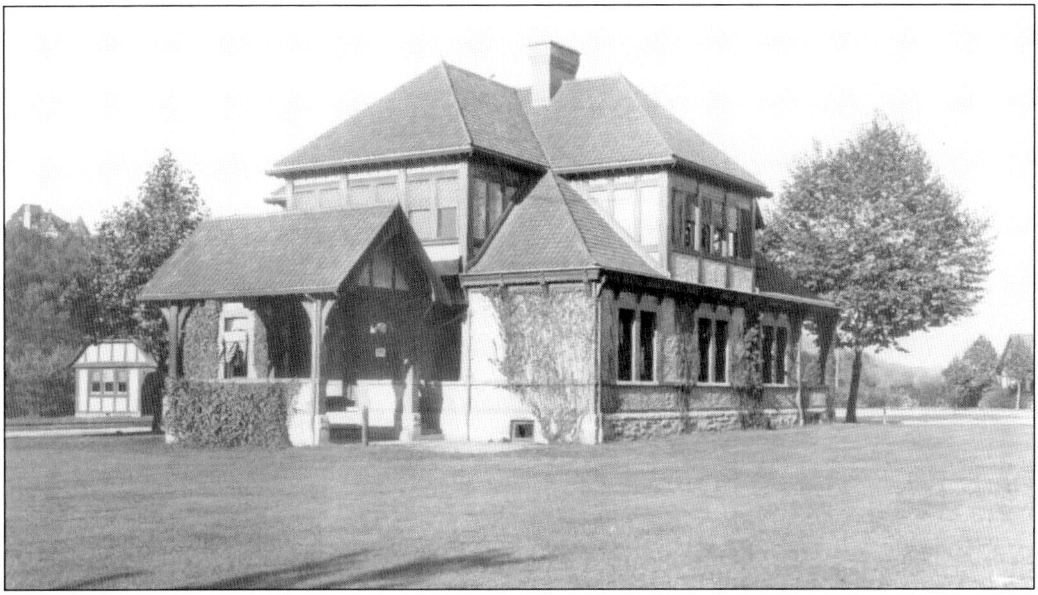

REAR VIEW OF BILTMORE OFFICE AND PORTE-COCHERE, C. 1906. From this office, estate superintendent Charles McNamee and later Chauncey Beadle conducted the general business affairs of the estate and Biltmore Village. The small half-timbered building across the street on the left was shared by the doctor's office and barbershop for many years and later was the first office of the Biltmore-Oteen Bank in the late 1920s. (National Park Service, Frederick Law Olmsted National Historic Site.)

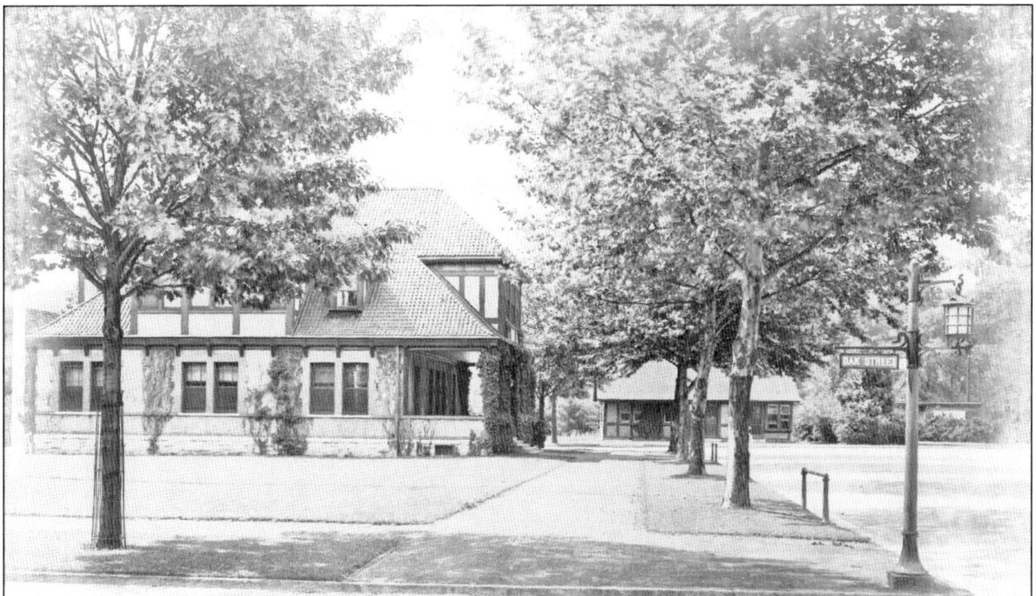

BILTMORE OFFICE FROM OAK STREET, C. 1910. The Biltmore Forest School opened in the fall of 1898 and held winter classes on the second floor. By 1925, a small garage had been added in the rear and was used by the Biltmore Village Fire Department. The city purchased the property in 1929 and converted the top floor into living space for firemen until 1975. The Biltmore Company leased the first floor until buying the building back in the late 1970s.

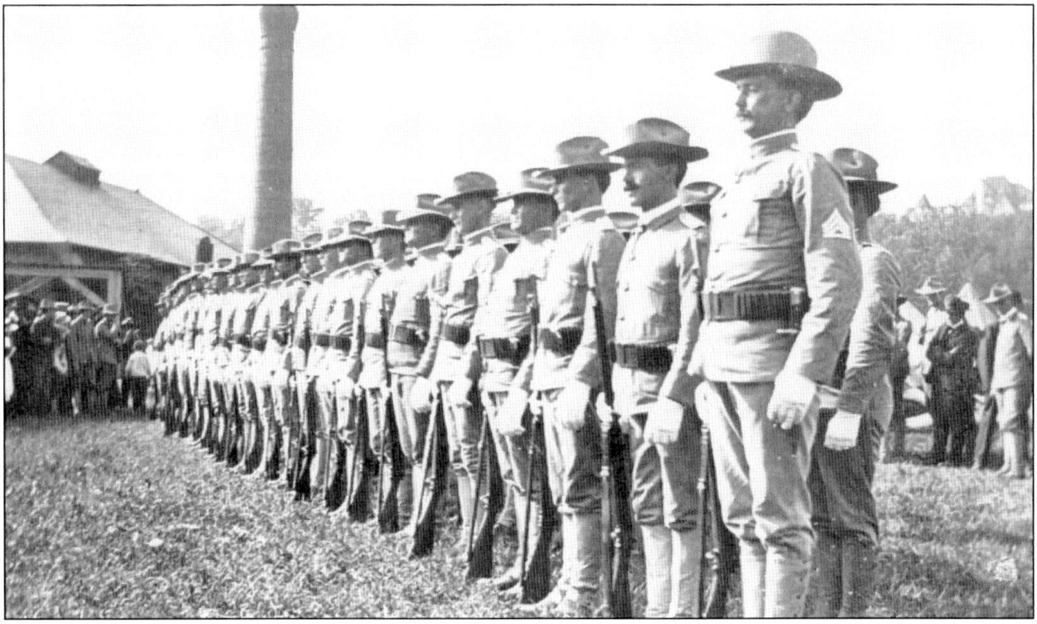

Drill Exercises during the Spanish-American War, 1898. The village greens were used for many different events over the years, including military operations. As seen in these images, a regiment of soldiers set up a temporary encampment for training during the Spanish-American War. The 1st Regiment of the National Guard (about 600 men) made a summer encampment for five days in August 1903. During both world wars, to aid the war effort, Edith Vanderbilt offered the military use of land and buildings for camps or training purposes. In June 1918, Chauncey Beadle advised Edith, "The United States, through Captain Streeman of the Quartermasters Department, General Hospital No. 12, Kenilworth, desires a lease on the dwelling No. 16 All Souls' Crescent (the former Rectory and recently occupied by Dr. Boyer) Biltmore, as Officers Quarters." A cottage and three stores in Biltmore Village were still being leased by the U.S. government in February 1920. (Both, North Carolina Collection, Pack Memorial Public Library.)

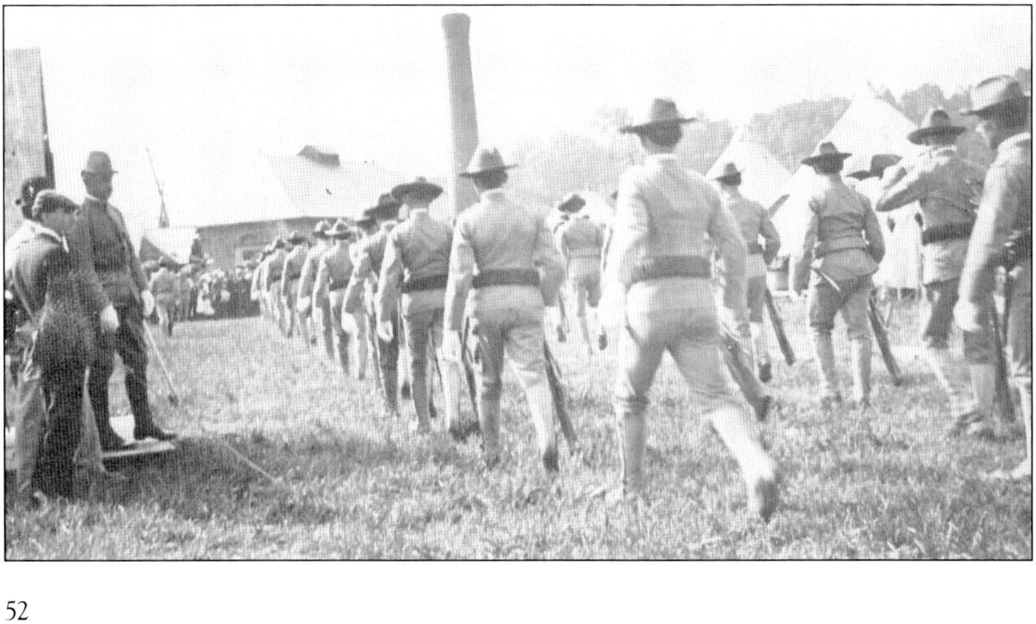

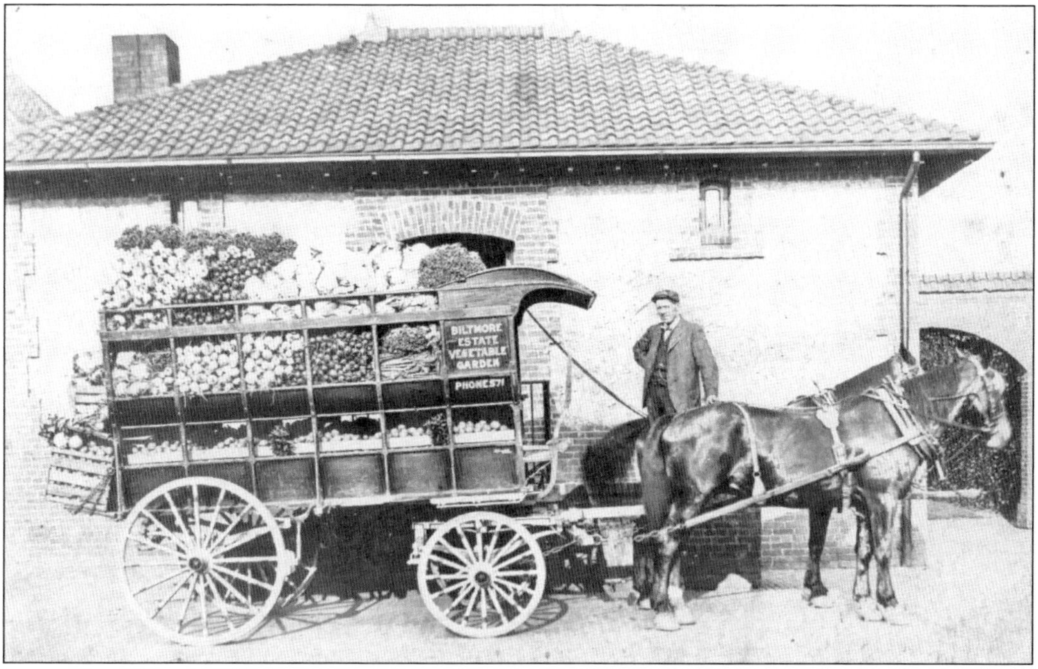

Biltmore Estate Vegetable Wagon, c. 1900. The Biltmore Estate Truck Farm, or Market Garden, grew extensive varieties of vegetables for sale in town and the surrounding communities. Biltmore Village grocers, restaurants, and area inns could be ensured of obtaining top-grade produce delivered fresh daily or as needed to supply their customers. The 1912 City Directory listed G. S. Arthur as manager of the Biltmore Vegetable Garden. (Estate of Agnes [Bell] Barber Blake.)

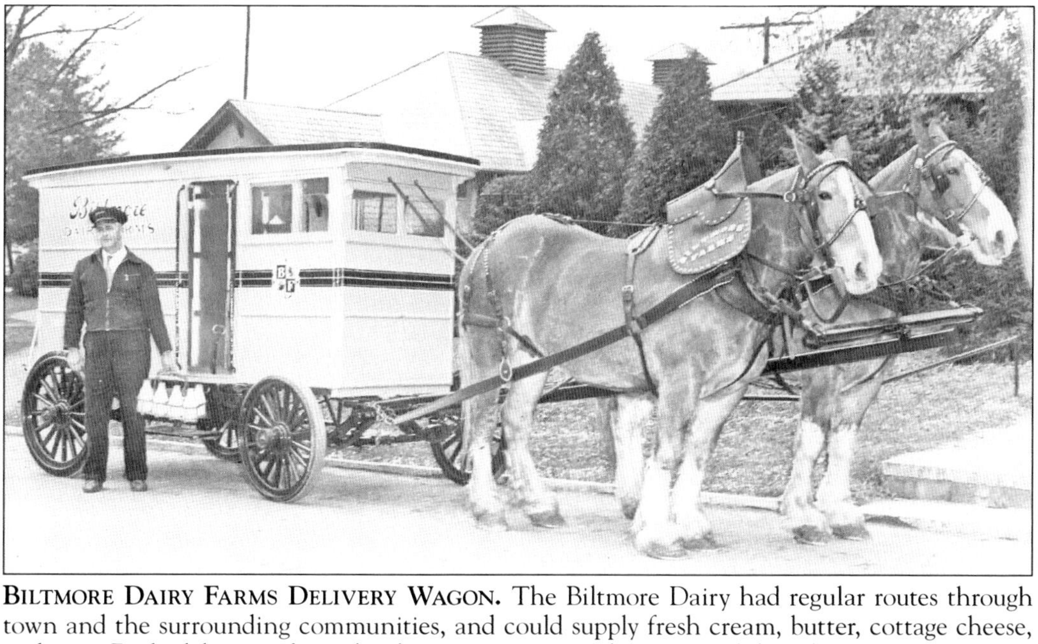

Biltmore Dairy Farms Delivery Wagon. The Biltmore Dairy had regular routes through town and the surrounding communities, and could supply fresh cream, butter, cottage cheese, and eggs. Daily deliveries from the dairy were promoted in some of the advertising for George Vanderbilt's rental cottages on Vernon Hill on the north side of the Swannanoa River.

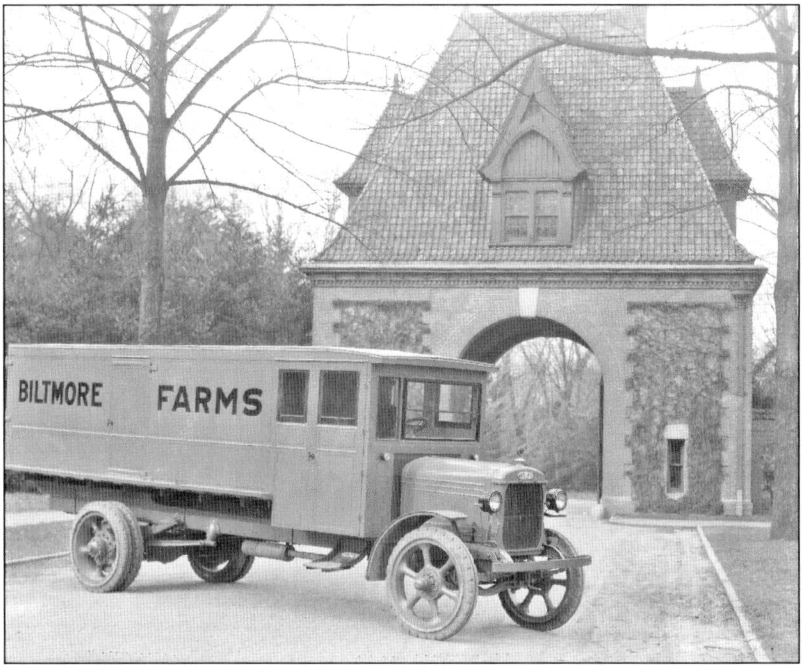

BILTMORE FARMS TRUCK, 1920. Transportation methods changed with time, but the Biltmore Dairy's service and quality of products maintained an impeccable record, and the farm's reputation continued to grow over the years. (E. M. Ball Collection, D. H. Ramsey Library, Special Collections, University of North Carolina at Asheville.)

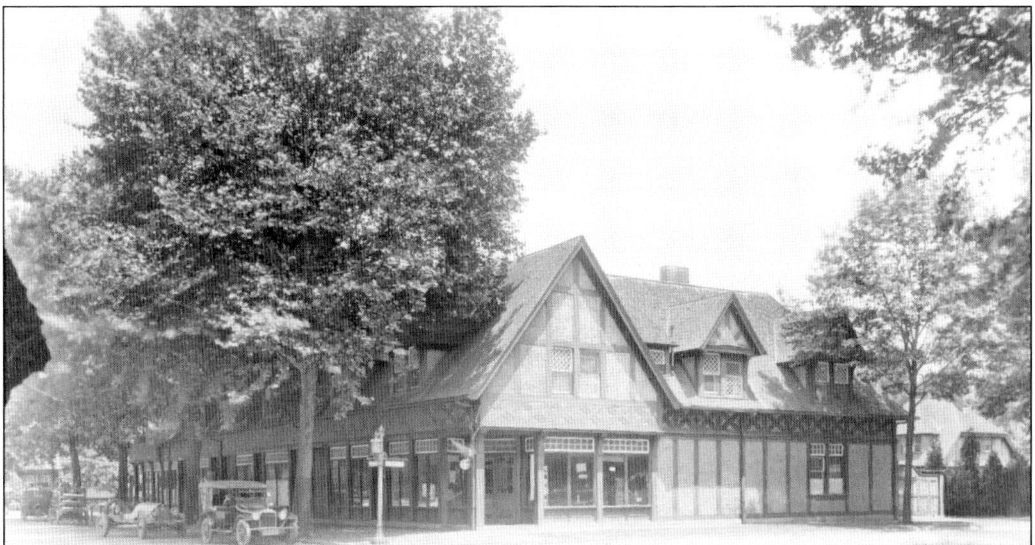

BILTMORE PLAZA STORES, 1920. The Biltmore Drug Store still occupied 10 Plaza at the corner of Oak Street after World War I. By 1917, the village fire department was located in the area in back of the store building facing Brook Street, in between the dwellings and the back of Plaza Shop No. 1. (William A. Barnhill Collection, Pack Memorial Public Library.)

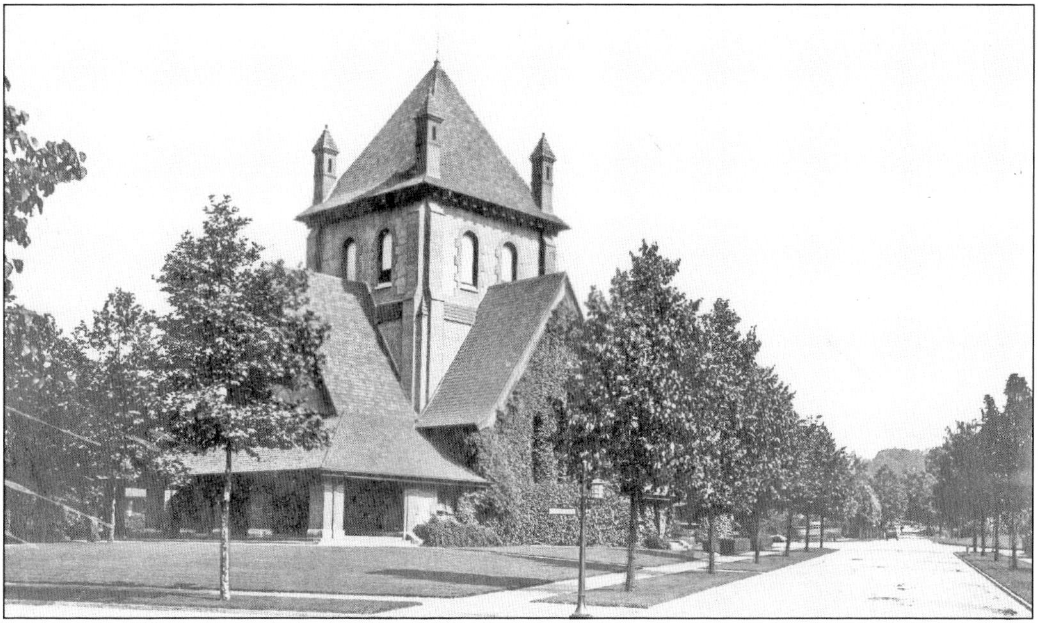

VIEW OF ALL SOULS CHURCH FROM THE CORNER OF ANGLE STREET AND BILTMORE ROAD, 1910. Marie Louise Boyer wrote in *Early Days: All Souls' Church and Biltmore Village*: "Mr. Vanderbilt was an ardent student of theology as well as a deeply religious man. . . . He erected, among the first buildings in his village, the church which he named All Souls. He hoped it would serve as a real spiritual influence in the community, a church to which everyone would feel welcome." (North Carolina Collection, Pack Memorial Public Library.)

VIEW OF ALL SOULS CHURCH FROM THE CORNER OF ANGLE AND SWAN STREETS, 1910. The only surviving church designed by Richard Morris Hunt, All Souls is cruciform in shape with an unusually short nave and a massive tower. The first weather vane on the tower was a cock, but was replaced by St. Hubert's stag with the cross between its antlers. The memorial windows of the church were designed by Maitland Armstrong and his daughter Helen of New York City.

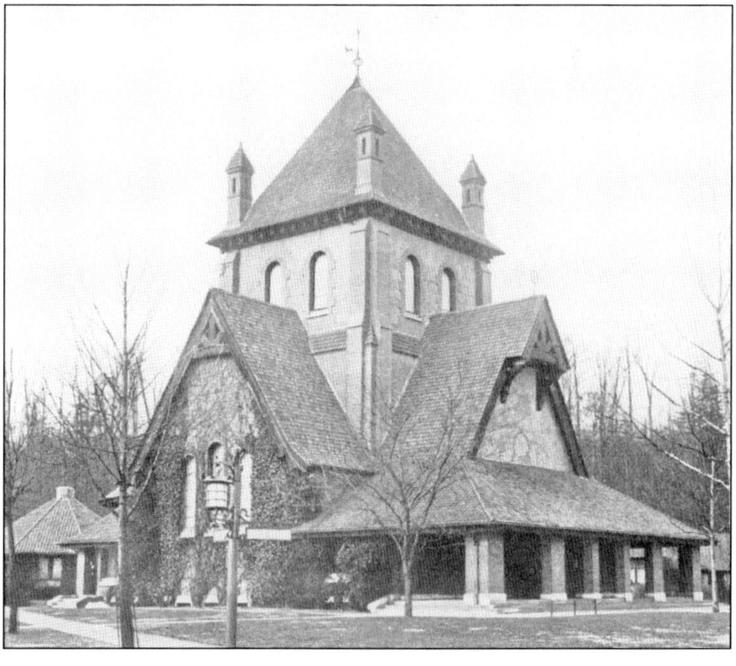

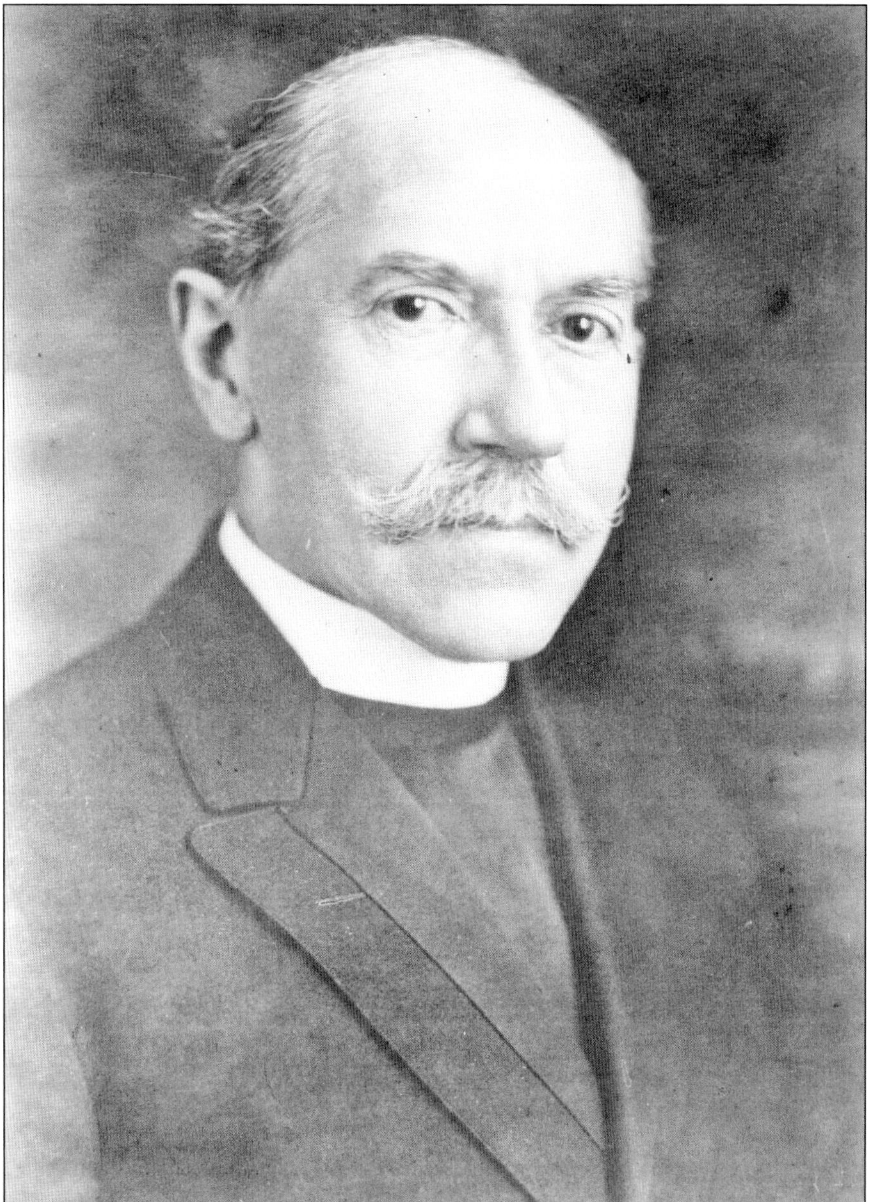

DR. RODNEY R. SWOPE. In late 1896, estate manager Charles McNamee wrote to the Episcopal bishop of North Carolina that George Vanderbilt sought "a young man who will be able to enter with great zeal into the arduous work of forming a new parish." On March 5, 1897, the vestry of All Souls extended a call to Dr. Swope in Wheeling, West Virginia, to become the rector of the church, and he began on May 1, 1897. Vanderbilt served as senior warden of All Souls Church, paid Dr. Swope's salary, and defrayed all expenses associated with running the church until Vanderbilt's death on March 16, 1914, in order that all offerings made at the services should be devoted solely to missionary and charitable purposes. As a result of Vanderbilt's generosity, Dr. Swope established and oversaw numerous missions during his nearly 20 years as rector of All Souls. He passed away not long after his retirement on November 30, 1917. (North Carolina Collection, Pack Memorial Public Library.)

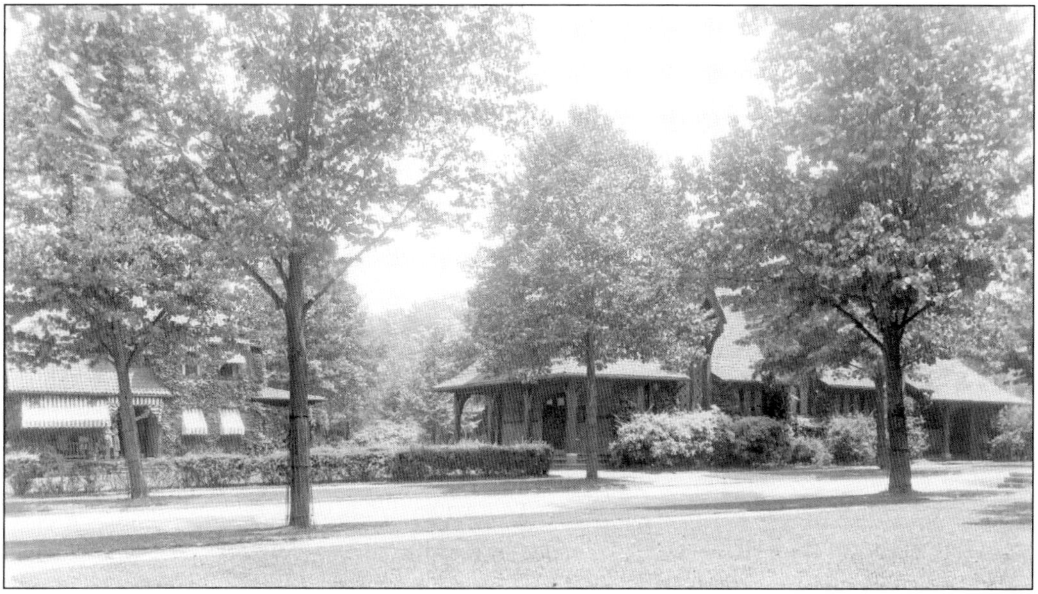

VIEW OF SUNDAY SCHOOL (PARISH HALL) AND RECTORY, C. 1920. All Souls Church established and operated a wide array of missions, educational classes, and clubs. The list of these parish offerings included: cooking, sewing, dressmaking, and kitchen garden classes, the Biltmore Village Club, the Gymnastics Club, the Boys Club, the Girls Club, the Neighborhood Club, the Mother's Club, the Happy Hour Club, and the Biltmore Orchestra. Many of the club meetings took place in the Sunday school building. (William A. Barnhill Collection, Pack Memorial Public Library.)

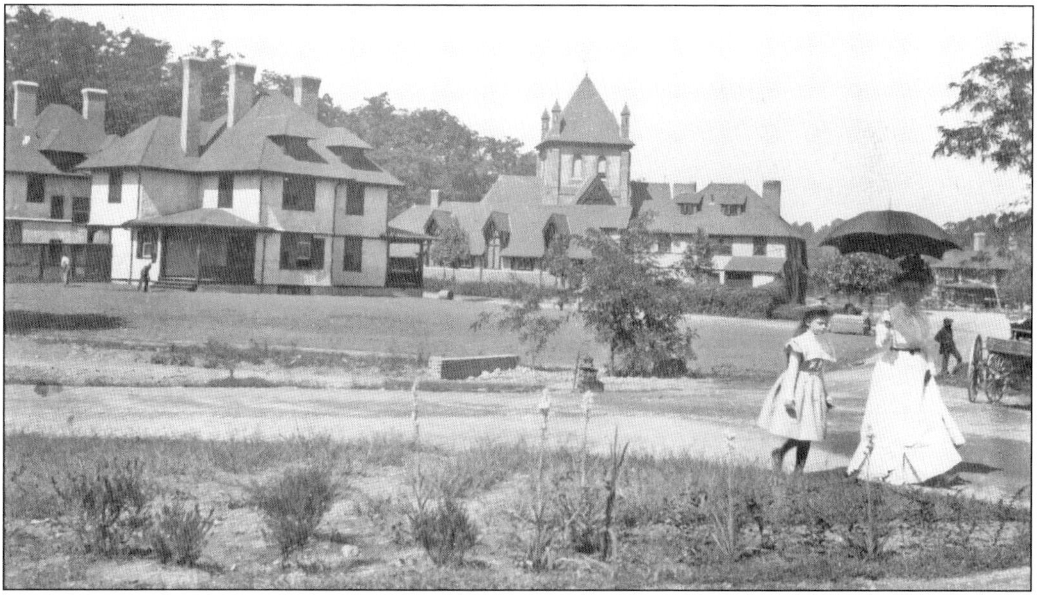

VIEW OF ALL SOULS CHURCH BEYOND SUNDAY SCHOOL, C. 1900. This view was taken from Village Lane near the intersection of Rectory Lane, which connected with Hendersonville Road and provided access to the new Rectory (not visible) and the two large cottages seen on the left. The ladies are believed to be Mrs. Rodney (Mary L.) Swope and her daughter Mary Louise Swope. (National Park Service, Frederick Law Olmsted National Historic Site.)

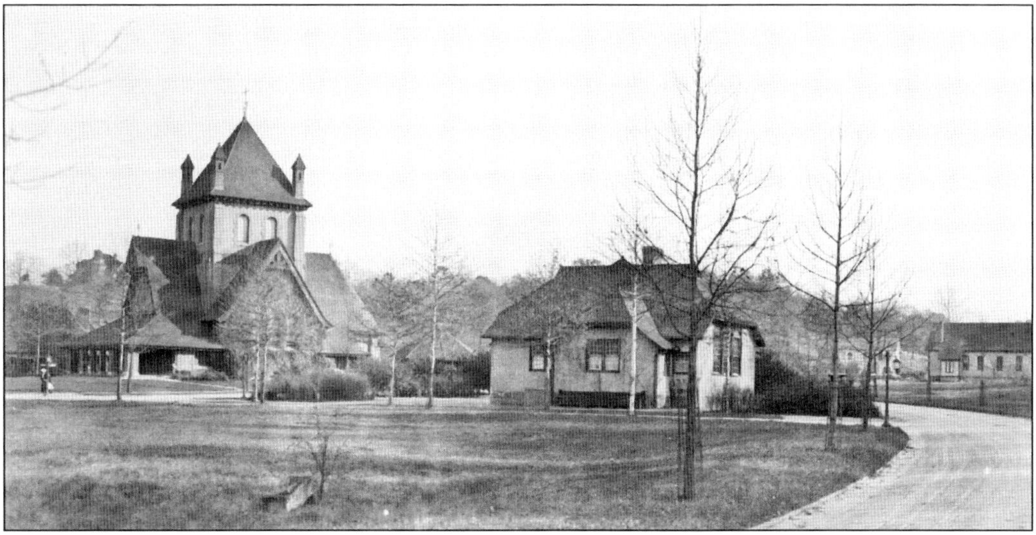

Biltmore Parish School and All Souls Church, c. 1900. The Biltmore Parish School had its origins in 1891 in one of the preexisting houses. Vanderbilt funded construction of the new school, designed by Richard Sharp Smith, in 1900 and authorized the construction of a large addition to the school, which was completed in 1902. (W. B. McEwen and Caroline Nichols McEwen Collection, D. H. Ramsey Library, Special Collections, University of North Carolina at Asheville.)

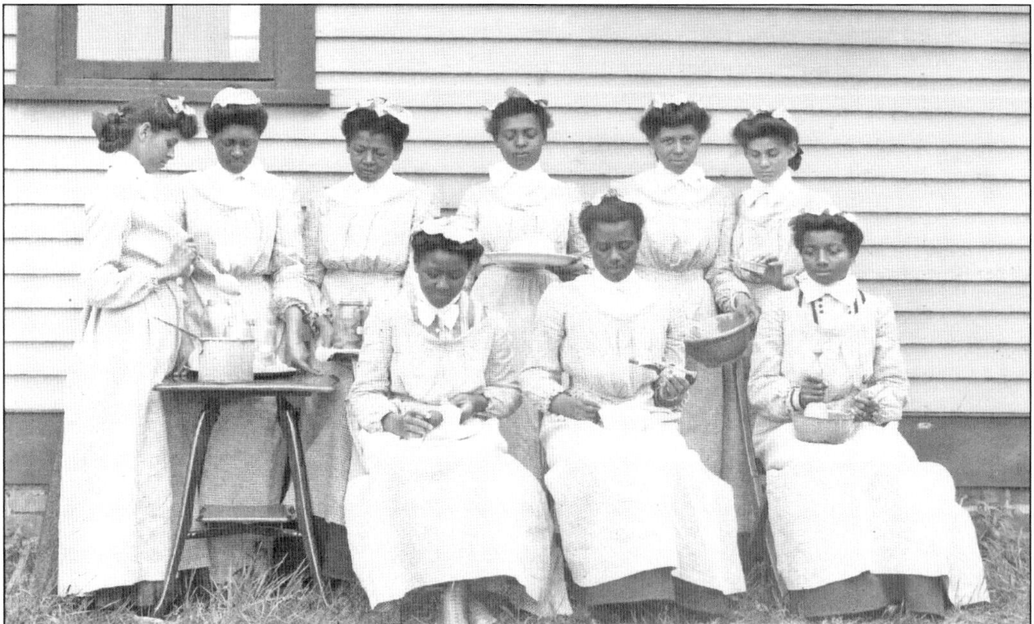

School of Domestic Science, 1900. Edith Vanderbilt established the School for Domestic Science to train young African American women in professional housekeeping. The school consisted of a laundry, a kitchen with individual work areas, a pantry, a dining room, and an assembly hall, and taught the practical application of housekeeping skills. Lessons included plain and fancy cooking, serving, waiting at table, care of the dining room and bedroom, washing and ironing, and soap-making.

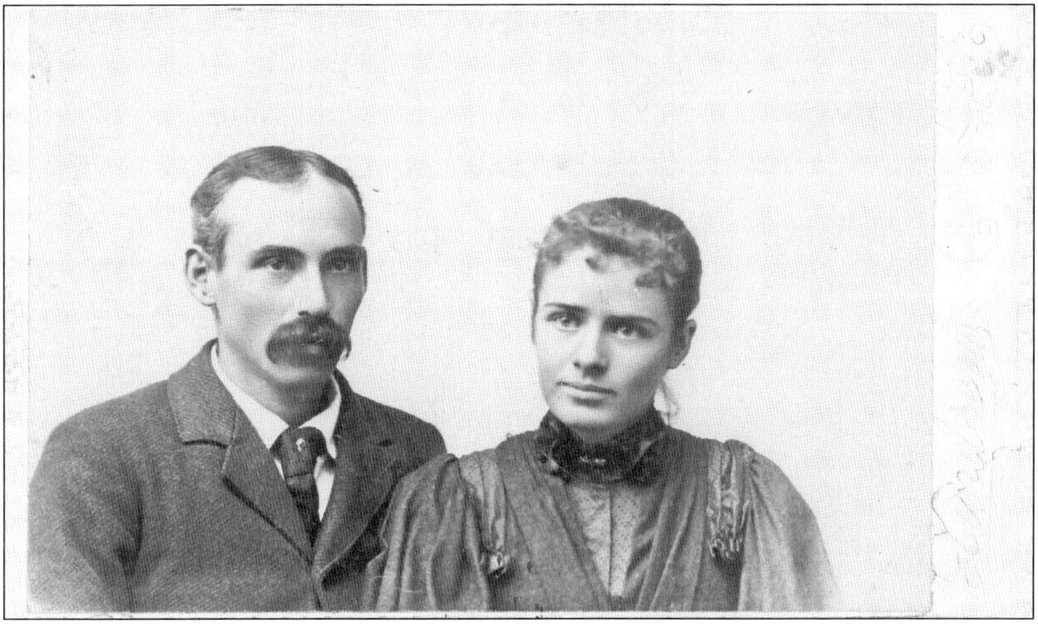

CHARLES (C. L.) BOYNTON AND FAMILY, C. 1905. Hired as a plant collector in 1896 for the Biltmore Nursery and Herbarium, C. L. Boynton moved to Biltmore from Highlands, North Carolina, to be close to his work. His brother, Frank E. Boynton, had worked for the nursery since 1893. George Vanderbilt approved the promotion of Frank in 1897 to be the "Guardian of the Biltmore Herbarium" and C. L. to be the "Chief Collector." Another botanist and acquaintance of the Boyntons', Prof. Thomas G. Harbison, left his job as the schoolteacher at the Highlands School to work with them. The 1902–1903 Asheville City Directory lists both F. E. and C. L. Boynton and T. G. Harbison as residents of South Biltmore. The residence of Charles and his wife, Ethel, pictured above, was on the east side of Hendersonville Road near Biltmore Village. The Boynton children, pictured below, are, from left to right, Charles, Linn, Gladys, and Amy. (Both, Davene Boynton Rusher.)

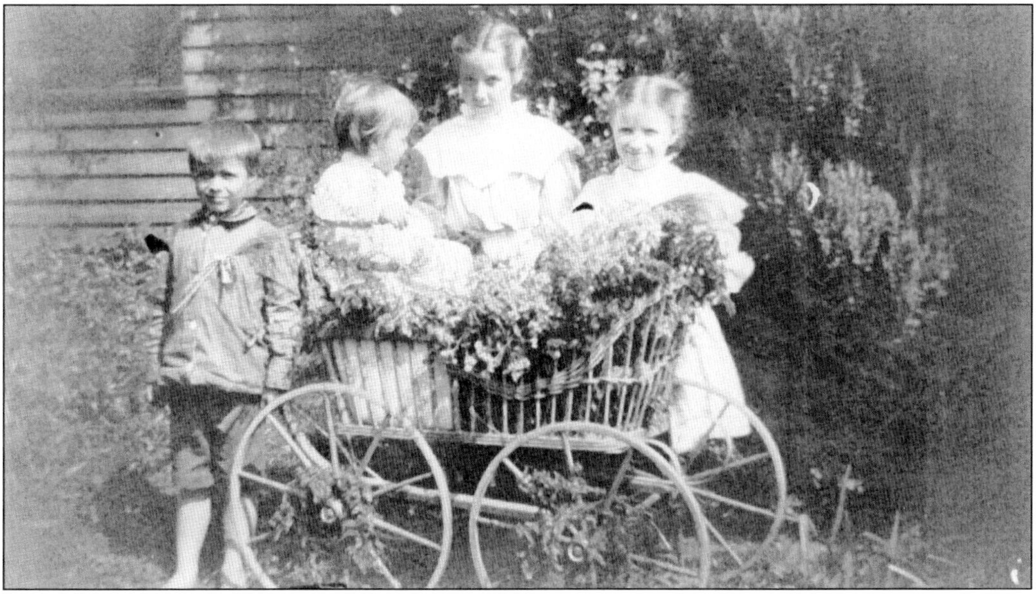

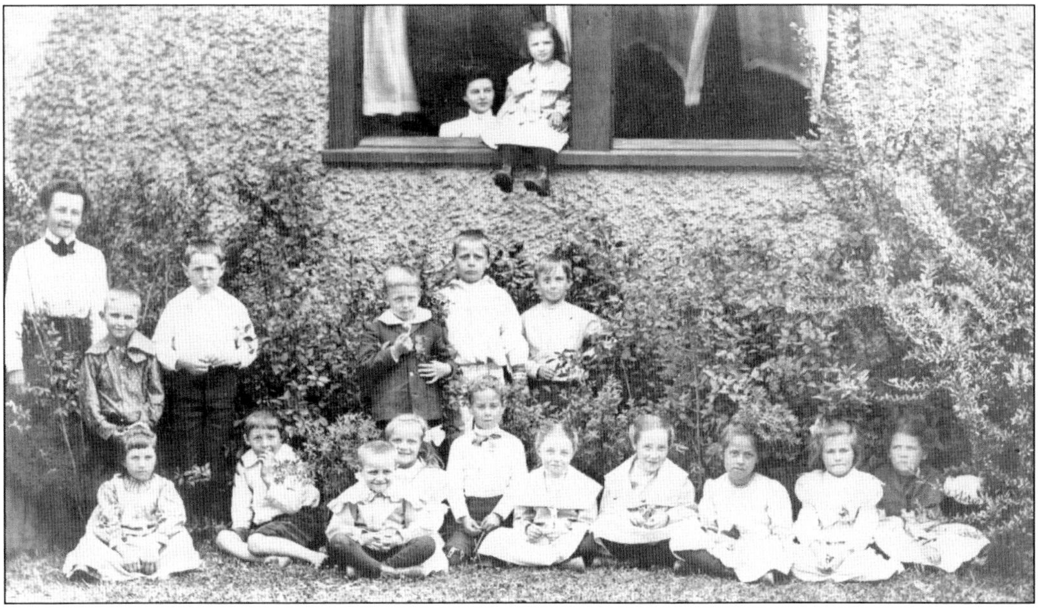

BILTMORE PARISH DAY SCHOOL, 1904. When class opened in October 1898, there were two teachers from Columbia University and 29 students, and attendance grew to 67 in the next months and increased each year thereafter. In 1904, there were 8 teachers and 126 pupils at the day school. Two of C. L. Boynton's daughters, Amy and Gladys, are seated sixth and seventh from left. (Davene Boynton Rusher.)

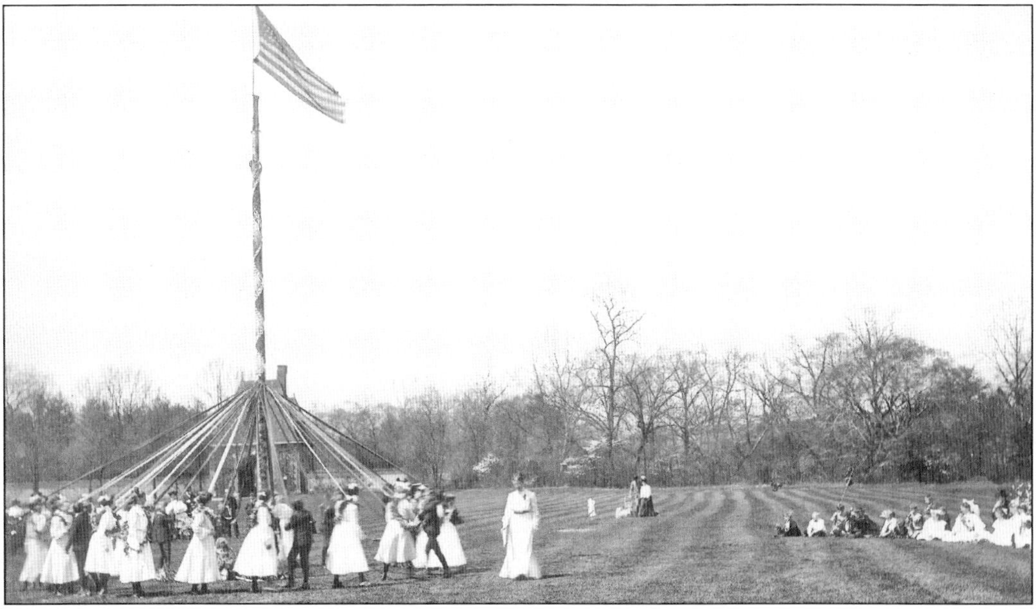

MAYPOLE DANCE ON VILLAGE GREEN, MAY 1, 1906. The Parish School utilized the village greens on either side of Lodge Street as a baseball field and for activities such as May Day celebrations, which included the erection of a Maypole and decorated throne for the May Queen. When U.S. president Theodore Roosevelt visited the estate in September 1902, the schoolchildren assembled on the village green in a tiled pavilion decorated with bunting and flags.

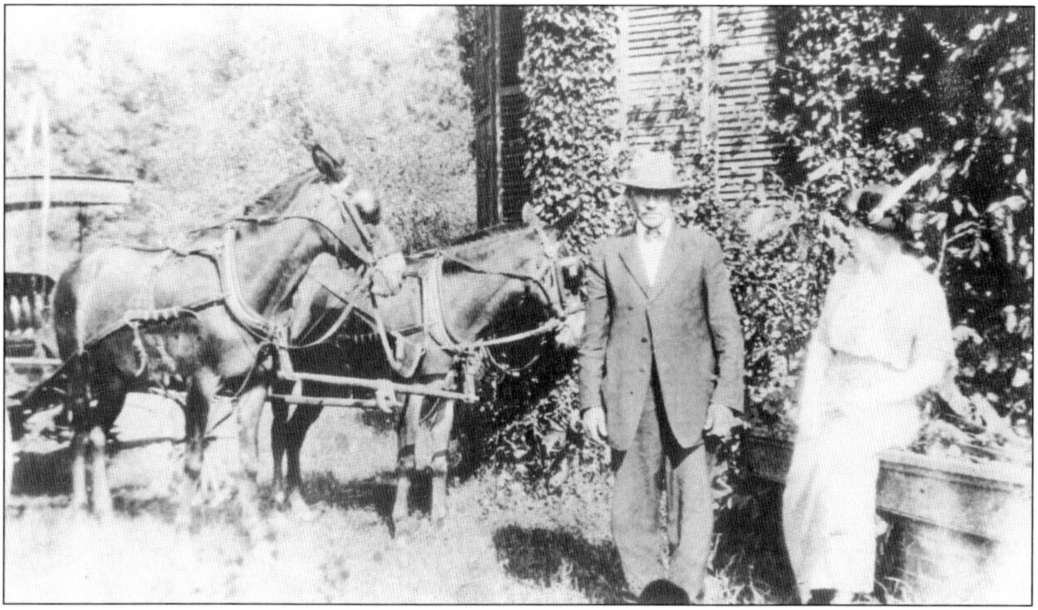

PINKNEY POINSETT SPAIN, C. 1900. Pinkney Spain raised pigs for market on his 51-acre farm near Browntown just south of Biltmore. He owned three teams of horses, which he hired out to work during the construction of Biltmore Estate. An enterprising man, he bought one- and two-seated carriages and arranged to pick up visitors at the Biltmore depot for driving tours of the estate on "pass" days. (Biltmore Village Historic Museum.)

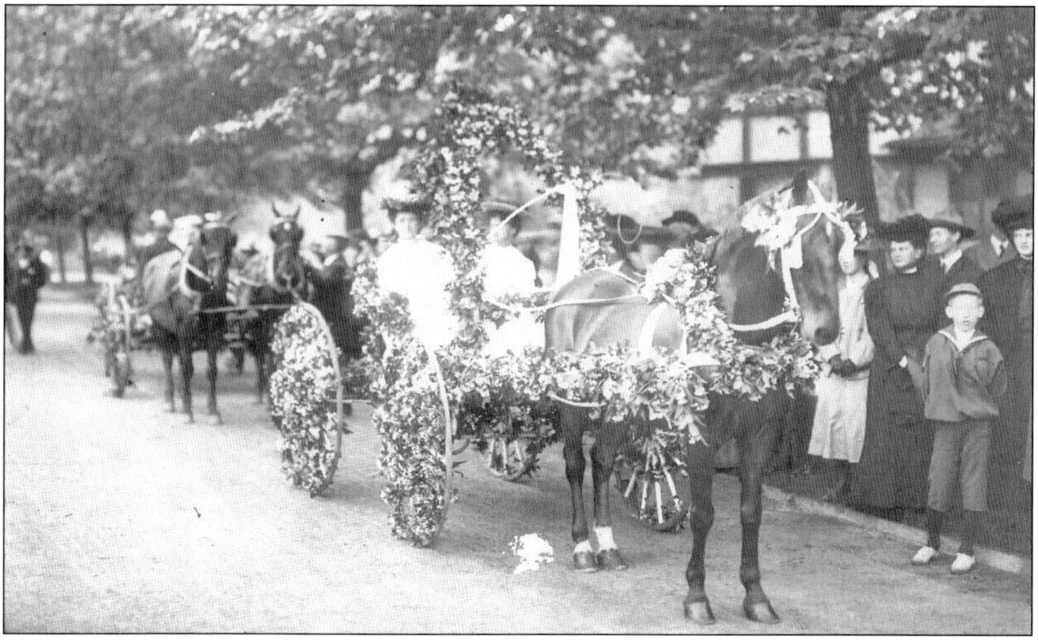

FLORAL PARADE, C. 1905. Edith Vanderbilt planned and held events in Biltmore Village like this parade, which featured carriages creatively decorated with flowers and greenery. On May 8, 1905, the *New York Times* printed an article titled "Floral Parade at Biltmore" that claimed, "Mrs. George Vanderbilt Plans for Show to Rival California's." Residents of Biltmore Estate, the village, and surrounding areas participated in these special occasions.

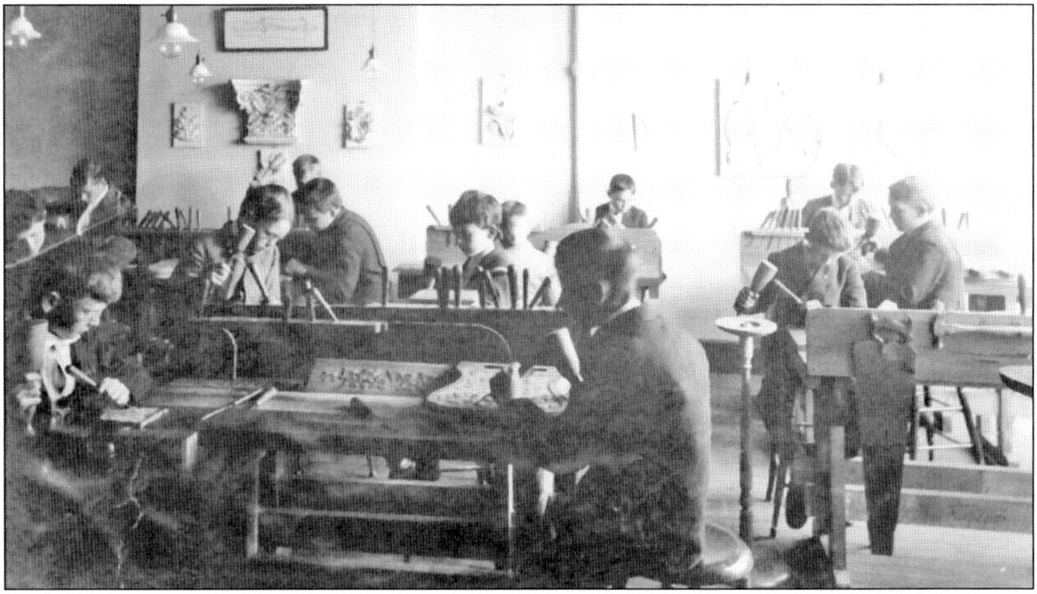

BOYS CLUB, C. 1903. Eleanor P. Vance, a member of All Souls Parish and an expert woodcarver, organized the Boys Club to teach interested boys how to carve wood. Edith Vanderbilt encouraged Vance and parishioner Charlotte L. Yale, a needle worker, to include girls as well, so it became the Boys and Girls Club. The club's mission was expanded to one of education and included classes in woodcarving, cabinetmaking, basketry, and weaving to teach marketable skills to the students.

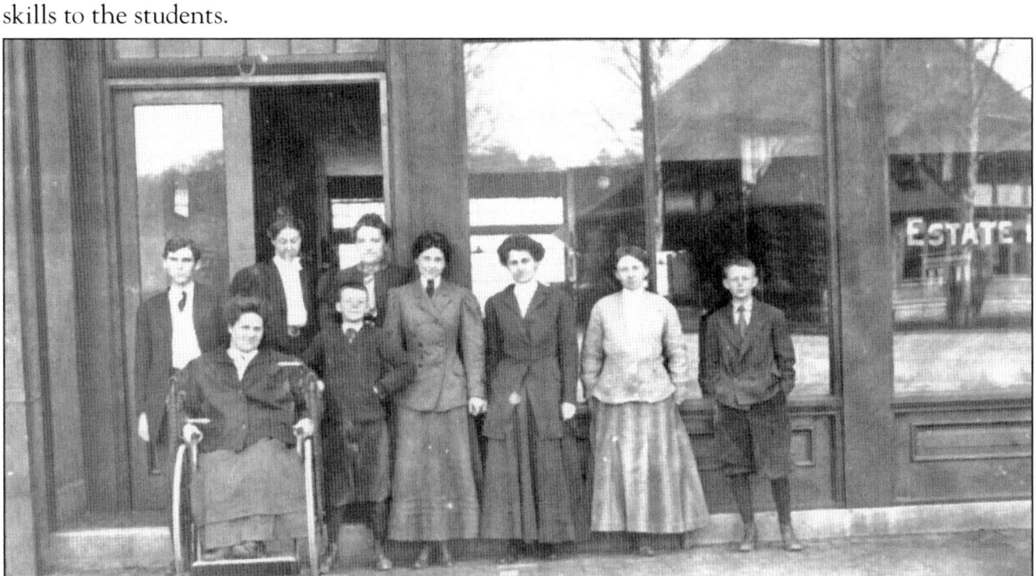

BILTMORE ESTATE INDUSTRIES, C. 1906. The older and more advanced students in the Boys and Girls Club were reorganized in 1905 as Biltmore Estate Industries, supported financially by Edith Vanderbilt and located at 8 Plaza. The new organization prospered and developed into a renowned cottage industry producing finely carved and turned decorative wood accessories and woolen dress goods for sale. From left to right are unidentified, Nell Lipe (in the wheelchair), three unidentified, Eleanor Vance, Charlotte Yale, and "Nannie" Clements. Those who are unidentified are student crafters. (Biltmore Village Historic Museum.)

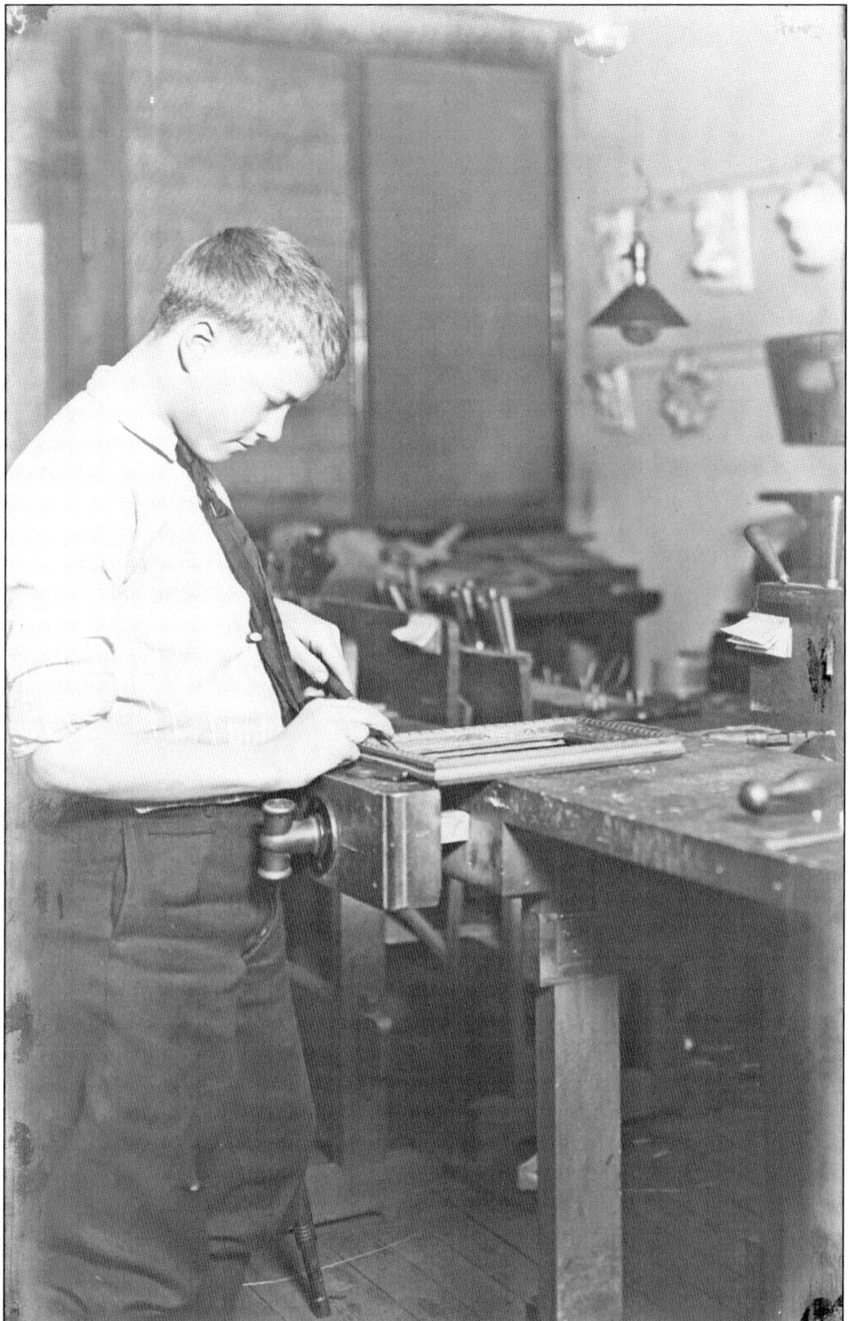

Robert A. (Bob) Stevens, c. 1906. Bob Stevens, born in 1898, carved animals out of potatoes and carrots that he displayed in his father James Robert (Jim Bob) Stevens's store in Biltmore Village. It is said that Edith Vanderbilt saw them and invited him to join the Boys Club, which became incorporated into Biltmore Estate Industries, to learn woodcarving. Bob, after serving in France with his younger brother Sam during World War I, returned to Biltmore Industries, which was purchased in 1917 by Fred Seely, and served as the general manager until his retirement. (John S. Stevens.)

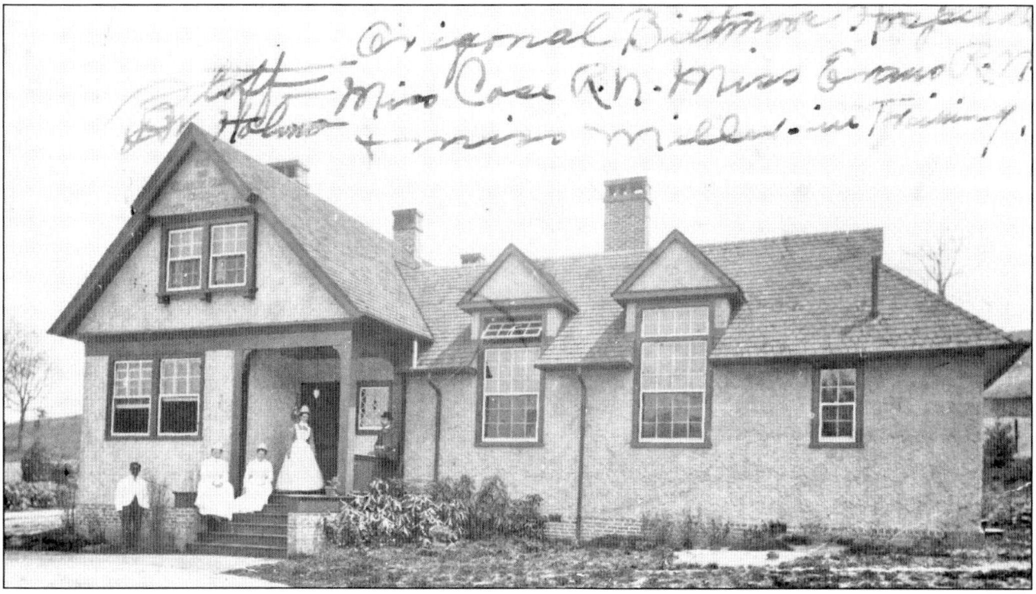

CLARENCE BARKER MEMORIAL HOSPITAL STAFF, C. 1900. The hospital was formally opened for inspection on September 4, 1900, with invitations being extended to the physicians of Asheville and surrounding areas, and opened for the reception of patients on September 6. Superintendent Adeline Orr reported 25 patients admitted during the first nine months of operation. In addition to her, an assistant nurse, a cook, a serving man, and a laundress had been hired. Where surgical cases required special care, additional trained nurses were hired at the patient's expense. Shown are, from left to right, a Mr. Washington, orderly; a Miss Case, R.N.; a Miss Eramo, R.N.; a Miss Miller, "in training;" and Dr. Lawrence E. Holmes. (Biltmore Village Historic Museum.)

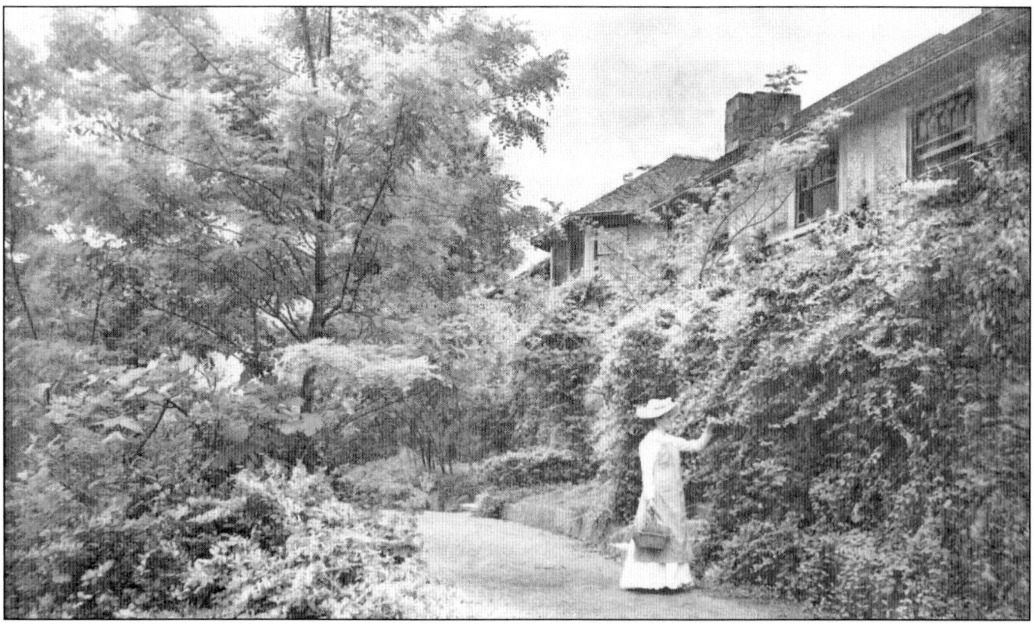

CLARENCE BARKER MEMORIAL HOSPITAL, 1901. John H. Tarbell photographed an unidentified lady admiring the honeysuckle shrubs in the lush landscape plantings around the hospital. (North Carolina Collection, Pack Memorial Public Library.)

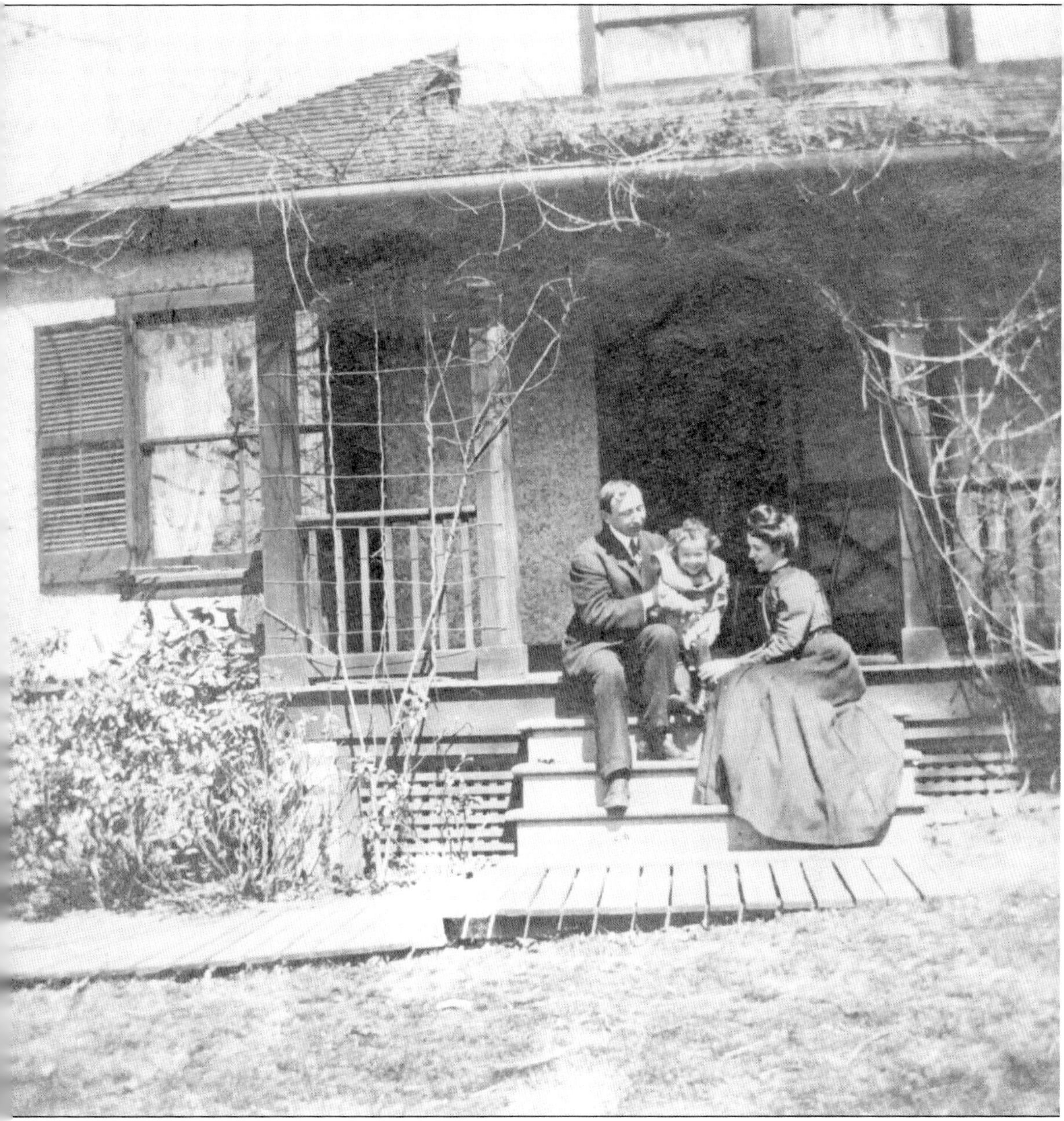

JULIAN P. KITCHIN, C. 1909. Kitchin, his wife, Hesta Reed Kitchin, and son Reed are shown sitting on the steps of a cottage. Kitchin was granted permission in January 1913 to use the reading room of the Village Book Club in the evenings to teach a class in shorthand and typewriting. He was active in the public affairs of Biltmore Village, serving on the board of trustees for the Firemen's Relief Fund of the Town of Biltmore. Kitchin resided at 2 Oak Street in 1917 and was mayor of Biltmore in the mid-1920s. When the City of Asheville annexed Biltmore Village, Oak and Short Streets were renamed to avoid confusion with streets in town with the same names. Oak Street became Boston Way, and Short Street became Kitchin Place. (North Carolina Collection, Pack Memorial Public Library.)

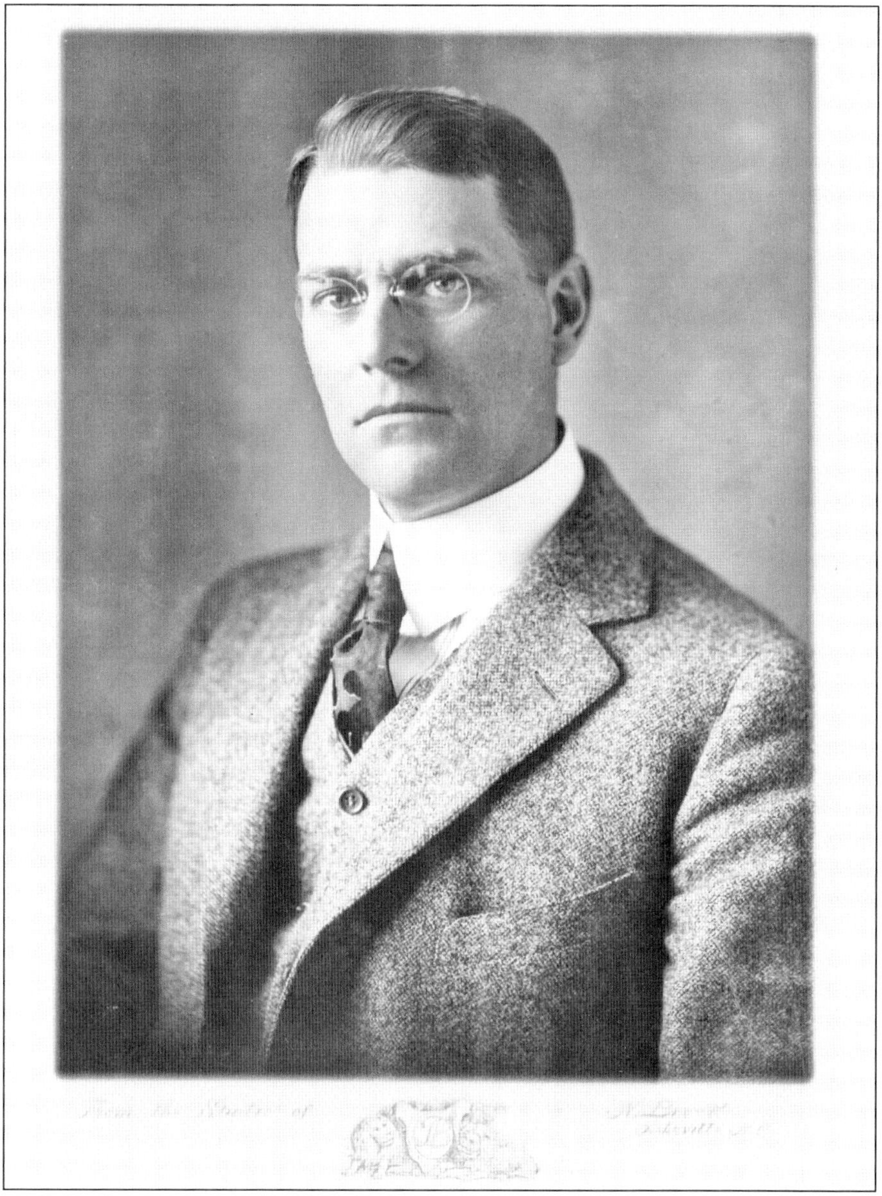

CHARLES EDWARD WADDELL. With a background in electrical engineering, Charles Waddell became superintendent of the Asheville and Biltmore Street Railway and Transportation Company, which was consolidated with the Asheville Electric Company. He was hired by Biltmore Estate superintendent Charles McNamee in January 1901 as an electrician and served as the estate's consulting engineer for a number of years. He established Charles E. Waddell and Company in 1902 and had many notable projects to his credit, some of which are illustrated in the publication *Twenty-Five Years of Engineering in Western North Carolina, 1902–1927*. A project of particular interest was his design and construction of the bridge that survived the flood of 1916. In 1925, he was awarded an honorary doctor of science degree from North Carolina State University, and he served as the first president of the American Society of Civil Engineers, North Carolina Section, from 1923 to 1924 and in the same capacity the following year. (Stephens/Waddell family.)

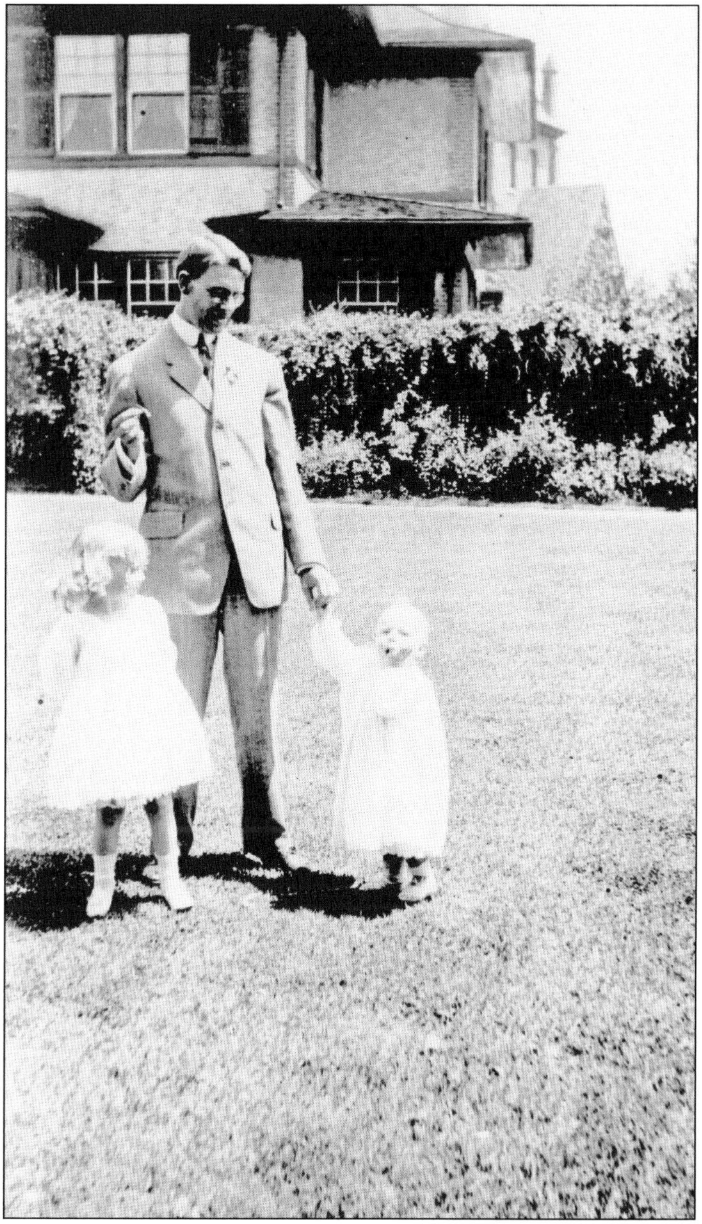

CHARLES E. WADDELL AND CHILDREN. Charles Waddell and his family lived in Biltmore Village and later for many years in Pinecliff, a cottage above the estate's Lodge Gate, where he continued to live after leaving the estate's employment. He was active in estate social affairs and All Souls Church. Waddell was selected to serve on the vestry by Dr. Rodney Swope and did so for 15 years, part of the time as head warden. In *Early Days: All Souls' Church and Biltmore Village*, published in 1933, Marie Louise Boyer wrote, "One does not speak of the Sunday School of All Souls without thinking of Mr. Charles Waddell. He became its Superintendent in 1902 and devoted himself untiringly to that phase of the work." Waddell was president of the Biltmore Hospital in the 1920s. He is pictured here with his son, Charles Edward Waddell Jr., and daughter, Eleanor Belknap Waddell Stephens, at their home in Biltmore Village. (Stephens/Waddell family.)

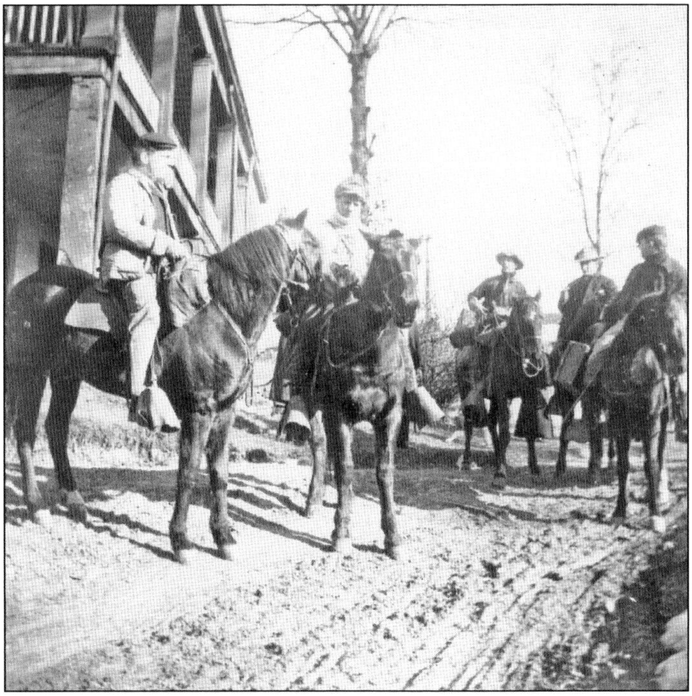

Dr. Clifton D. Howe and Biltmore Forest School Students, c. 1905. From left to right are Dr. Howe, Perry Emigh, Guy Gooding, Jack D. Mylrea, and Perry M. Wilson on horseback at the Forest Hill Inn. Winter classes were held in the Biltmore office in the village, and students were responsible for finding their own room and board around Biltmore. (North Carolina Collection, Pack Memorial Public Library.)

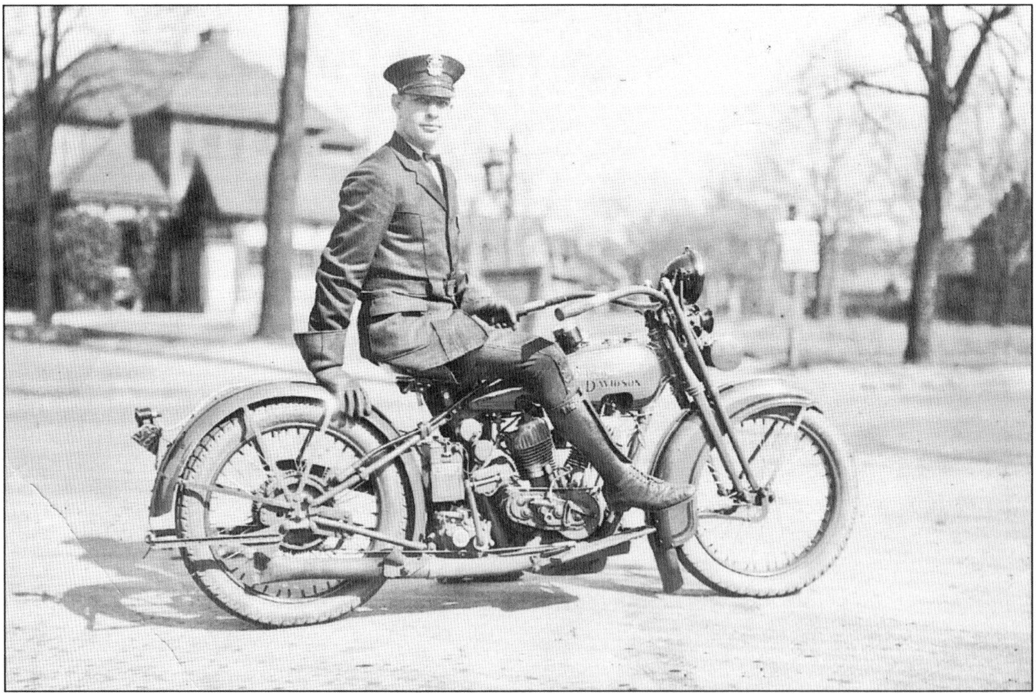

Daniel Baker Lipe, 1859–1934. Daniel Lipe worked as a carpenter on Biltmore Estate for a few years during construction of Biltmore House. Daniel, his wife, Julia Francis Lipe, and their seven children lived in the area of South Biltmore. While mayor of South Biltmore in 1912, Lipe was the proprietor of the Biltmore Shop near the bridge that offered "general blacksmithing, buggy and carriage painting, and horse-shoeing services." (Donated by Catherine Baker Lipe.)

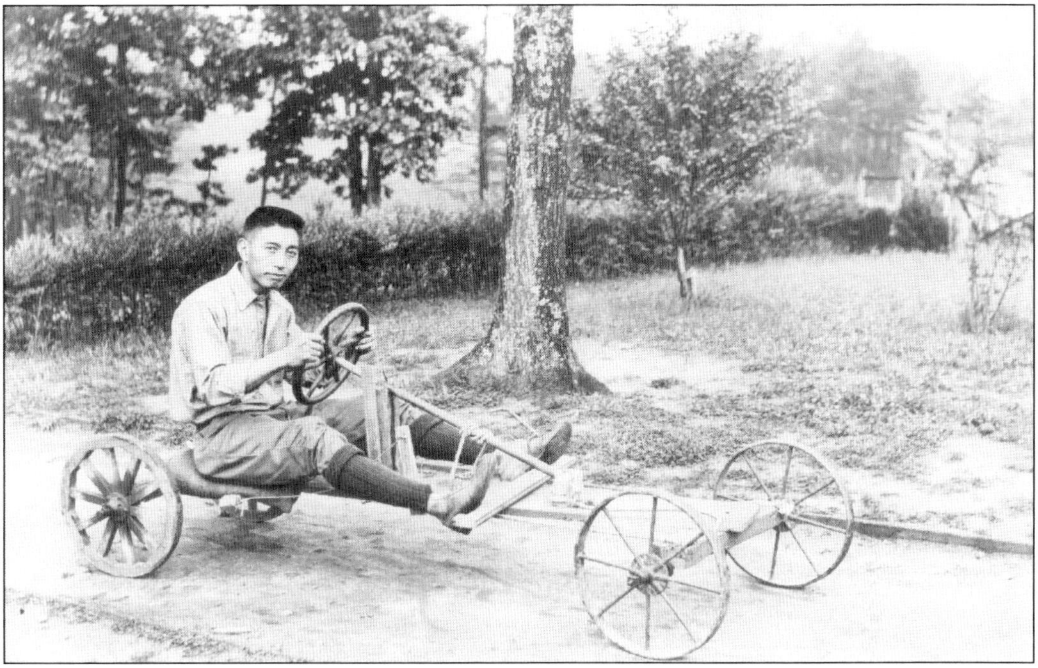

GEORGE MASA, C. 1915. Photographer George Masa is seated on a go-cart that appears to have been fabricated from spare parts. Masa lived with the Oscar Creasman family for a few years between 1915 and 1920 at 615 Brookshire Street in South Biltmore. Oscar Creasman worked as a cabinetmaker for Biltmore Estate during that time period. (North Carolina Collection, Pack Memorial Public Library.)

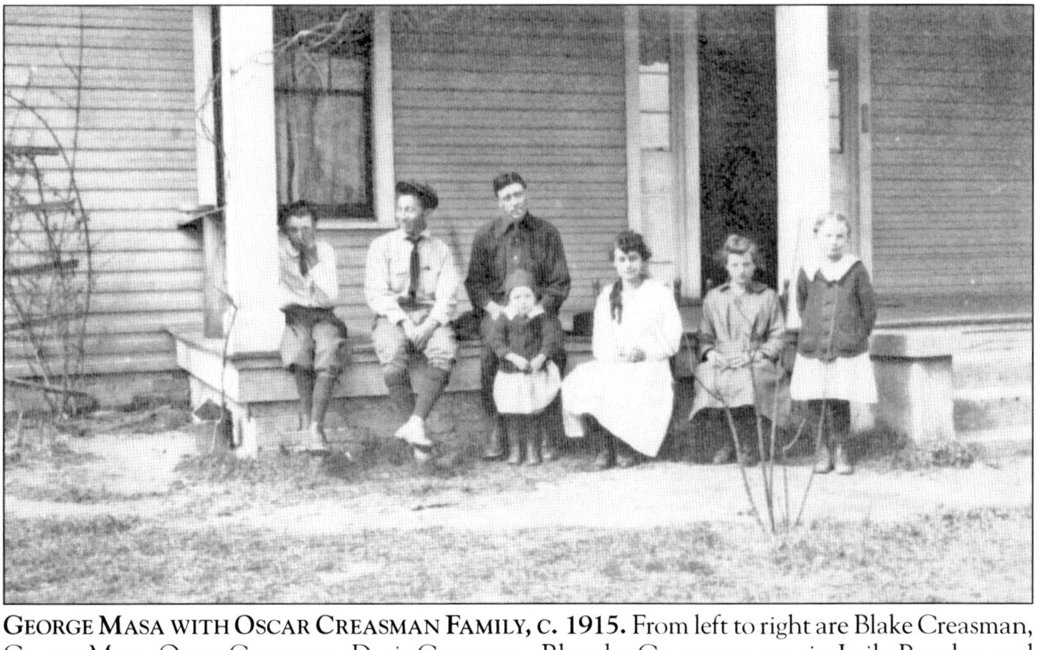

GEORGE MASA WITH OSCAR CREASMAN FAMILY, C. 1915. From left to right are Blake Creasman, George Masa, Oscar Creasman, Doris Creasman, Blanche Creasman, cousin Leila Pressley, and Ruby Creasman as identified by Jeanne Creasman Lance, daughter of Oscar Creasman. (North Carolina Collection, Pack Memorial Public Library.)

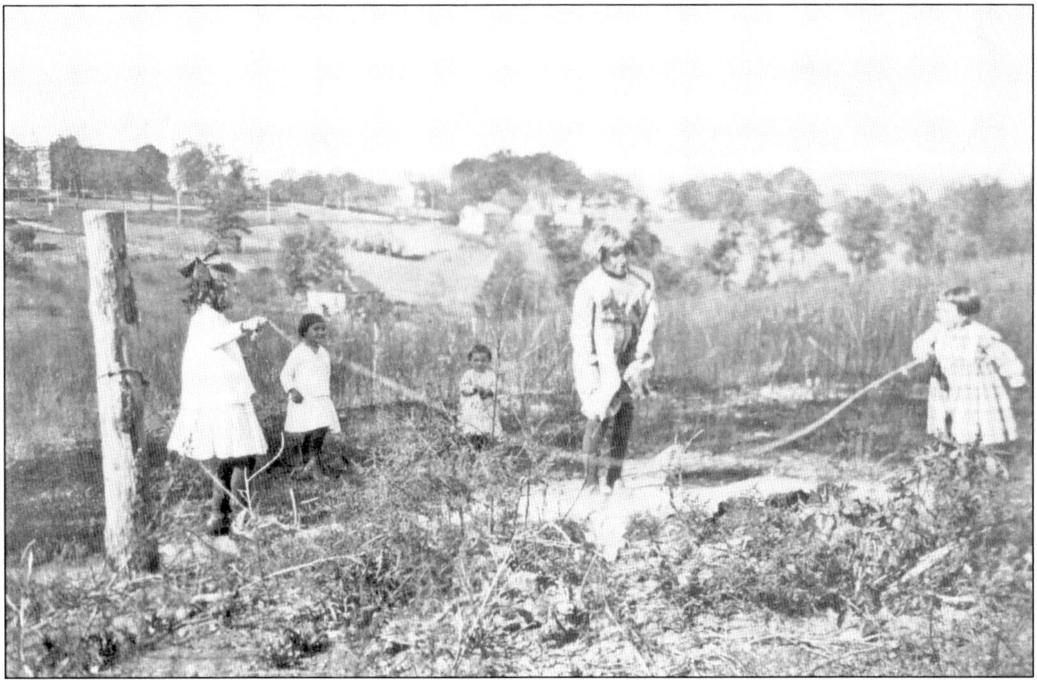

RUBY CREASMAN AND FRIENDS, C. 1915. Ruby Creasman, aged seven or eight years old, is jumping rope with four younger girls in a field near the Creasman home in South Biltmore. Several houses and a larger structure, believed to be the Biltmore School, can be seen in the background. (North Carolina Collection, Pack Memorial Public Library.)

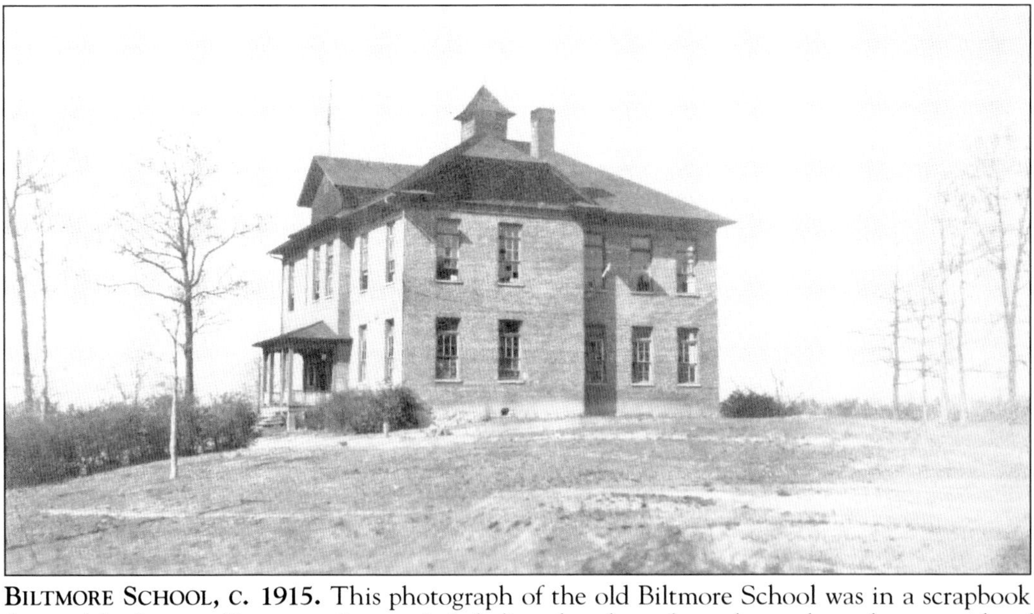

BILTMORE SCHOOL, C. 1915. This photograph of the old Biltmore School was in a scrapbook donated by Jeanne Creasman Lance. It is believed to have been located on the east side of Hendersonville Road opposite the Biltmore High School that replaced it around 1920. The Asheville City Directory of 1902–1903 lists a "South Biltmore Graded School;" it might be referring to this one. (North Carolina Collection, Pack Memorial Public Library.)

Four

Where Life Is Worthwhile

Asheville and the surrounding region's reputation as a resort locale with the "healthiest climate in the country," picturesque mountain scenery, hot springs, and grand hotels that boasted the latest in modern conveniences and recreational amenities was well known and widely promoted in large city centers in the North as well as the South. Advertisements in newspapers, magazine articles, and other publications like Harriet Sawyer's *Souvenir of Asheville or Sky-Land* in 1892 and *Lindsey's Guide Book to Western North Carolina* promoted the town and Western North Carolina with appealing slogans as the "Land of the Sky," "Health-seeker's Paradise," "Poet's Dream," and "Madonna in the Mountains." For many of the same reasons that attracted George Vanderbilt to visit the area, others came from far and wide to enjoy all the area provided. The area's popularity spurred the building of resorts like the Hotel Belmont at Sulphur Springs, Oakland Heights Hotel, Battery Park Hotel, and Kenilworth Inn. The city's progressive growth brought one the country's first and finest electric street railway systems, which connected the depot with the town square and branch lines to the area's major resorts and attractions. There were two light companies, a gas company, a telephone exchange, and a number of prominent and skilled physicians. Asheville boasted excellent private and public school systems, and well-known finishing schools for girls and prep schools for boys flourished in the area. Other amenities included a public library and reading room, several banks, and numerous manufacturing and other businesses. As the population increased, Asheville became "justly celebrated for the beauty and salubrity of its suburbs," one of the most attractive being the town of Victoria on a hill north of Biltmore Village where George Vanderbilt constructed his country residences on Vernon Hill. It was considered that "no visitor's sight-seeing trip around Asheville was complete until he was driven through Victoria and given the opportunity to see its beautiful roads, planting and landscaping, its charming homes with their green lawns at all times in perfect order." (From the *Anti-Extension Plain Dealer*, Volume I, Asheville, North Carolina, April 23, 1929.) As a result of the area's prosperity and wide acclaim, Kenilworth Inn and other establishments sometimes used the phrase "Where Life Is Worthwhile" to make their advertisements more appealing.

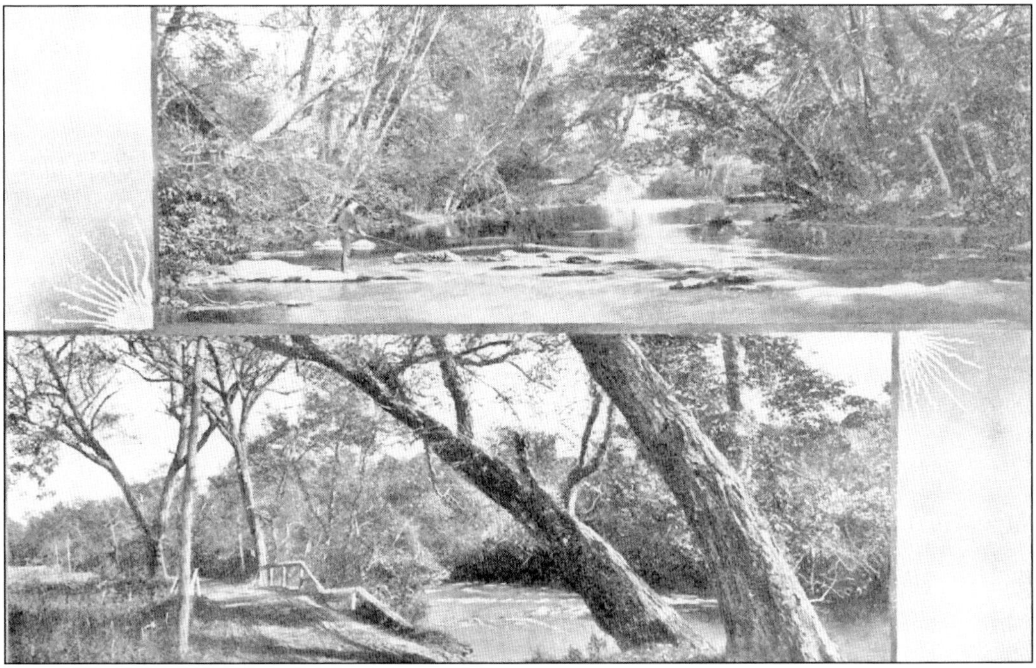

SWANNANOA RIVER, 1900. This small tributary of the French Broad River originates in the high reaches of the Black Mountains barely 20 miles away. Writer Fanny C. W. Barbour, in *A Palace in "The Land of the Sky"* (June 1895), stated, "Its fame has been sung and its loveliness portrayed by poets and authors without number." The river's scenic beauty attracted both fishermen and amorous couples to the popular "Lovers' Bridge," as seen in these images from Biltmore Photogravures, H. T. Rogers, 1900.

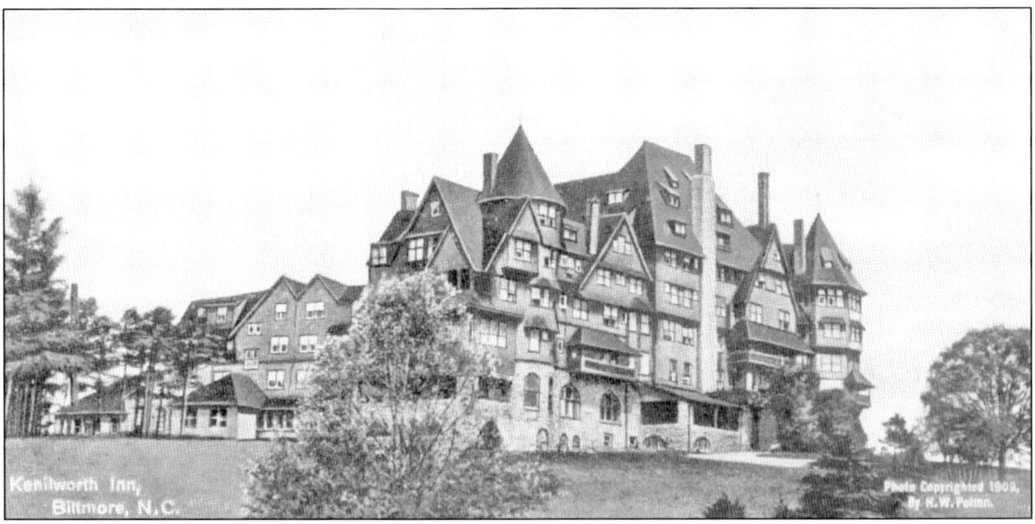

KENILWORTH INN, 1909. The *Souvenir of Asheville or the Sky-Land* (1892) proclaimed, "A park of one hundred and sixty acres immediately surrounds Kenilworth Inn, twenty acres of which is in a velvety lawn . . . the breadth of view . . . is remarkable. . . . A superior cuisine, the purest water, no back rooms, rare views from every room, electric lights, elevator, billiards, bowling, tennis, laundry and livery." A later advertisement used the slogan, "Where Life Is Worthwhile." (Hal Branch.)

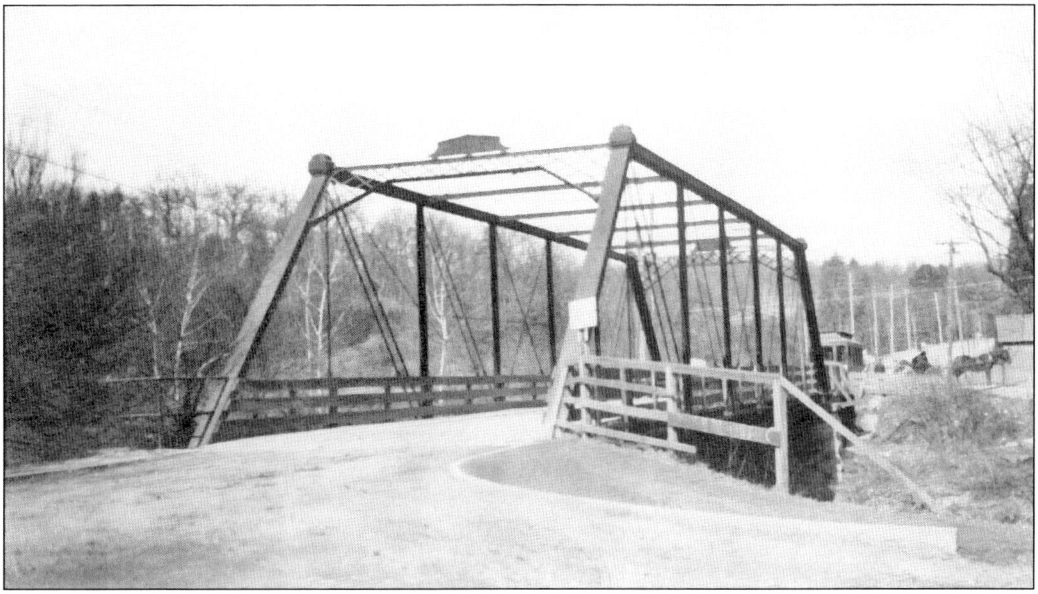

BILTMORE BRIDGE, C. 1905. This iron bridge crossed the Swannanoa River on the road from Biltmore to Asheville, known variously as South Main Street, the Biltmore Road, and later Biltmore Avenue. In this view looking north toward Asheville, a streetcar at the end of the Biltmore Electric Street Railway line can be seen to the left of the horse carriage. (Biltmore Village Historic Museum.)

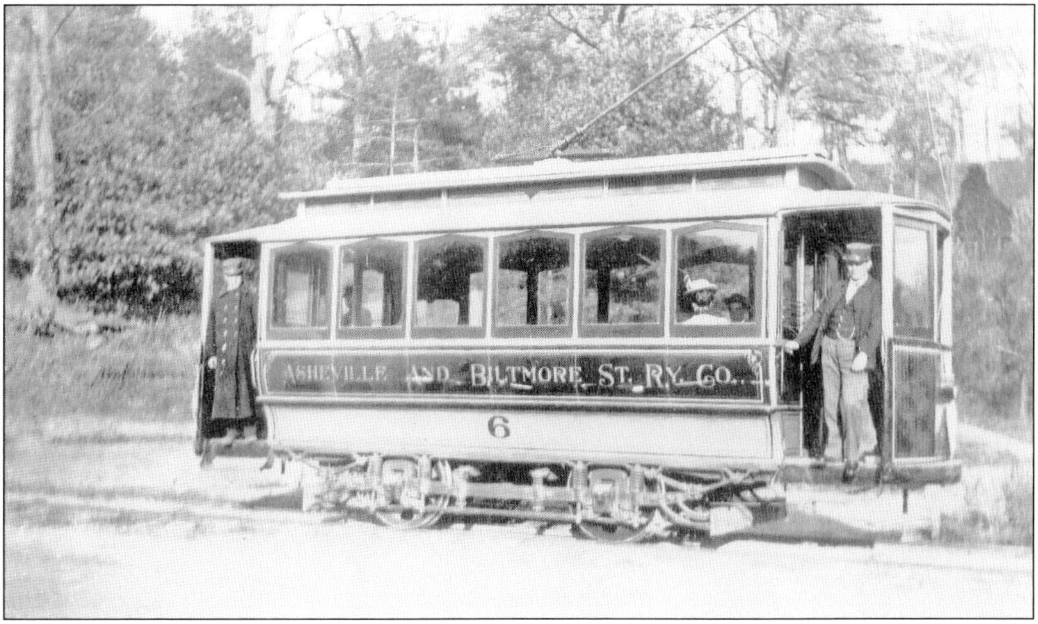

ASHEVILLE AND BILTMORE ELECTRIC STREET RAILWAY. On February 1, 1889, Asheville began operation of one of the first electric street railways in the United States. As early as February 1892, Biltmore Estate was investigating the cost of an electric railway from Biltmore Station to the Asheville Court House. Streetcar No. 6 ran the line between Asheville and Biltmore that was constructed between 1897 and 1898. (North Carolina Collection, Pack Memorial Public Library.)

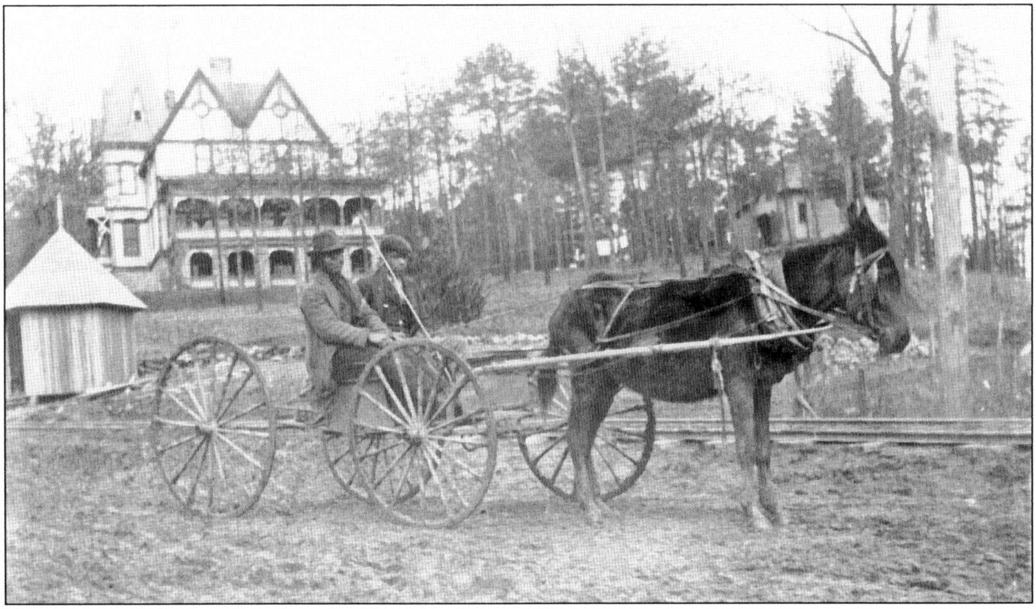

WILLIAM E. BREESE HOUSE, 1899. A prominent banker from Charleston, South Carolina, Breese moved to Asheville in 1885 for the health of his son, who had contracted tuberculosis. Breese, who played a leading role in the city's late-19th-century development, founded the First National Bank of Asheville in 1885 and helped to finance the Spartanburg to Asheville Railroad. His house, known as Swannanoa Hill, is seen on South Main Street just north of Biltmore and the Swannanoa River. (Louis Weeks's photograph donated by Howard C. Weeks.)

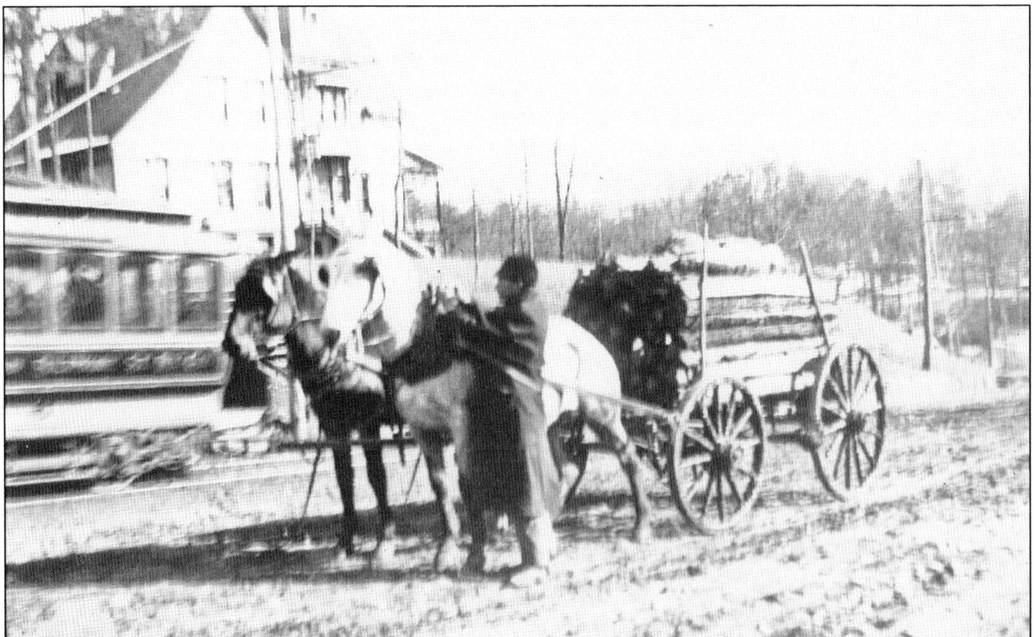

STREETCAR AND WAGON, 1899. A streetcar on the Asheville and Biltmore Electric Street Railway whizzes by the William E. Breese house and a wagonload of wood pulled by a team of mules on the way to Asheville. (Louis Weeks's photograph donated by Howard C. Weeks.)

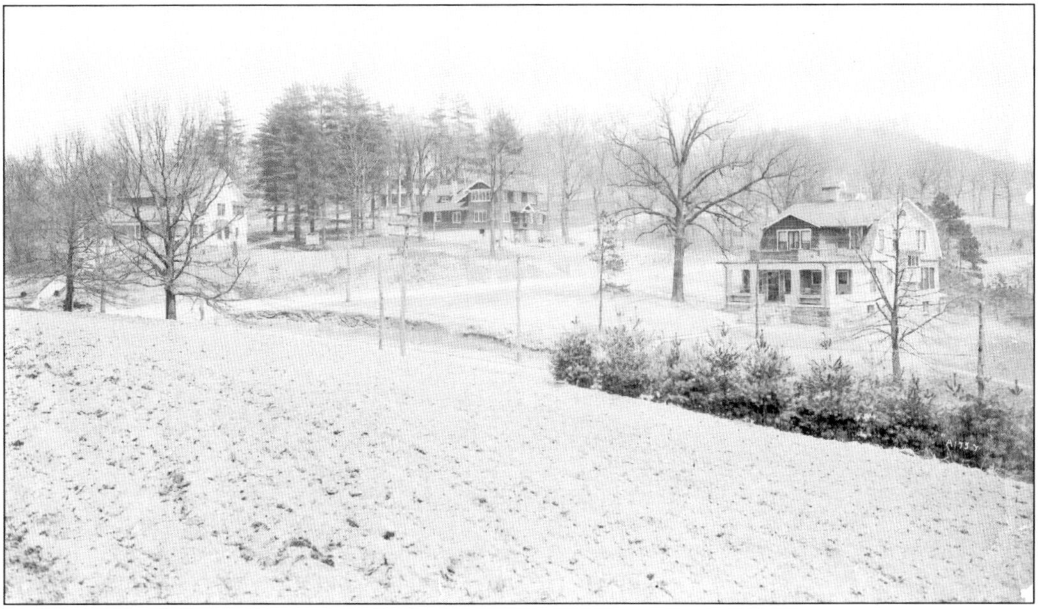

FOREST HILL INN. Mrs. W. Talbot Penniman operated her family home as an inn, which was described in a 1912 Asheville City Directory advertisement: "Buried deep in a forest of virgin growth, yet within close access by electric car to every part of the city of Asheville, is that well-known old colonial house, Forest Hill. . . . Most popular place in the suburbs to stop when spending the summer or winter in Asheville." It was "far enough out of the city to be removed from the noise and dirt and other objectionable features yet near enough to have the advantages of city water, telephones, free delivery of mail, and the service of the street car line," with a schedule of every 15 minutes. There were extended views over the Swannanoa Valley, Kenilworth Park, the Vanderbilt Estate, and stretches of the principal mountain ranges and peaks. The two-story columned porch is visible through the trees in the top photograph. (Both, North Carolina Collection, Pack Memorial Public Library.)

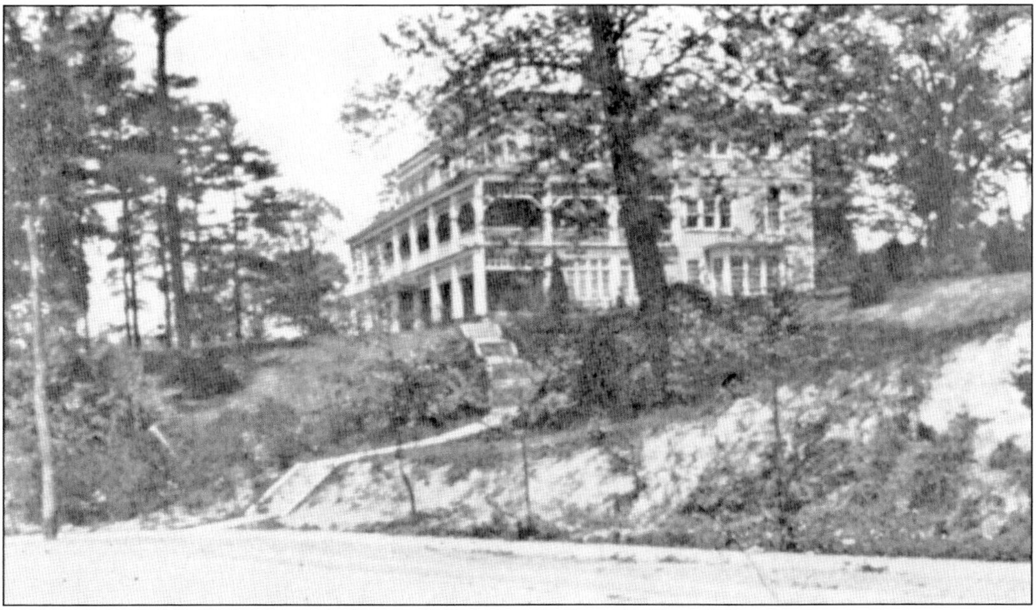

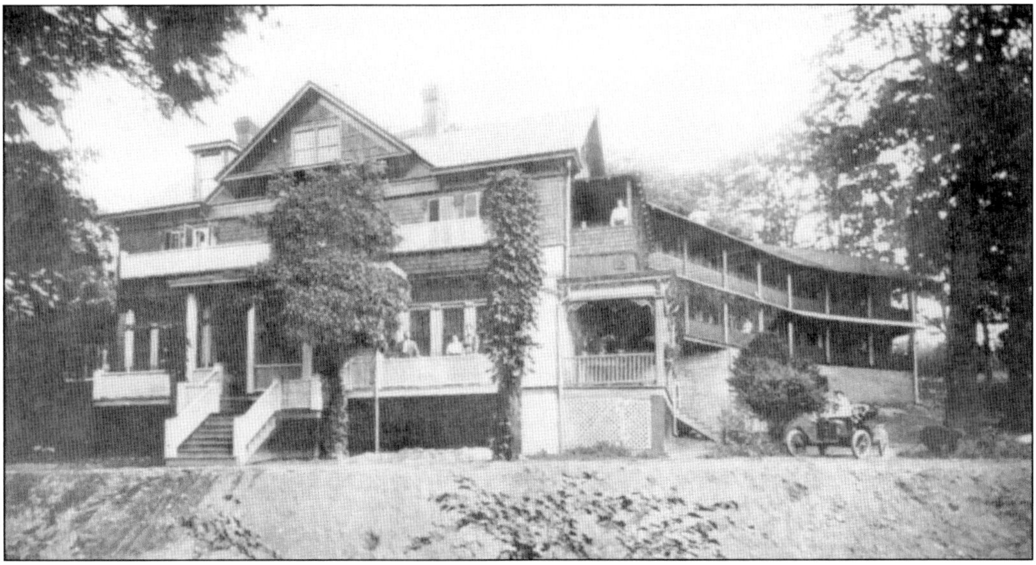

ASHEVILLE-BILTMORE SANITARIUM, C. 1910. At the beginning of the 20th century, Asheville was known as a popular health resort for patients with tuberculosis and other lung ailments, and numerous sanatoria were established. The Asheville-Biltmore Sanitarium on South Main Street near Kenilworth promoted " 'In and Out Door Sleeper' accommodations. The original out-door-life rooms for night and day in any season and climate" in the *Souvenir Directory to the Land of the Sky*. (North Carolina Collection, Pack Memorial Public Library.)

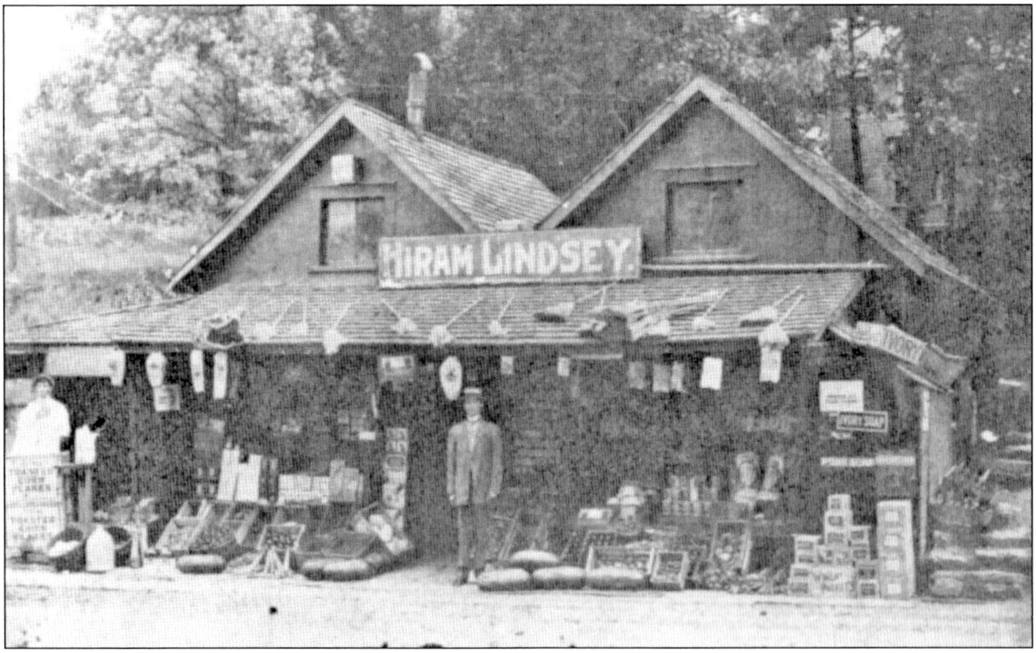

HIRAM LINDSEY'S STORE, 1901. Located on the east side of South Main Street (450 South Main Street then and later 458) near Victoria Road, Hiram Lindsey's General Store advertised Ivory Soap and Toasted Corn Flakes. There were a number of other proprietors from 1912 as long as the store existed, possibly until the late 1940s. (North Carolina Collection, Pack Memorial Public Library.)

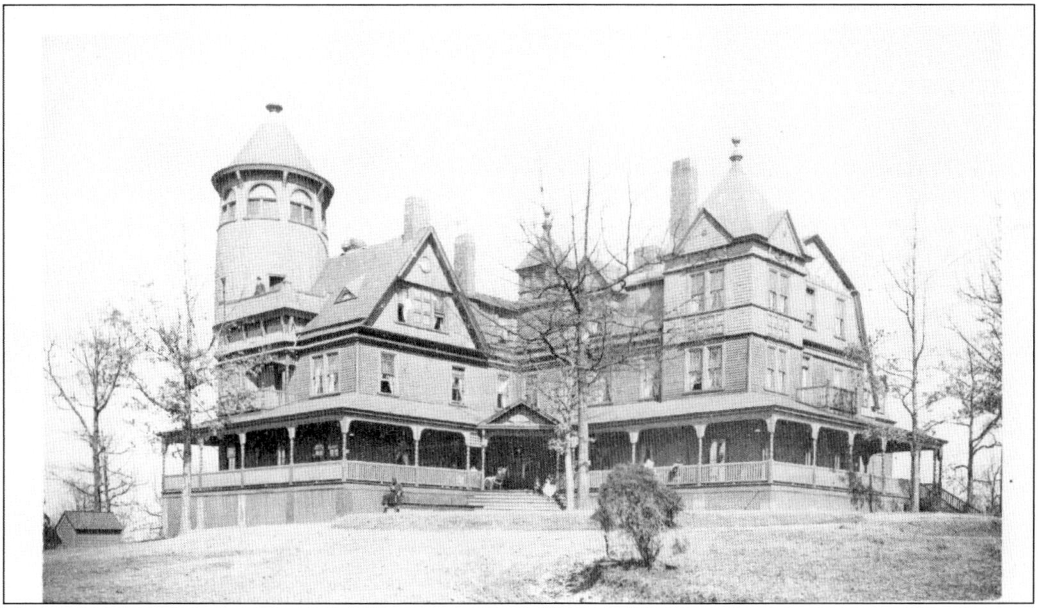

Oakland Heights Hotel, c. 1895. This large three-story wooden-frame building was constructed in the Victoria Settlement for $110,000 in 1889 for Alexander Garrett, who deeded it to his son, Robert U. Garrett, in 1891. The hotel featured extensive verandas and a famous water tower. In 1896, the 80-room structure became the Oakland Heights Health Resort, a sanatorium directed by doctors Paul Paquin and Samuel Westray Battle that was famous for therapeutic baths. (North Carolina Collection, Pack Memorial Public Library.)

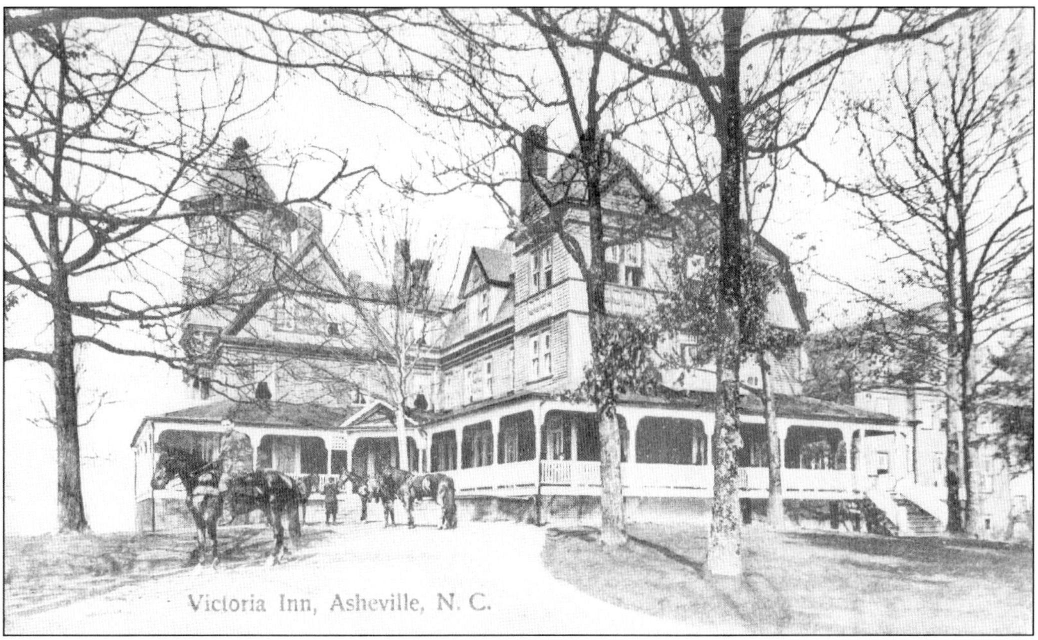

Victoria Inn, c. 1909. Oakland Heights became the Victoria Inn around 1909. The tower on the left in this postcard was a landmark and was advertised by the inn as holding "30,000 gallons of pure mountain water." Other noted features of the inn included a circular room with 16 windows atop the tower and spacious verandas. (Hal Branch.)

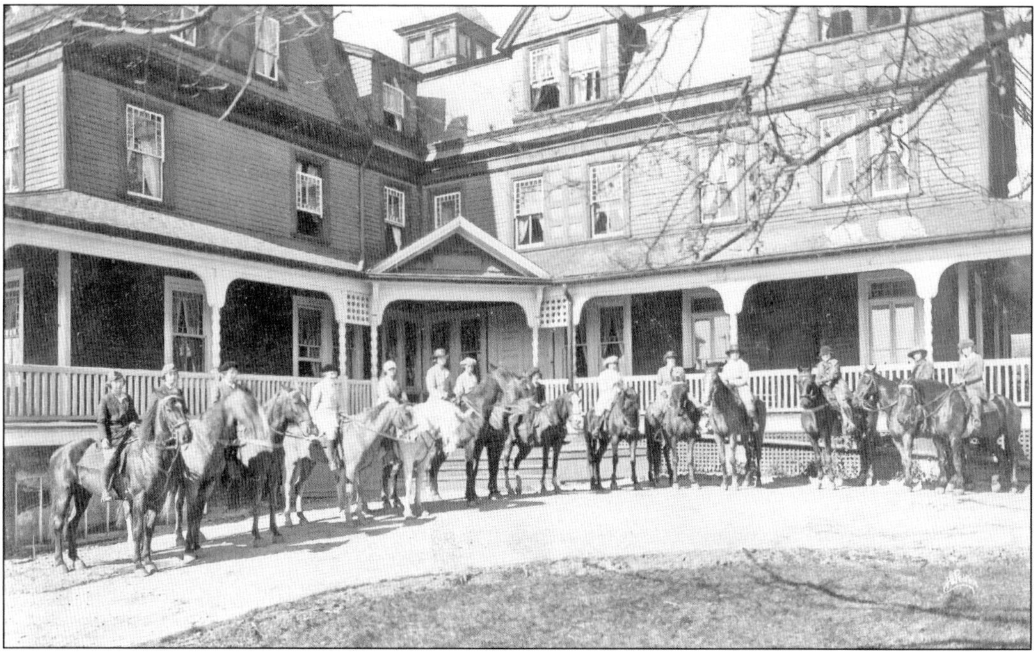

RIDING PARTY, C. 1909. A riding group poses for a photograph in front of the Victoria Inn before heading out to explore the town and countryside. The former Oakland Heights Hotel and Health Resort was situated on a hill above the confluence of the Swannanoa and French Broad Rivers and convenient to Asheville by way of Victoria Road and South Main Street. (North Carolina Collection, Pack Memorial Public Library.)

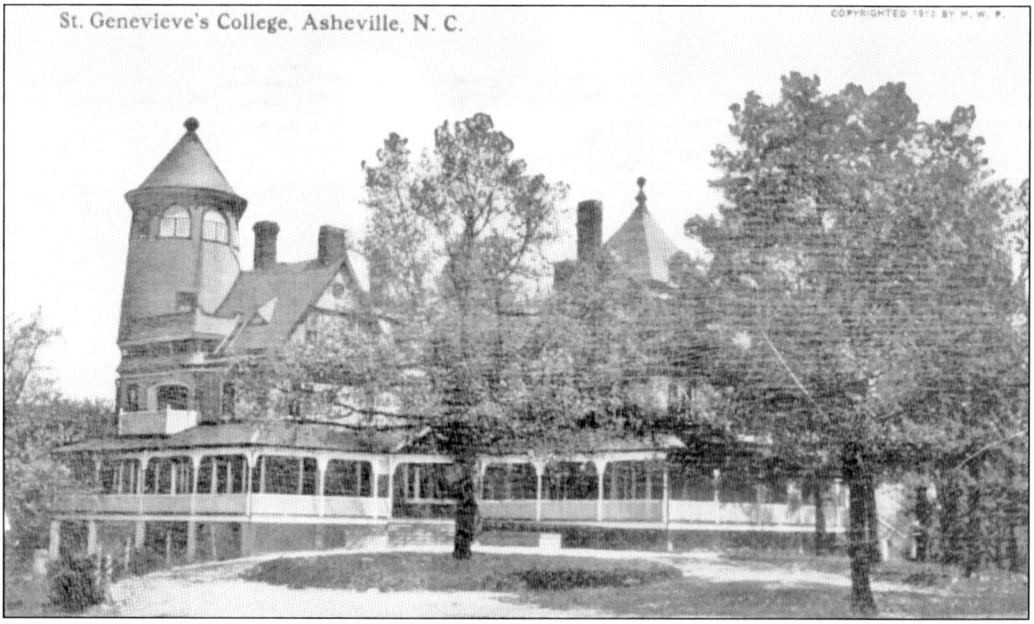

ST. GENEVIEVE'S COLLEGE, C. 1910. After a fire in 1910, the former Victoria Inn was sold to the Sisters of Christian Education for St. Genevieve's College, a boarding and day school for ladies that became St. Genevieve of the Pines school in 1922. Victoria Hall was used by the school for classrooms and as a convent for the sisters before it was razed in 1963. (Hal Branch.)

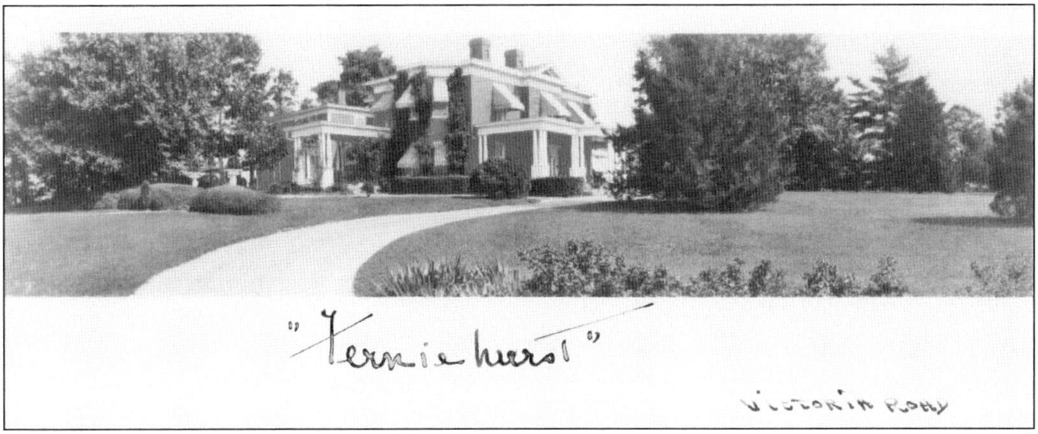

FERNIHURST. Col. John Kerr Connally, a Confederate veteran, and his wife, Alice, built a summer home called Fernihurst around 1875 on a hilltop just south of the Smith-McDowell House. This brick Italianate-style house, named after the Kerr family castle in Scotland, originally included 25 rooms. In 1933, new owner John P. Curran and architect Henry Irven Gaines razed several frame additions, leaving the original soft brick house. (North Carolina Collection, Pack Memorial Public Library.)

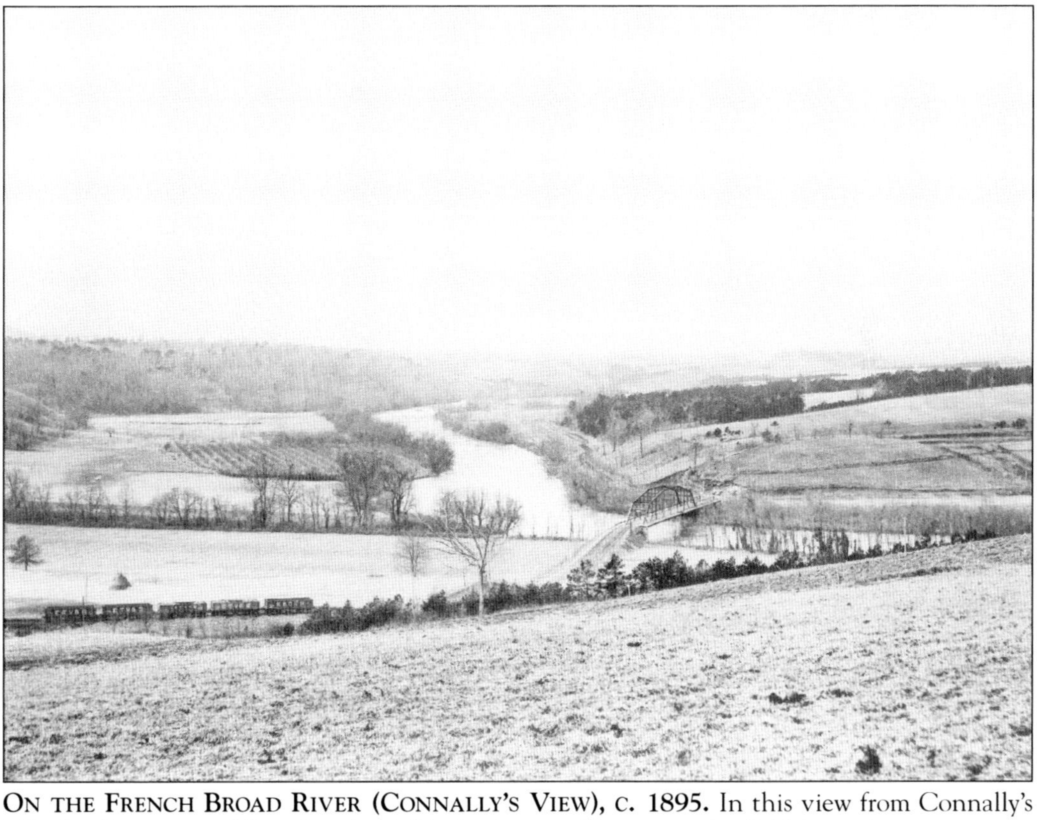

ON THE FRENCH BROAD RIVER (CONNALLY'S VIEW), C. 1895. In this view from Connally's hill, the Swannanoa River, barely visible in the tree line across the field from the train, enters the French Broad at the left of the bridge. The cultivated fields and wooded hills on the left became part of Biltmore Estate. (From *Art Work of Scenes in North Carolina*, North Carolina Collection, Pack Memorial Public Library.)

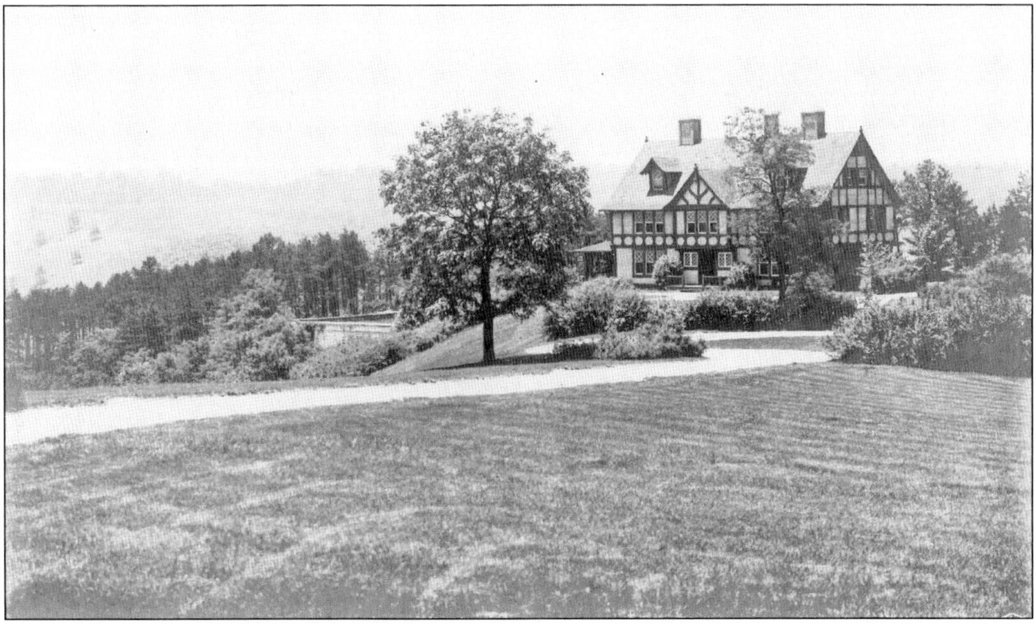

SPURWOOD, C. 1900. George Vanderbilt built Washington Cottage (later renamed Knollacre) in 1895 and began plans for improving Victoria Road and building five additional country residences on nearby Vernon Hill. Designed by Richard Sharp Smith, they were constructed in 1900. Spurwood, shown here, had 14 rooms and rented for $300 per month or $2,200 per year. (North Carolina Collection, Pack Memorial Public Library.)

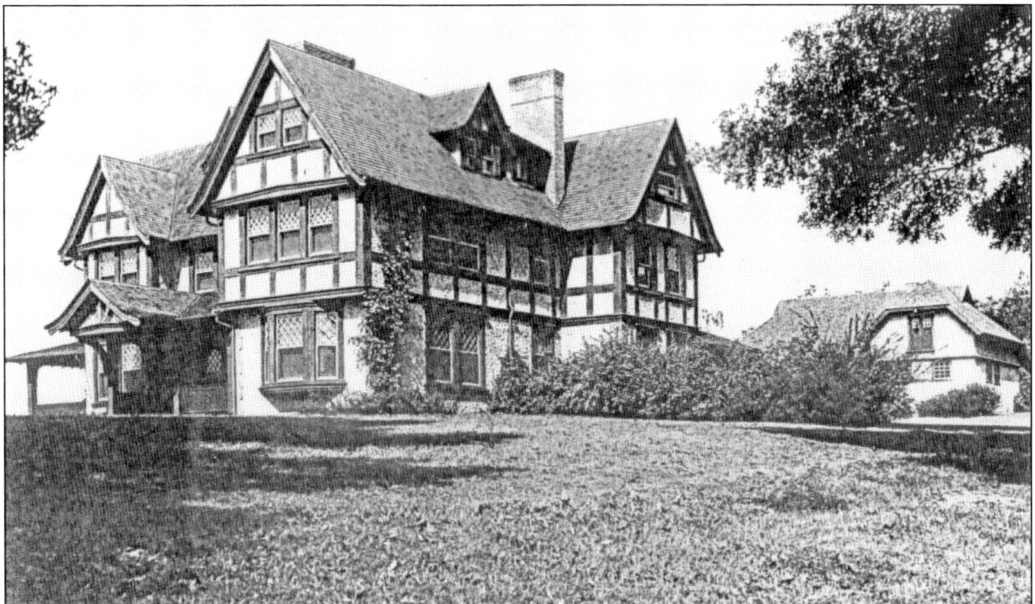

SUNNICREST, C. 1900. Similar in construction to Spurwood, with a gabled roof and exterior finish of half-timbers in-filled with roughcast or pebble dash, Sunnicrest was of similar size and amenities, and was rented furnished for $350 per month or $2,500 per year. Frances Hodgson Burnett, author of *Little Lord Fauntleroy* and later *The Secret Garden*, and her party rented Sunnicrest for two months in the winter of 1904.

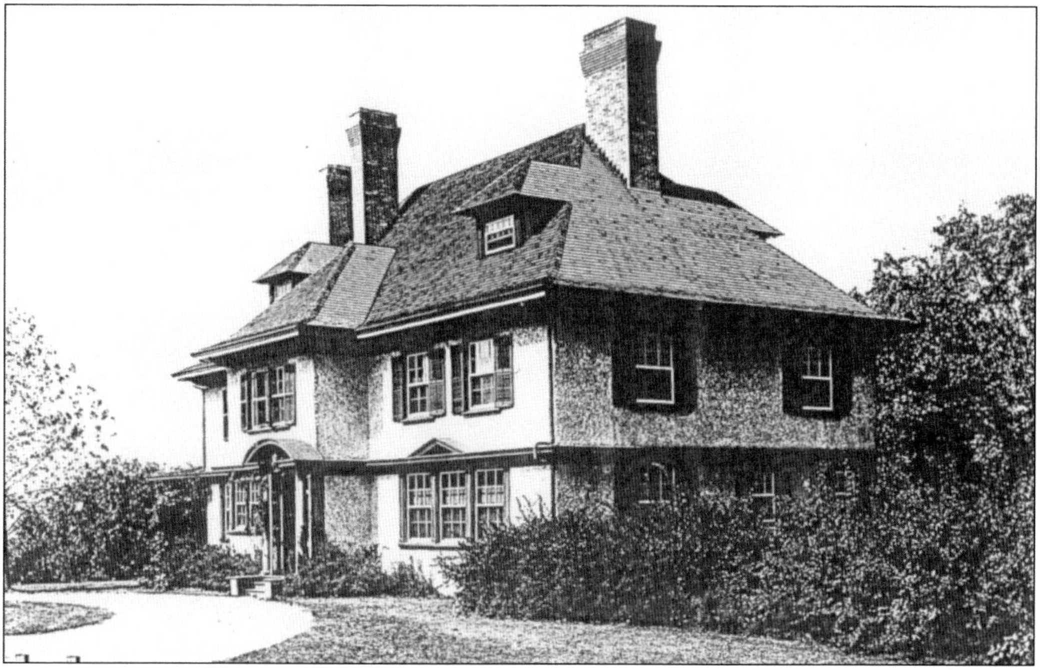

WESTDALE, C. 1900. The roughcast exterior of Westdale and its hip roof was similar in style to the two large cottages Richard Sharp Smith designed between All Souls Crescent and Rectory Lane in Biltmore Village. It included a large parlor, reception hall, dining room, kitchen, and butler's pantry on the first floor, five bedrooms, a bathroom, and a hall on the second, and four chambers, a storeroom, and a bathroom in the attic.

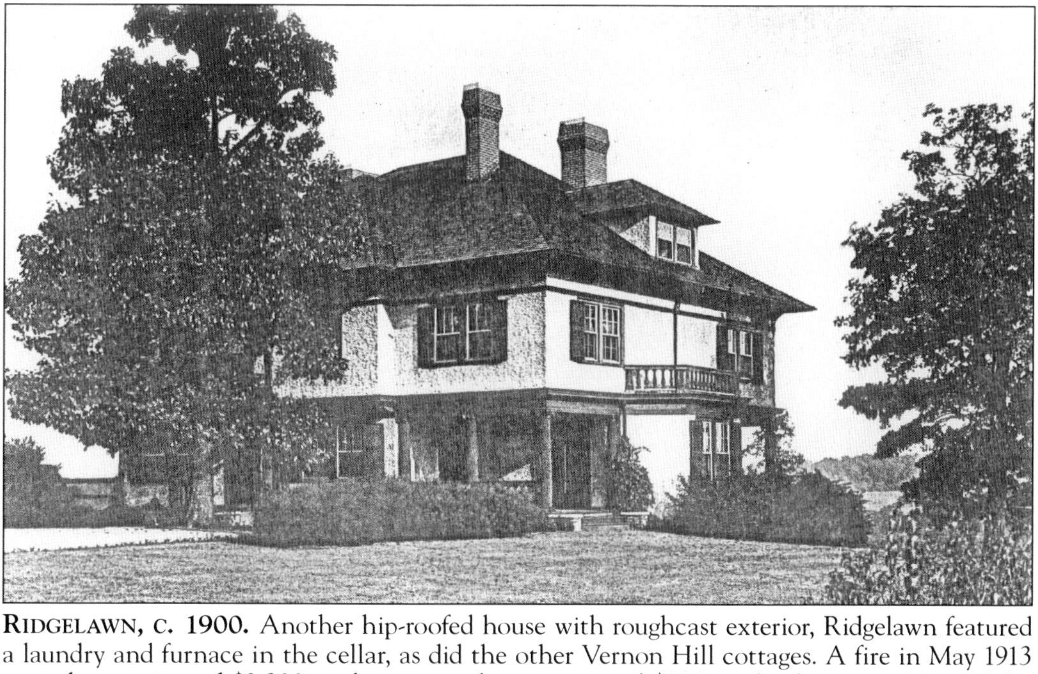

RIDGELAWN, C. 1900. Another hip-roofed house with roughcast exterior, Ridgelawn featured a laundry and furnace in the cellar, as did the other Vernon Hill cottages. A fire in May 1913 caused an estimated $2,300 in damage to the cottage and $200 to the furniture. Most of the damage was due to water and was repaired in quick order.

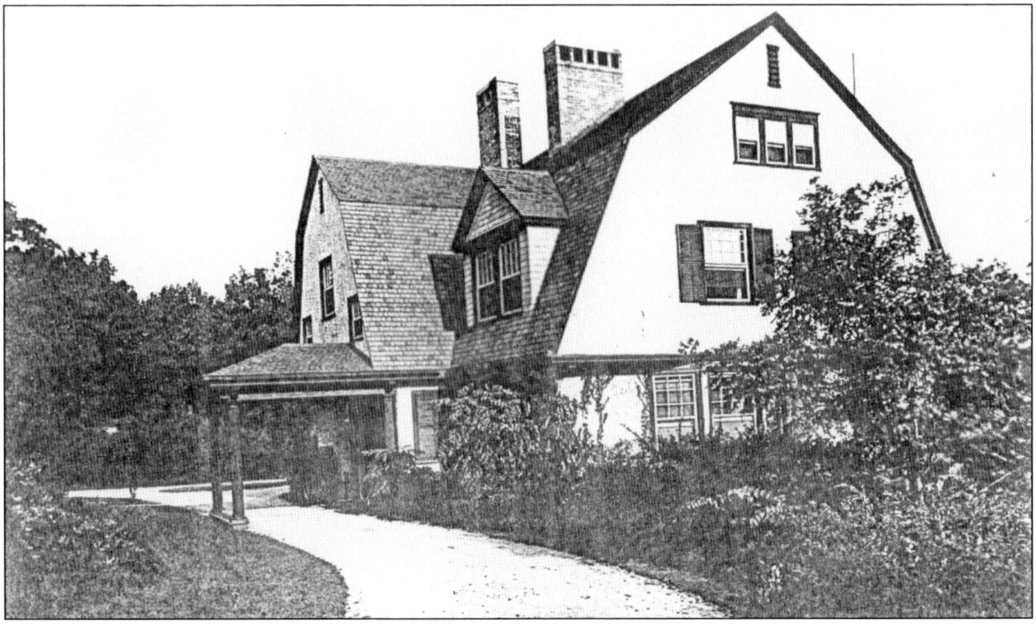

HILLCOTE, C. 1900. Different in style from the other Vernon Hill cottages, Hillcote featured gambrel roof lines at right angles to each other, was smaller, and rented for less. In response to a request from a prospective tenant wishing to know if rent for Hillcote could be lowered, George Vanderbilt wrote, "There is nothing as comfortable as this house in Asheville and by the year $1,600 or at rate of $133 per month is also far better than anything else."

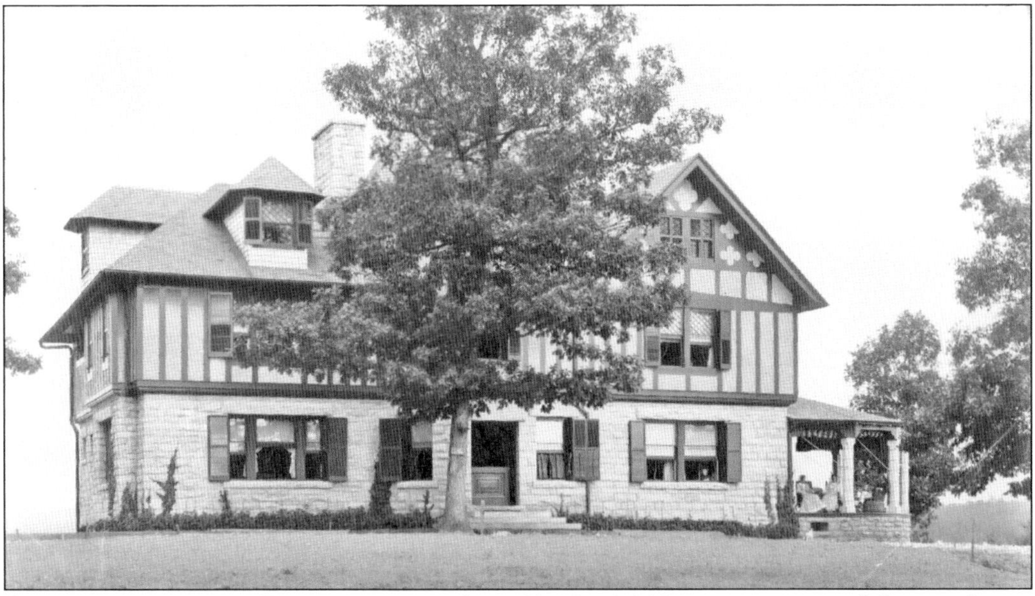

OLD FORD, C. 1900. Estate superintendent Charles McNamee constructed his residence, Old Ford, on the north side of the Swannanoa River in Victoria in 1890–1891. It was situated near Victoria Road, once part of the Buncombe Turnpike, which crossed the Swannanoa at Davidson's Ford. The crossing was later known as Patton's Ford and finally Old Ford, which probably inspired McNamee's choice for the name of his house. McNamee was later mayor of the town of Victoria.

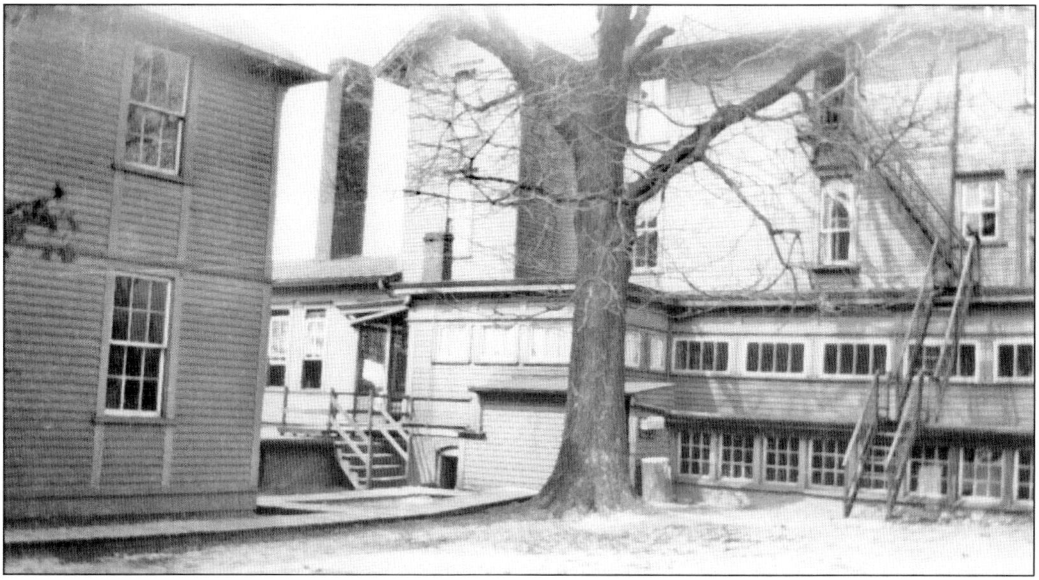

PEASE MEMORIAL HOUSE. Rev. Louis McKendrick Pease established the Asheville Home Industrial School near South Main Street on October 5, 1887. Pease, recognizing the importance of hand as well as head and heart training, had previously erected a building in 1885 for an industrial school for black women on College Street that he deeded to the Women's Board of Home Missions of the Methodist Episcopal Church. (North Carolina Collection, Pack Memorial Public Library.)

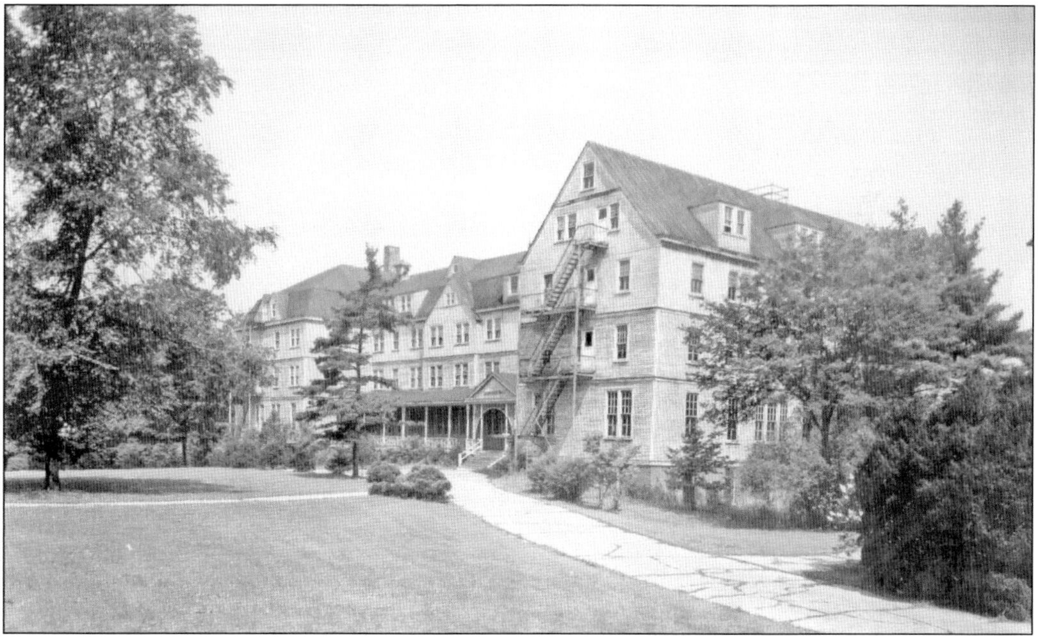

ASHEVILLE NORMAL AND COLLEGIATE INSTITUTE. THE Asheville Normal School, as it was often called, opened in 1887 as a project of the Home Missions Board of the Presbyterian Church on land donated by the Pease family. Lawrence Hall, seen in this rear view, was named for Dr. Thomas Lawrence, the first director of the school. (North Carolina Collection, Pack Memorial Public Library.)

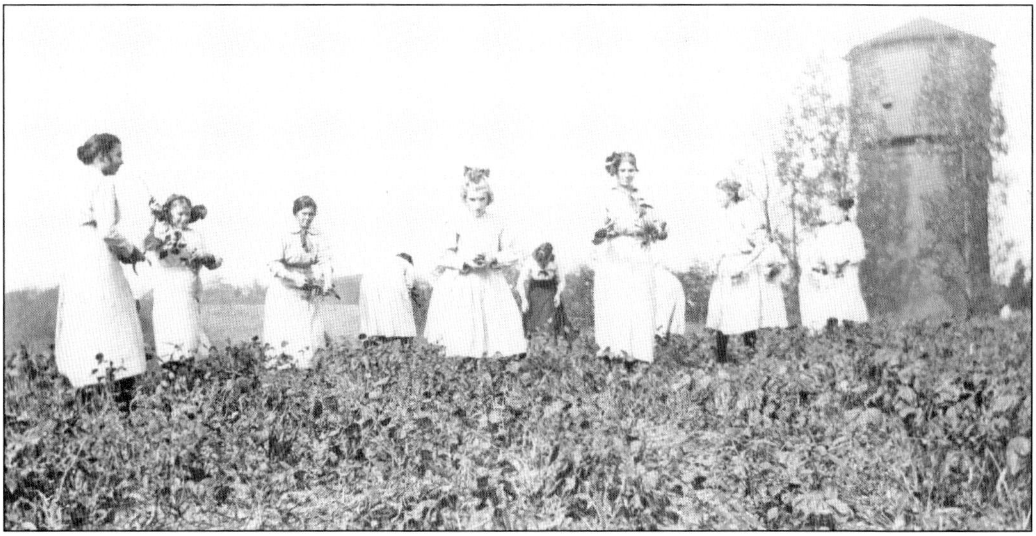

ASHEVILLE NORMAL STUDENTS, C. 1918. The Asheville Normal and Collegiate Institute was one of many women's schools that flourished in Western North Carolina in the late 19th and early 20th centuries. Most were finishing schools and did not have the service mission of the Asheville Normal Teacher's College, as it came to be known. Working with the YWCA and Presbyterian Board of Home Missions, the school encouraged its students to make individual efforts to contribute to the surrounding communities. The motto of service meant that graduates integrated themselves into whatever community hired them to teach, joining churches, participating in the community's special projects, and stimulating the community to higher ideas. The above photograph shows students working in the school garden, used to supplement food supplies, and a silo in the right background. Below, students are building a wooden structure in 1918. (North Carolina Collection, Pack Memorial Public Library.)

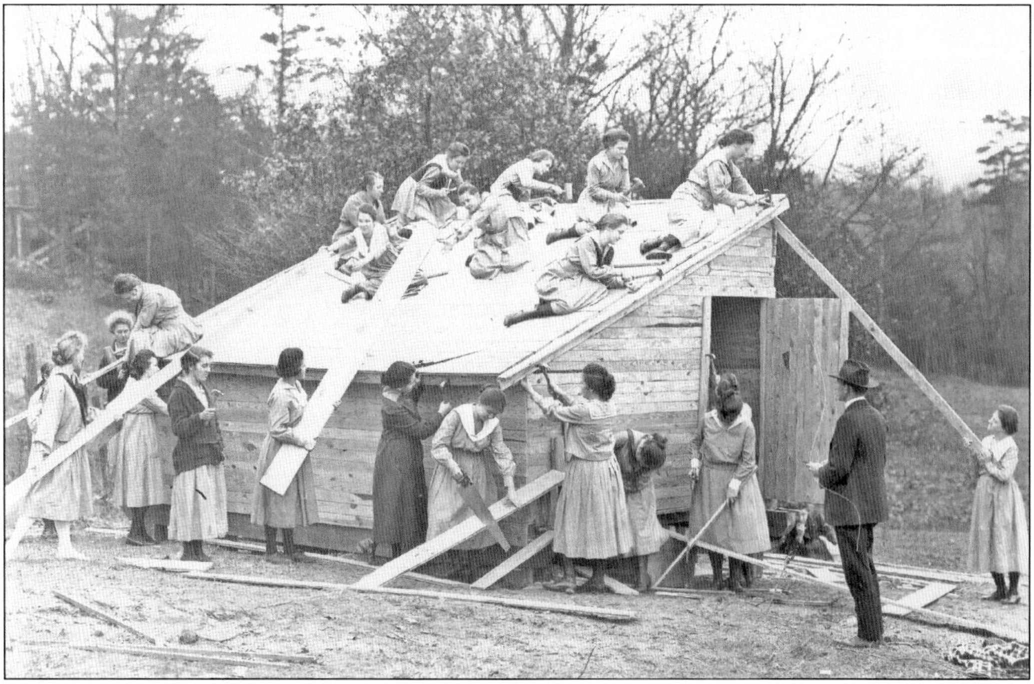

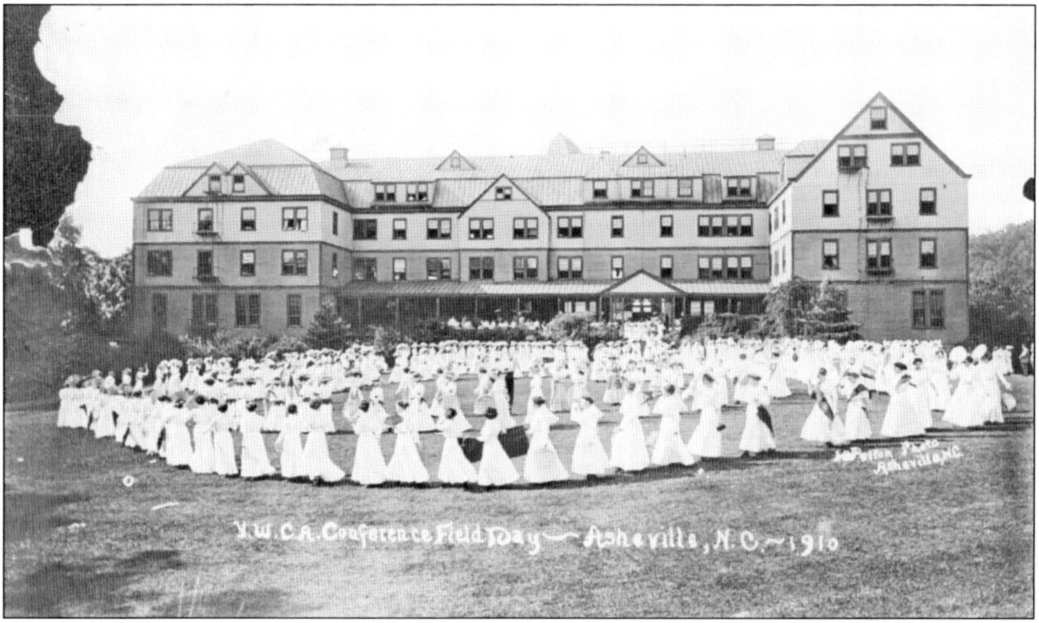

LAWRENCE HALL, ASHEVILLE NORMAL AND COLLEGIATE INSTITUTE, 1910. The campus and buildings of Asheville Normal and Collegiate Institute played host for many events through the years. In the above Herbert W. Pelton photograph of a YWCA Conference Field Day held on the campus of Asheville Normal, the elegantly dressed women carry pennants and parade in a circle while onlookers watch from the porch of Lawrence Hall in the background. Below, members of the Southern Presbyterian Synod are shown at a meeting at the Asheville Normal hosted by Dr. Thomas Lawrence. About a hundred people, mostly men, are gathered on the porch, steps, and lawn in front of Lawrence Hall. (Both, North Carolina Collection of Pack Memorial Public Library.)

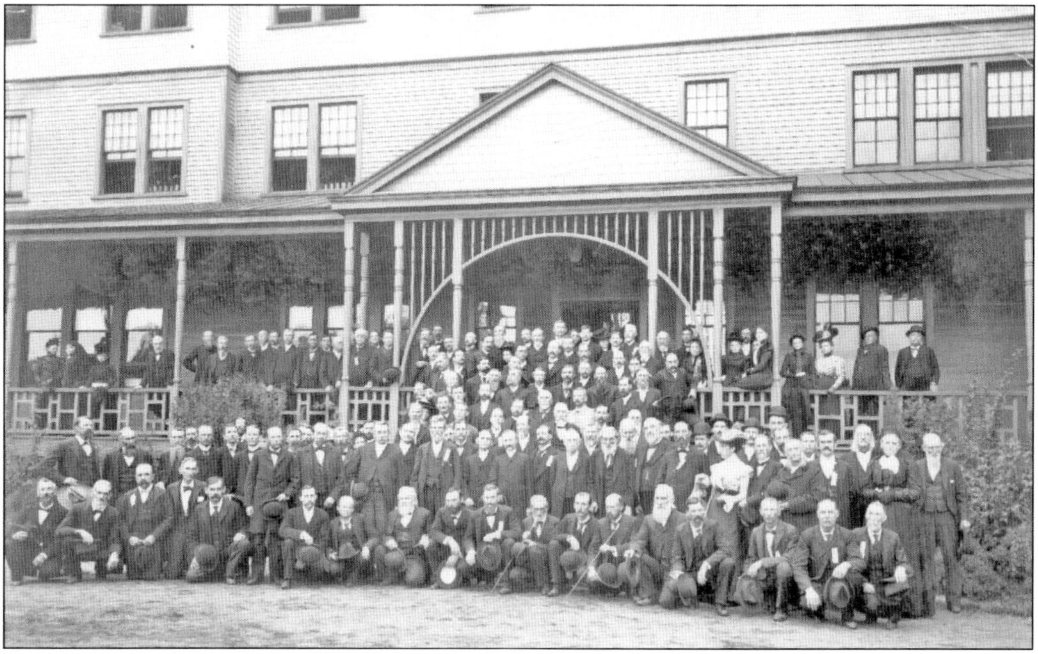

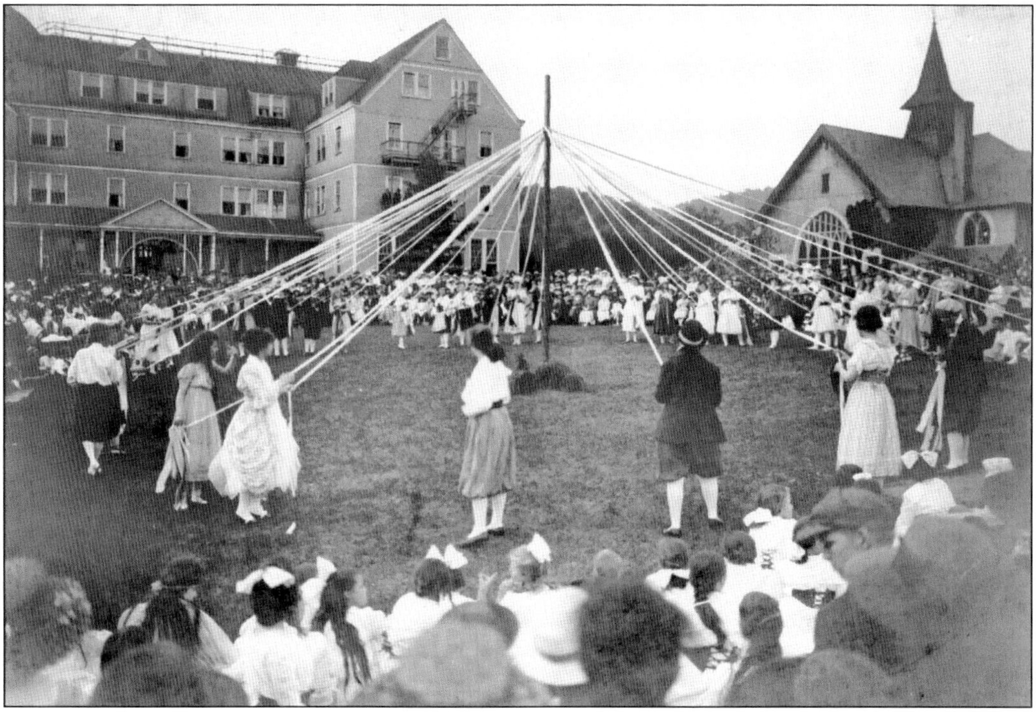

May Day Celebration at Asheville Normal and Collegiate Institute, 1919. Families and friends gather to watch the popular May Day celebration held on the campus of the Asheville Normal School in the above Herbert W. Pelton photograph. In the Pelton photograph below, students in flowing white dresses perform around the Maypole in celebration of May Day. By 1918, the school, with 14 faculty members, had graduated 570 women since it opened in 1887. (Both, North Carolina Collection, Pack Memorial Public Library.)

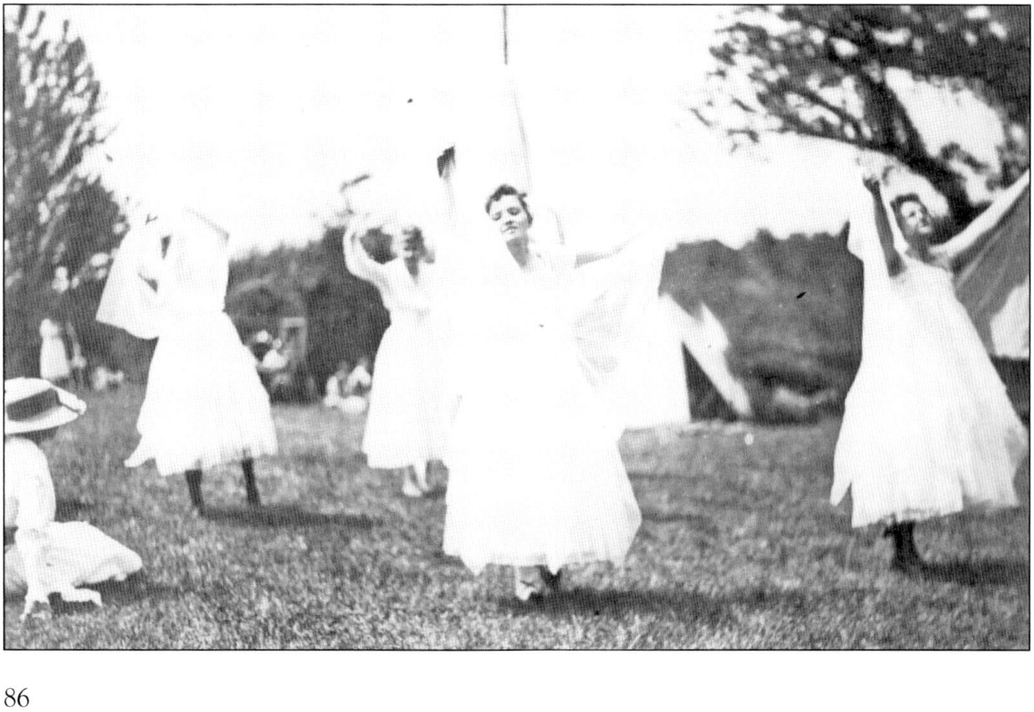

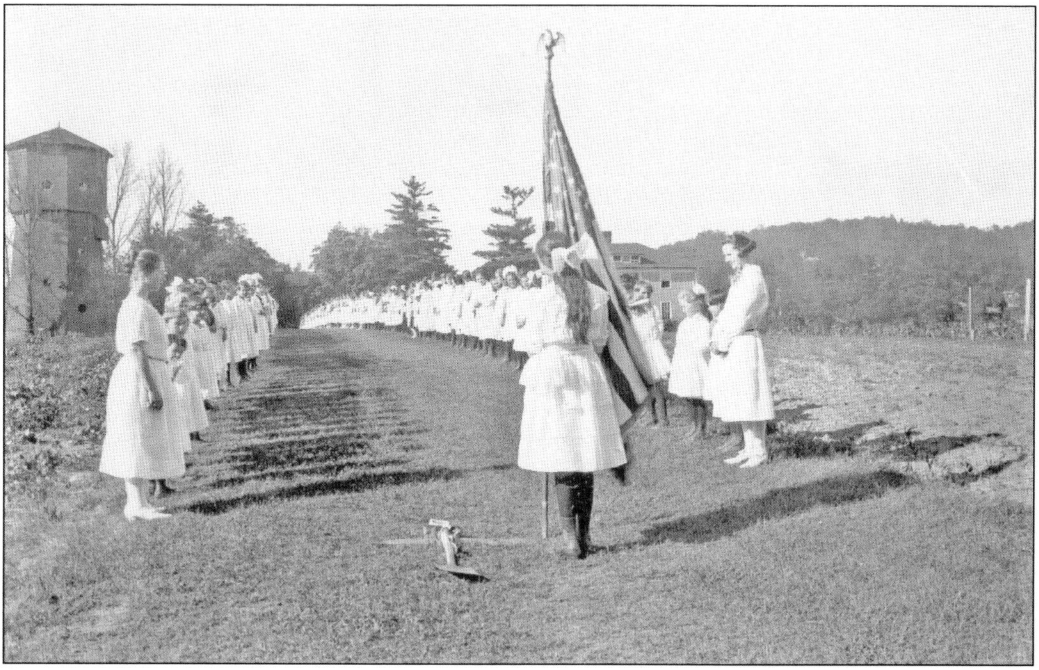

GROUND-BREAKING CEREMONY, 1920S. In the above photograph, students are lined up before a flag bearer for ground-breaking ceremonies for the Florence Stephenson Hall on the campus of Asheville Normal. The hexagonal tower, sometimes referred to as the "silo," is seen on the left. In the photograph below, the gentleman is believed to be Dr. John E. Calfee, president of the college since 1916, leading the procession at the ground-breaking ceremonies. Pease Hall is seen in the right background. (Both, North Carolina Collection, Pack Memorial Public Library.)

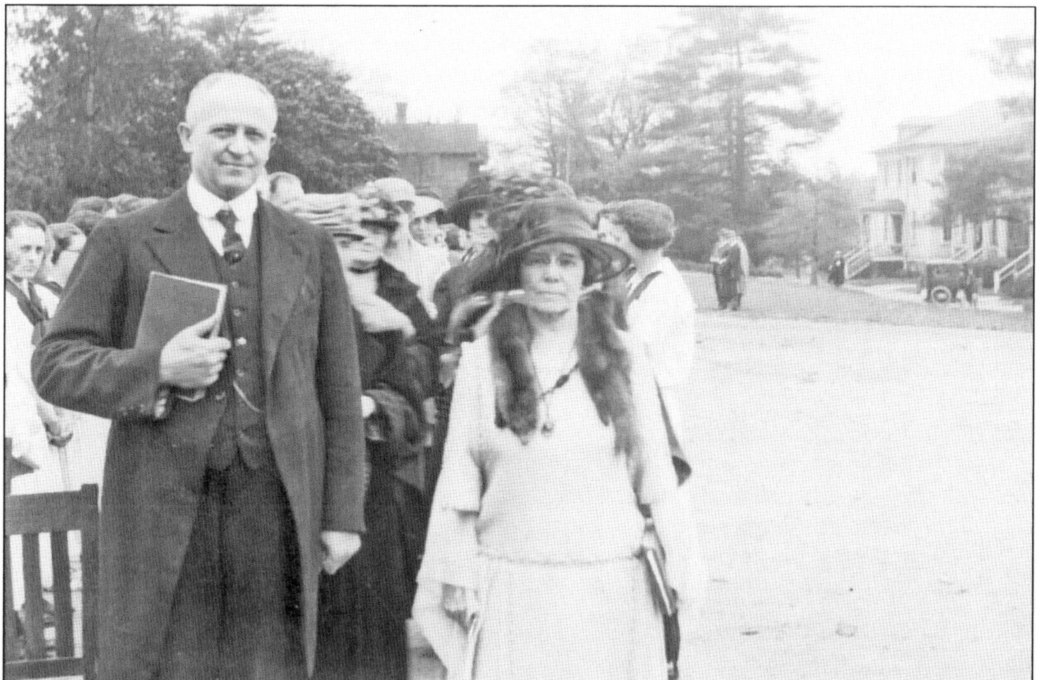

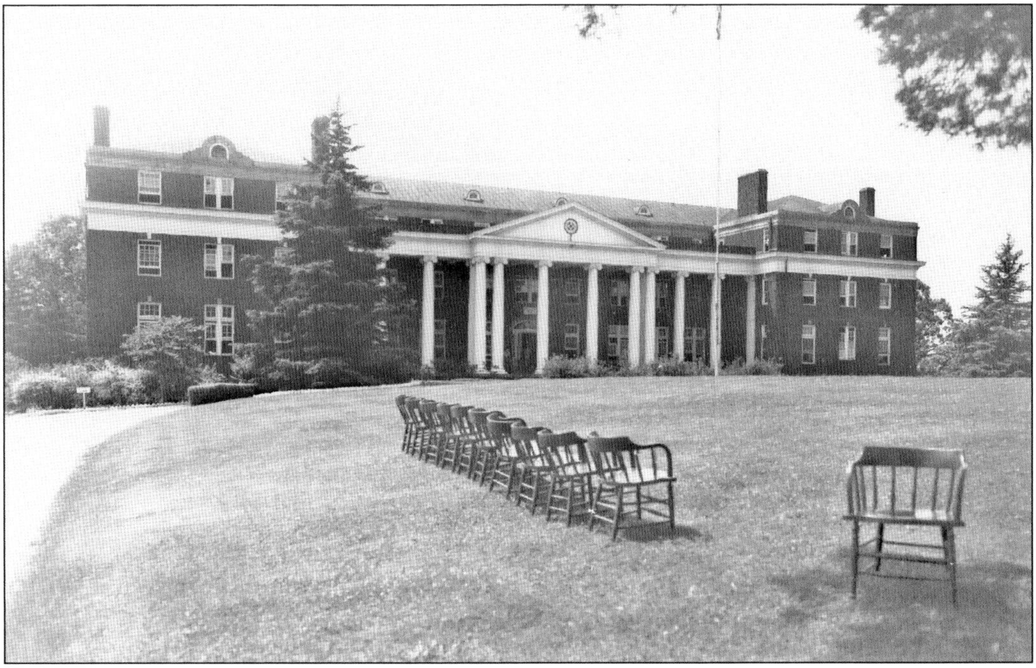

CAMPUS BUILDINGS, ASHEVILLE NORMAL AND COLLEGIATE INSTITUTE, C. 1930. Stephenson Hall, seen above, was built around or before 1930 and was named for Florence Stephenson, the first principal of Asheville Normal. Norburn Hospital, originally established in 1928 on Montford Avenue by Dr. Russell Lee Norburn and his brother Dr. Charles Norburn, acquired the campus in 1946. Prior to obtaining the Asheville Normal property, the hospital had struggled to survive through the Depression, when few of their patients could afford to pay their medical expenses. Pease Hall, in the photograph below on the campus of Asheville Normal, was built in 1908 and was remodeled in 1925 to function as a dormitory for seniors. This building became the nurses' home when the property was acquired by Norburn Hospital, which was eventually taken over by Memorial Mission Hospital. (Both, North Carolina Collection, Pack Memorial Public Library.)

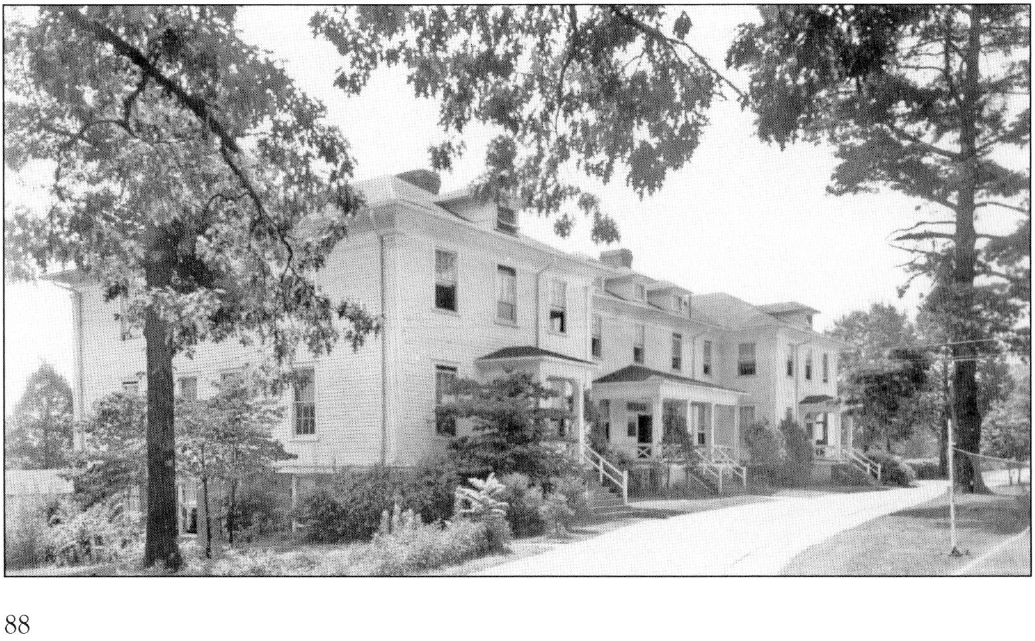

Five

The Changing Face of Biltmore

No town or place is frozen in time and secure from inevitable change, nor should it be. George Vanderbilt's untimely death on March 6, 1914, was the beginning of a long chain of events that started changing the face of Biltmore. Vanderbilt's death left his widow, Edith Vanderbilt, faced with making decisions concerning the management of Biltmore Estate, Biltmore Village, and the Vernon Hill cottages. She sold approximately 87,000 acres of Pisgah Forest to the federal government for national forest purposes, completing negotiations begun by her husband before his death. Edith sought the legal counsel of Judge Junius G. Adams to help her and the trustees of Vanderbilt's estate assess the assets, liabilities, and future prospects during this critical period. Then the devastating flood of July 16, 1916, struck and prompted a new look at plans. Among other things, Adams recommended that Biltmore Village and land on the north side of the Swannanoa occupied by the Biltmore Nursery be sold, but plans were put on hold when the country was drawn into World War I. The occupation of the new Kenilworth Inn by the U.S. General Hospital and the presence of the military in the village through the war years changed everyday life in the area as the war affected life everywhere. On April 1, 1920, all of Biltmore Village except for All Souls Church, the hospital, rectory, parish house, and train station was sold to George Stephens and the Appalachian Realty Company. Stephens in turn began selling various parts of the village over a period of time. The Great Depression set the village back severely, as it did Asheville and the whole country. As each decade passed, Biltmore Village continued to change and experienced periods of growth as well as periods of being at a standstill. Floods in 1928 and 1940 and another world war, as well as the building boom that followed, each played a role in the changing face of Biltmore.

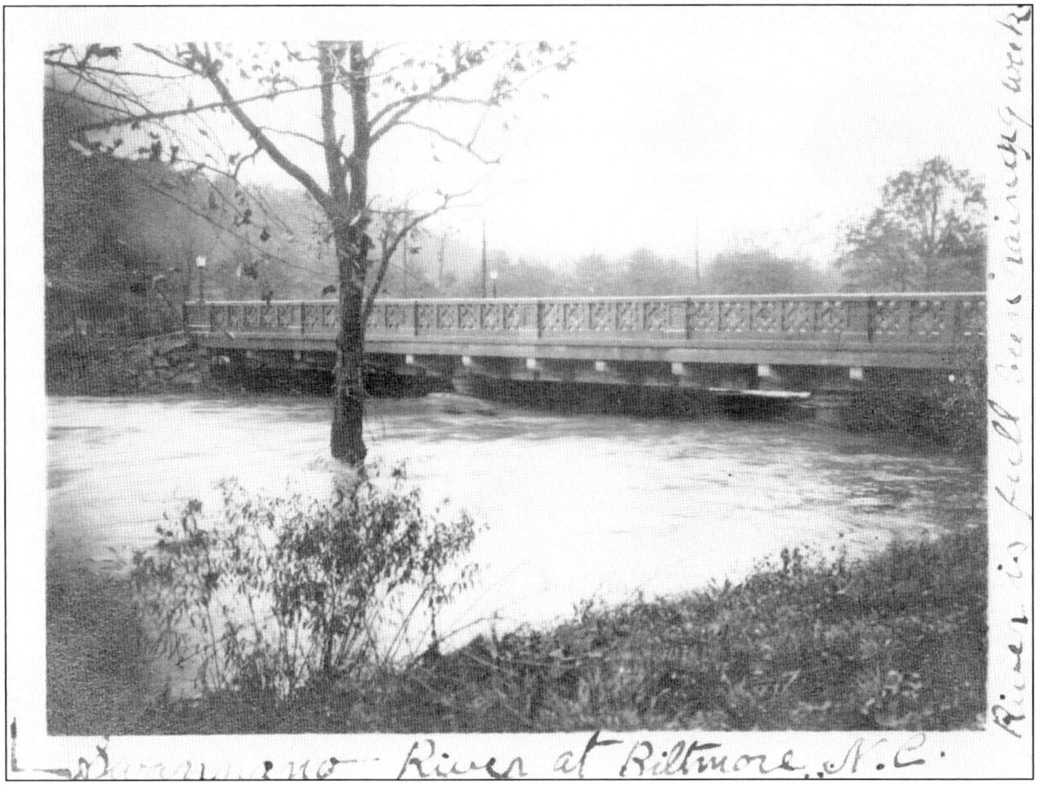

BILTMORE FLOOD, JULY 16, 1916. Settlements along the banks of the Swannanoa and French Broad Rivers endured major floods in 1796 and 1845, and in the devastating 1852 flood, lives were lost and existing bridges were washed away. Another flood occurred in 1901. In the above photograph, believed to have been taken by George Masa, floodwaters are again rising near the newly built Biltmore Bridge. Framed by the double row of power poles marking Biltmore Avenue, the view below was taken from atop a streetcar looking across the swollen Swannanoa River toward Biltmore Village and the tower of All Souls Church. The small building visible at center was the waiting room at the terminus of the electric street railway line that had floated into the street. (Both, North Carolina Collection, Pack Memorial Public Library.)

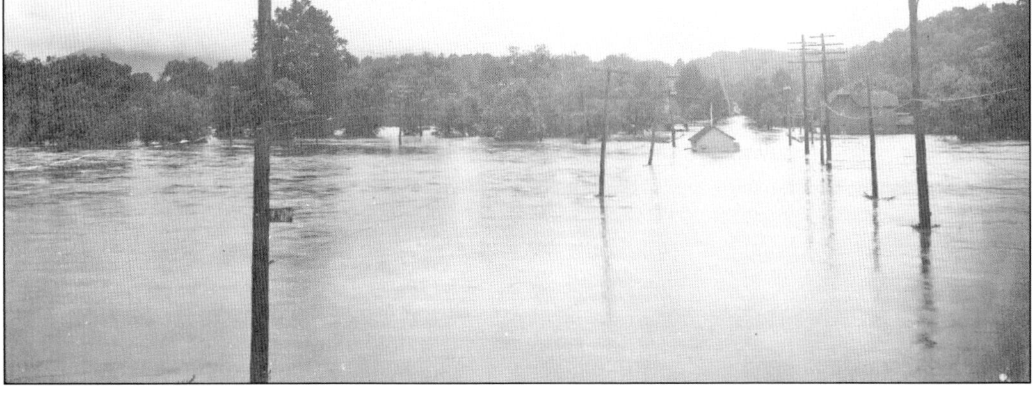

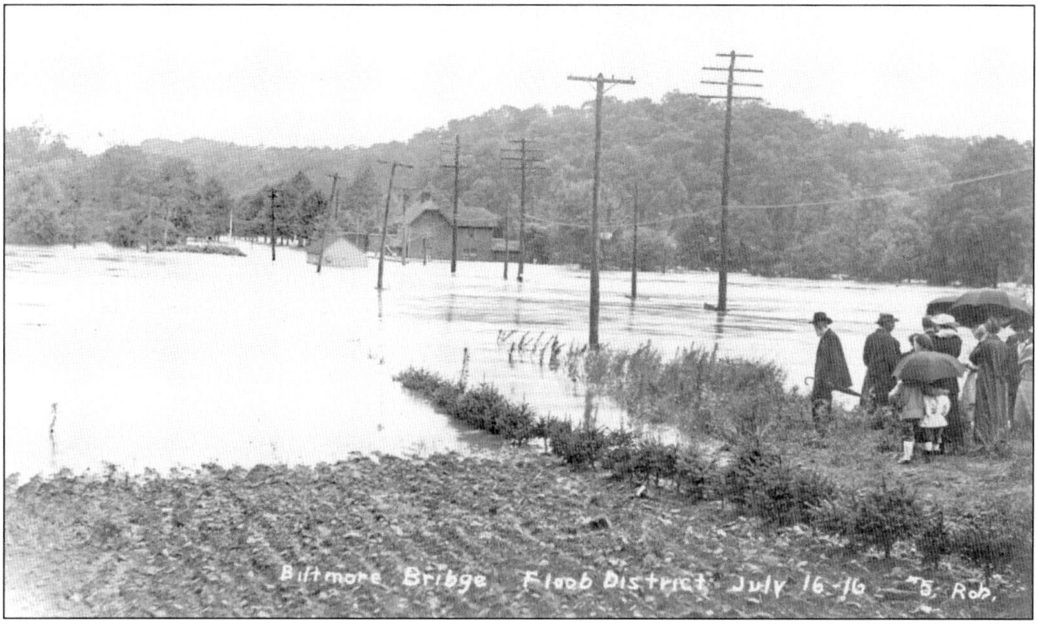

BILTMORE FLOOD, JULY 16, 1916. In the above image by John G. Robinson, curious onlookers are gathered near the end of the electric street railway line near the Swannanoa River. The waiting room is in the center of Biltmore Avenue just ahead, and debris is lodged on the bridge railings beyond. The residence of Capt. J. C. Lipe and family is readily visible on the opposite, or south, bank of the river. Below, receding waters reveal both triumph and tragedy. The bridge designed by engineer Charles E. Waddell and constructed a few months before came through the flood with little damage except for the pole lights, which had to be replaced. On the south bank of the river to the right, little remains of the Lipe residence that sat across from the brick store building. (Both, North Carolina Collection, Pack Memorial Public Library.)

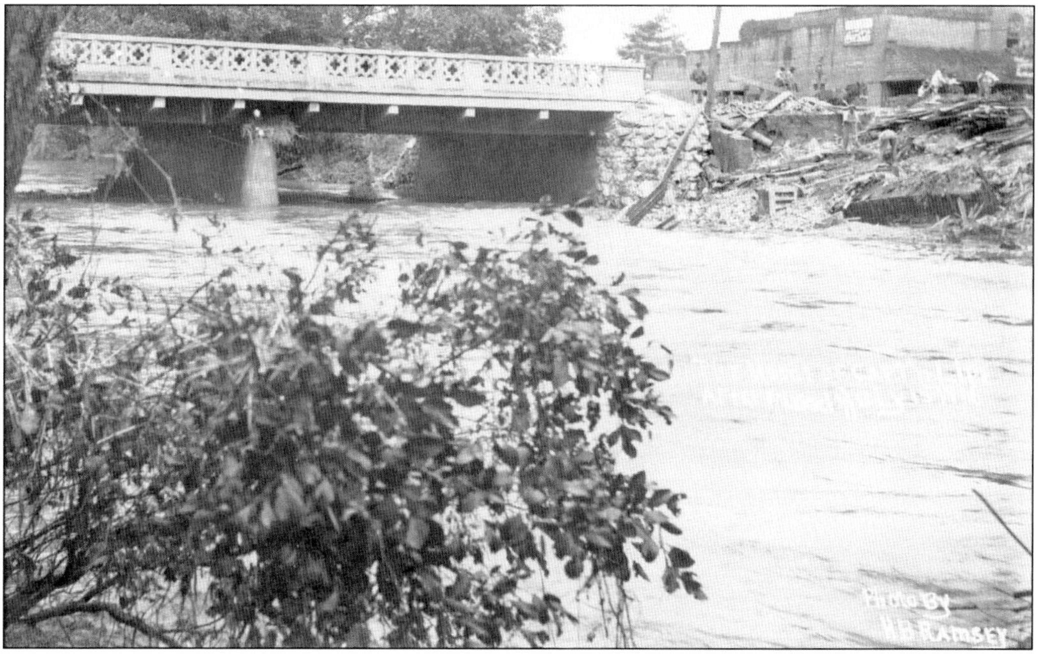

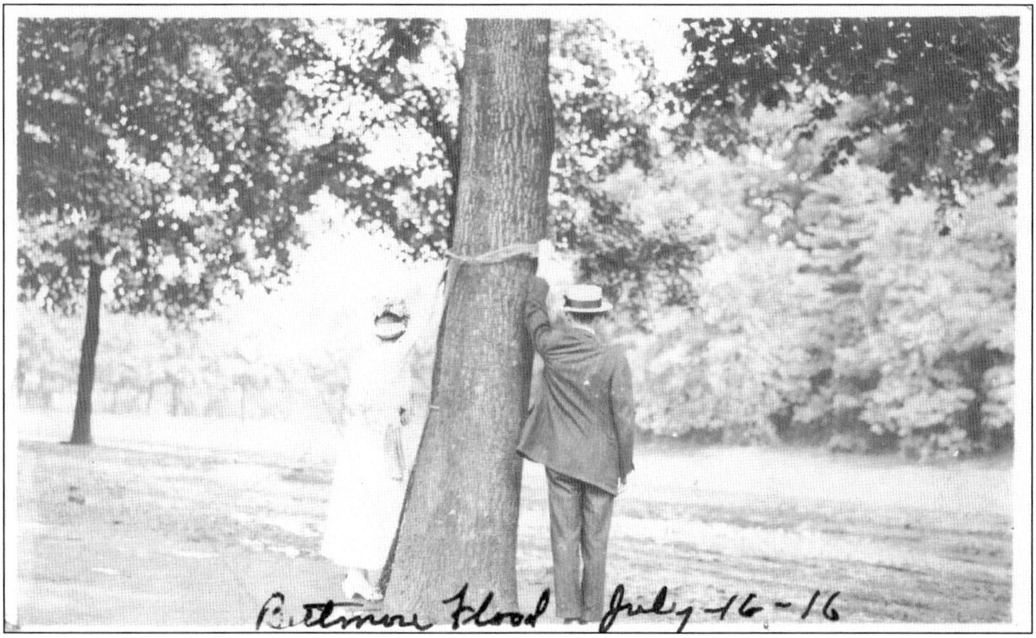

AFTER THE FLOOD, JULY 1916. In the above photograph, a man and a woman are marking the height of the floodwaters on a tree in the village green area adjacent to the Swannanoa River and near the Biltmore Estate entrance. Here Biltmore fireman Capt. James Cornelius Lipe lost his life while trying to save his daughter Kathleen; two nurses, Vickie Foister and Charlotte Walker; and Charlotte's 15-year old sister, Marion. After hours of clinging to this tree and failed rescue attempts, all were swept away and drowned except Kathleen. The force of the floodwaters collapsed the wall between the south side of the Lodge Gate and the adjoining hillside, as seen in the image below. (Both, North Carolina Collection, Pack Memorial Public Library.)

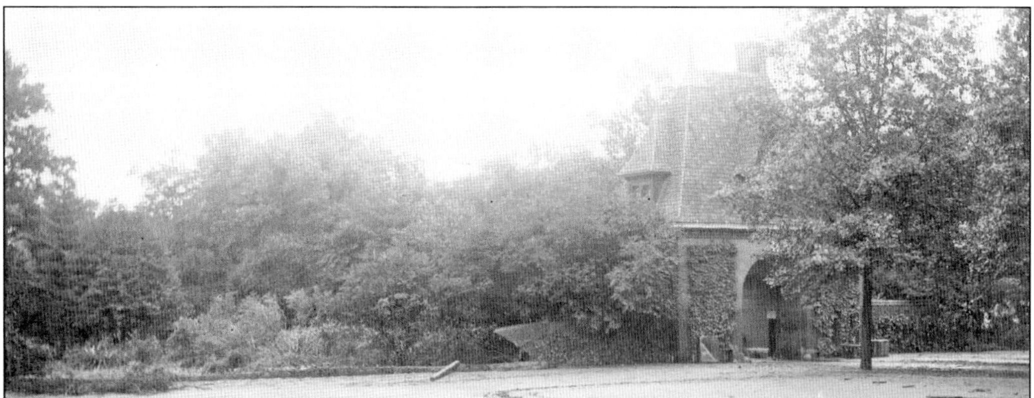

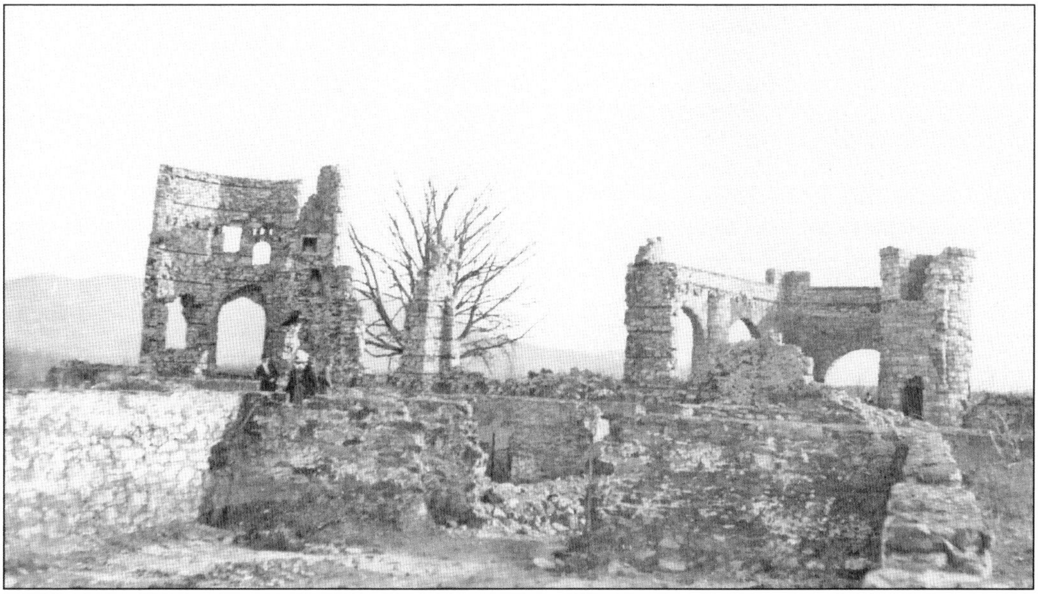

KENILWORTH INN RUINS, C. 1913. The original Kenilworth Inn burned on April 14, 1909. Although no guests lost their lives in the fire, the hotel manager died, and owner Sen. Joseph M. Gazzam narrowly escaped. Not having adequate insurance to cover such a total loss, Senator Gazzam sold the 151-acre property to James M. Chiles and his partners in 1912. (North Carolina Collection, Pack Memorial Public Library.)

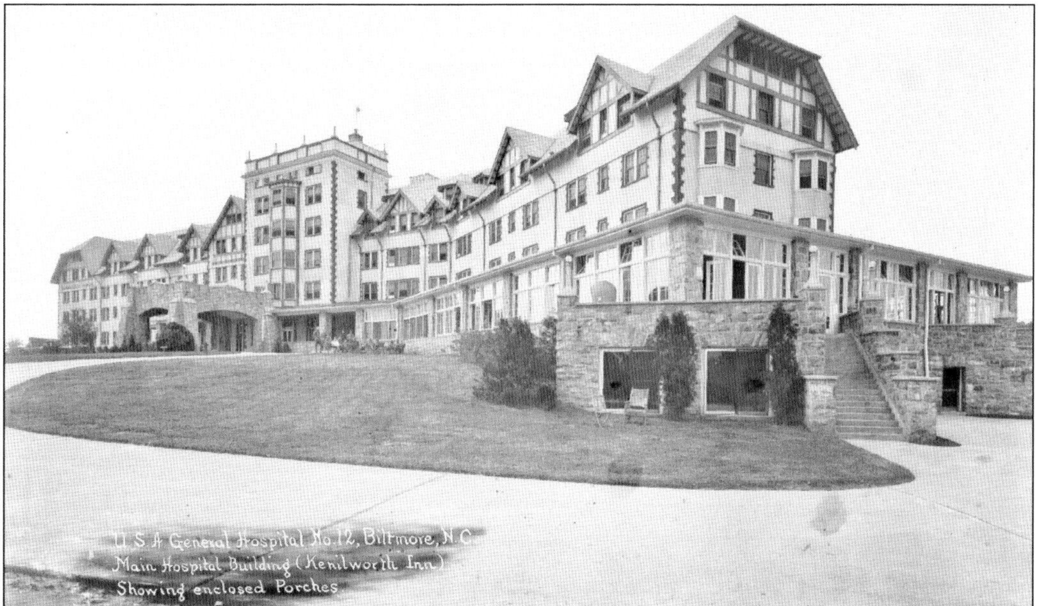

U.S. GENERAL HOSPITAL NO. 12, BILTMORE, NORTH CAROLINA, C. 1918. James M. Chiles and the Kenilworth Park Company were in the process of constructing a magnificent new inn to replace the one that burned down when the U.S. government commandeered the new Tudor Revival–style structure as an army convalescent hospital during World War I. (E. M. Ball Collection, D. H. Ramsey Library, Special Collections, University of North Carolina at Asheville.)

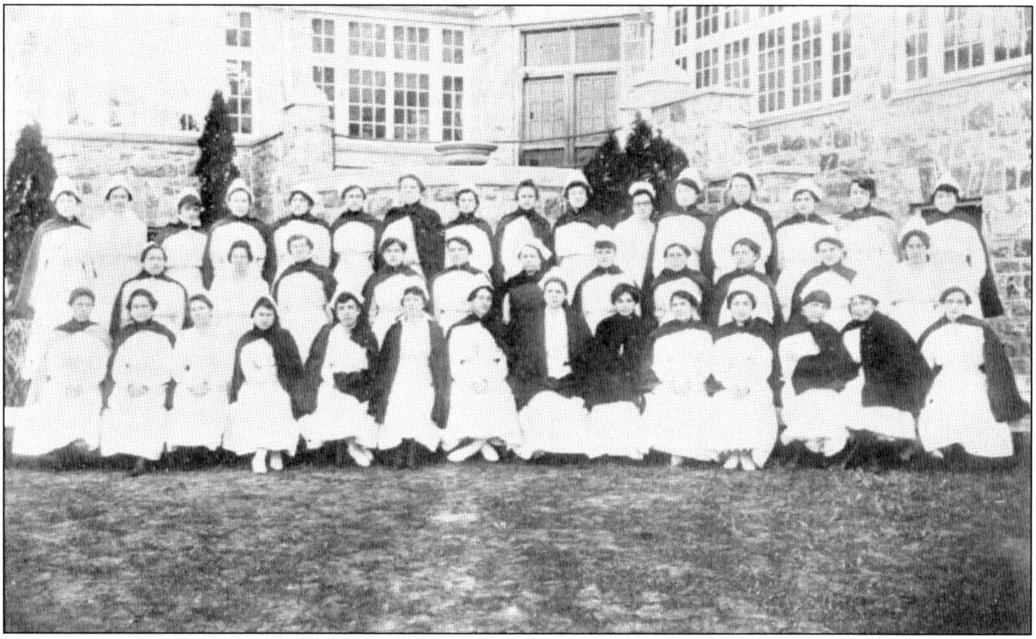

PART OF THE NURSING STAFF, C. 1918. During the time the Kenilworth Inn was used as a U.S. General Hospital, a large staff of officers and enlisted personnel, including the nurses shown here, was stationed at the hospital to care for wounded patients. Various houses in Kenilworth, Biltmore, and the surrounding areas were used to house officers and staff, including 16 All Souls Crescent, the former rectory in the village. (Hal Branch.)

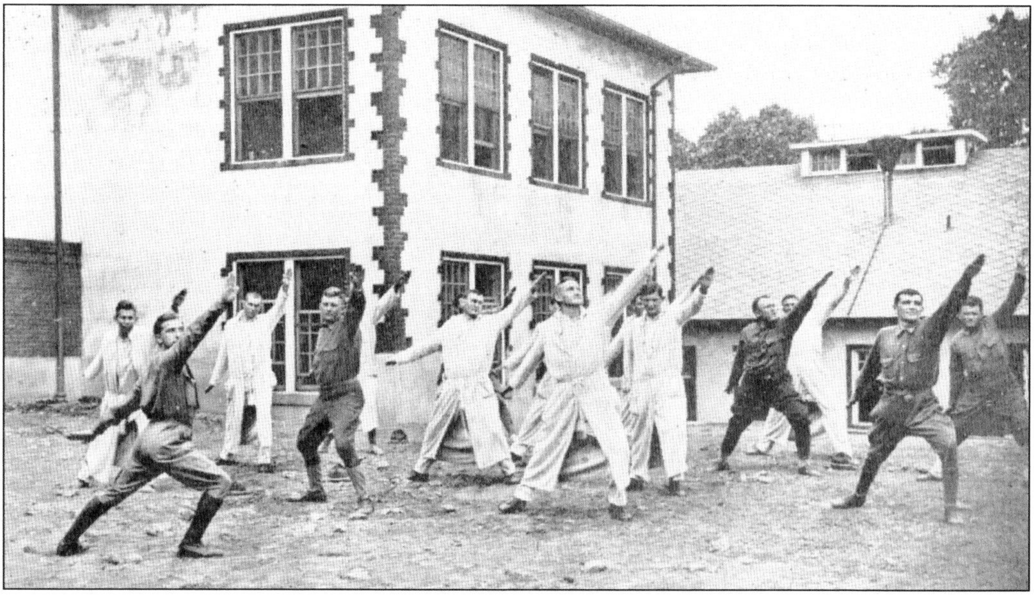

PATIENTS AT EXERCISE, C. 1918. Various activities, including therapy and exercise, helped the patients to recover from their wounds. The village greens in Biltmore, as well as the grounds at Kenilworth, were used for military drills, formations, and other activities for officers and enlisted staff. Edith Vanderbilt also allowed military personnel to visit the grounds of Biltmore Estate. (Hal Branch.)

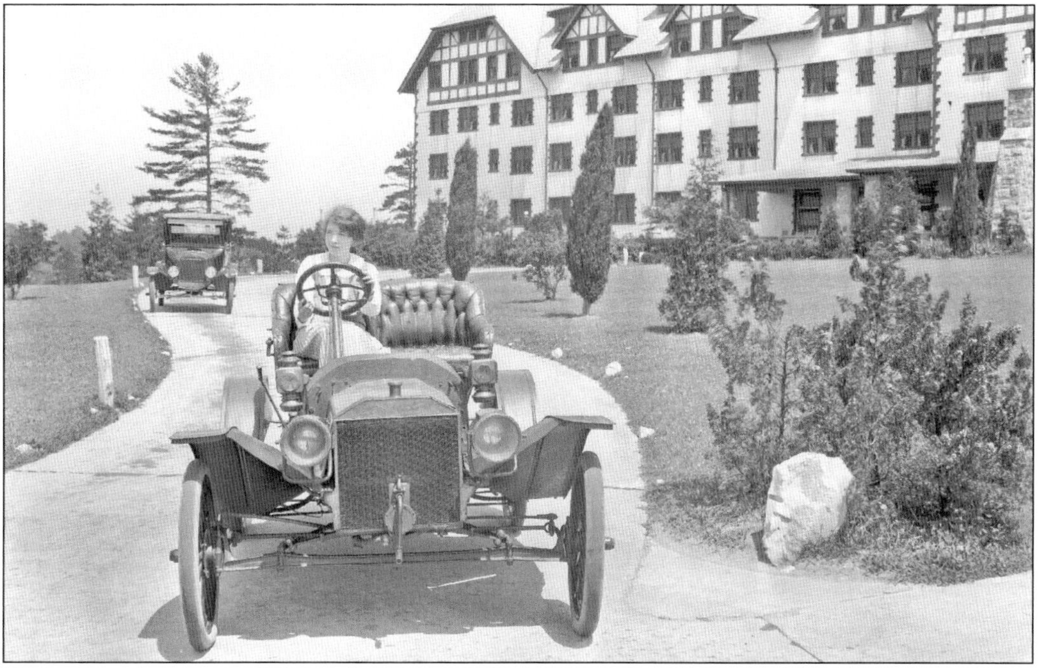

Kenilworth Inn, c. 1923. After the war, James M. (Jake) Chiles fulfilled his dream that "A new and better Kenilworth will rise, Phoenix-like, from its ashes" and completed the inn, the rival of the best that Asheville had to offer. It took three years to restore the inn from alterations made by the government and to add finishing architectural details for the March 1923 opening. Kenilworth Inn, which could accommodate 500 guests year-round, was a much-needed hostelry to support Asheville's growing numbers of visitors and vacationers. Like Grove Park Inn, it sat atop a hill in the midst of woodlands and beautifully landscaped grounds, and offered guests a quiet and peaceful setting while providing quick and easy access to the city for shopping, entertainment, and business. (Both, E. M. Ball Collection, D. H. Ramsey Library, Special Collections, University of North Carolina at Asheville.)

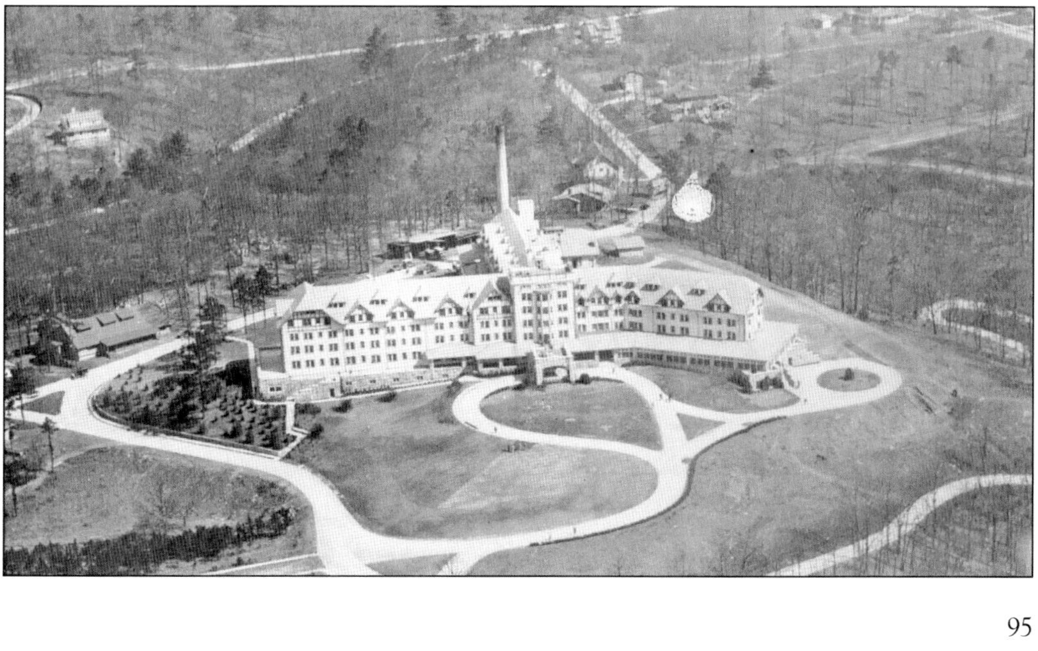

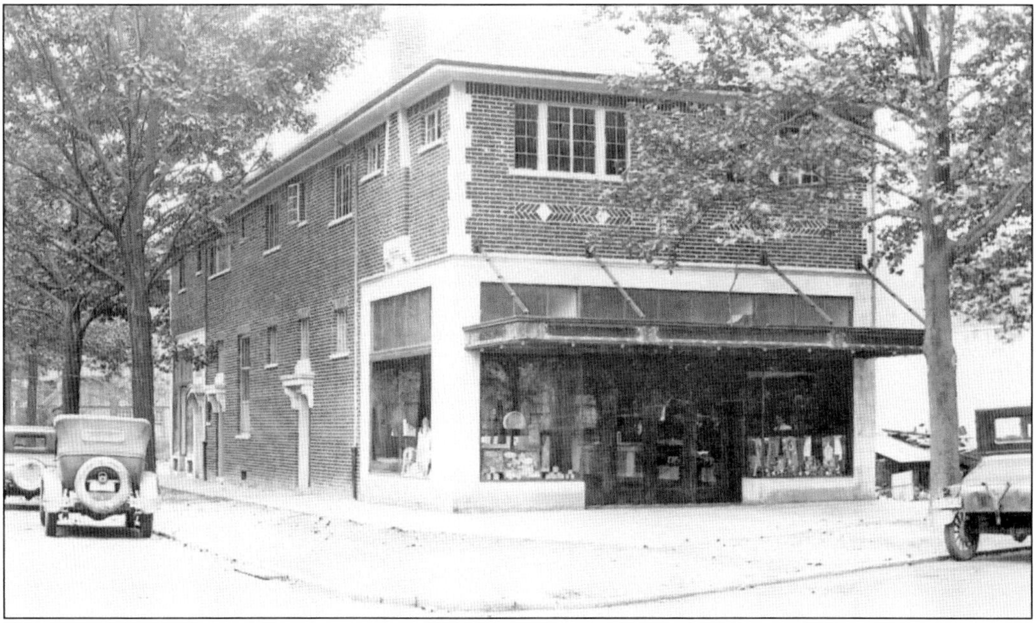

BILTMORE DRUG STORE, C. 1926. After Edith Vanderbilt's sale of the village to George Stephens and the Appalachian Realty Company in 1920, new businesses and growth began to occur. The Biltmore Drug Store, operated by Dr. Lloyd M. Jarrett, was a landmark in the village, having occupied 10 Plaza in the original store building since it opened in early 1901. The advertising pamphlet for the new store stated, "Introducing the New Biltmore Drug Store: Built to Serve Greater Asheville, In Biltmore, Corner of Oak and Short Streets On the Plaza." The new drugstore featured "ample parking space, delivery anywhere in Asheville, a real prescription service under the experienced care of a licensed druggist, and Buncombe's finest fountain (and we make no reservations)." The exterior of Biltmore Drug Store is seen above, and the soda fountain and cigar stand are pictured below. (Both, North Carolina Collection, Pack Memorial Public Library.)

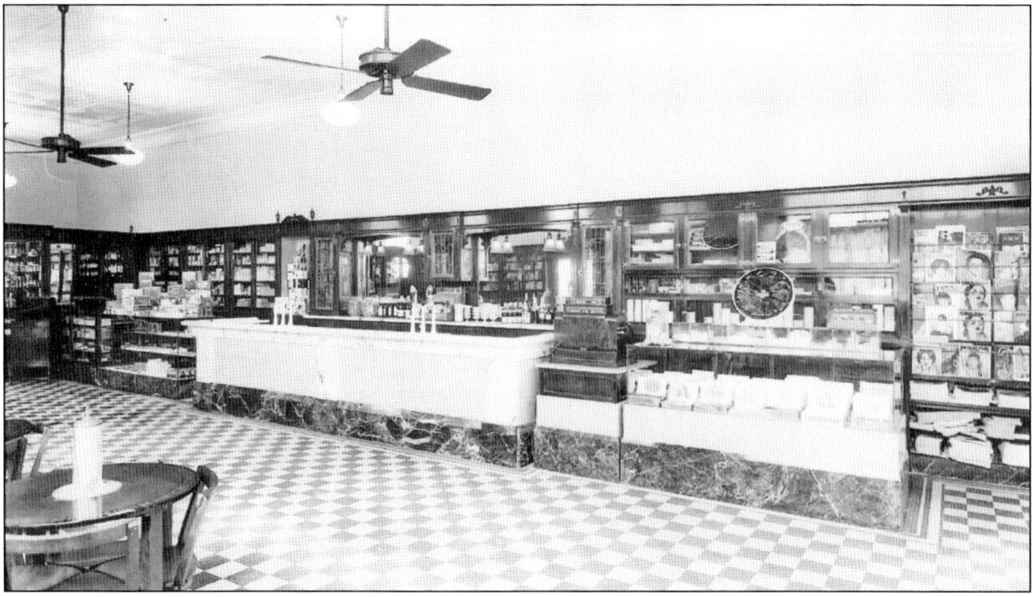

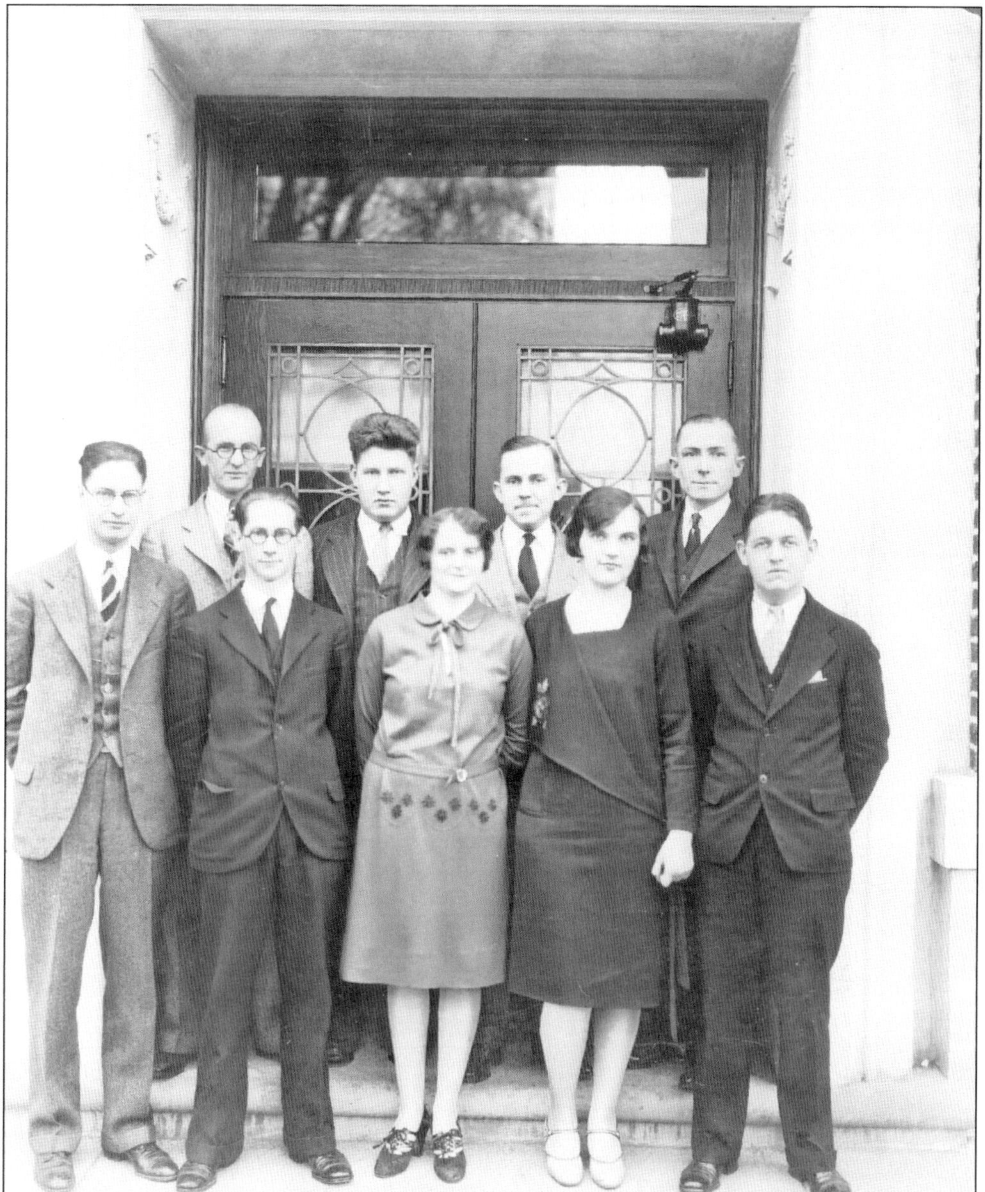

BILTMORE-OTEEN BANK, c. 1928. The Biltmore-Oteen Bank first operated out of the small half-timbered building on Lodge Street just west of the passenger station in the mid-1920s until this new building was constructed in its place. The bank leased office space with a fireproof vault at the corner of Oak Street and Plaza in 1926. The old bank building was moved farther west and turned at right angles with Lodge Street to make room for the two-story Georgian Revival structure that features English bond brickwork and classical ornamentation. Pictured in the group in front of the new bank is William Crown on the left in the first row, T. C. Harrell third from the left in the second row, and businessman Walter A. McGeachy on Harrell's right. McGeachy, a Mason and member of Biltmore Lodge No. 446, planned a special lodge room upstairs in his new McGeachy building, designed by local architect Ronald Green and completed in 1928 on the west side of the Plaza. (Biltmore Village Historical Museum.)

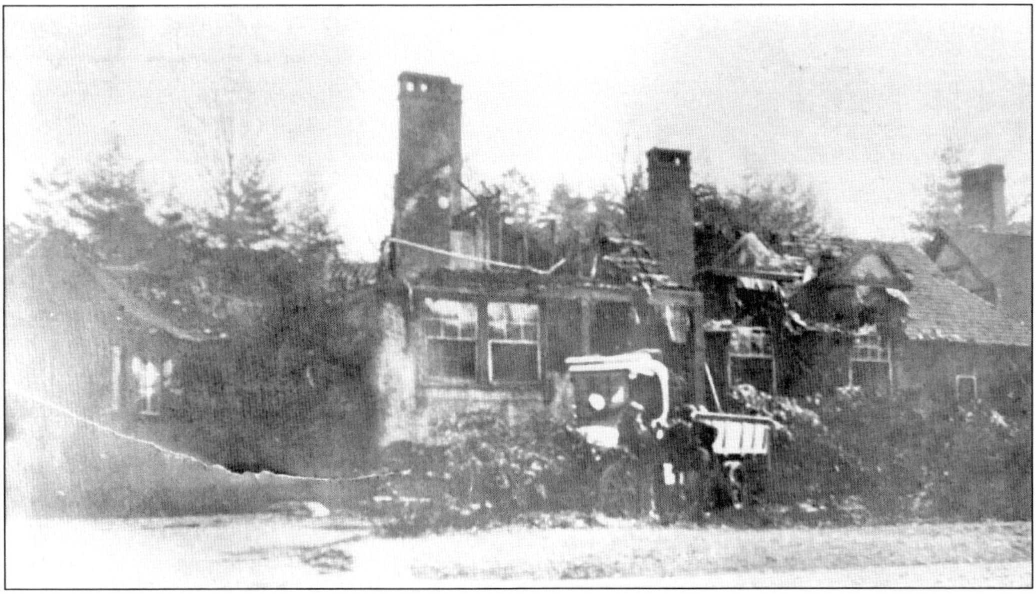

BILTMORE HOSPITAL FIRE, 1921. A severe fire loss at the hospital on January 1, 1921, prompted Edith Vanderbilt to offer 15 acres on a knoll between Hendersonville Road and Brandon Hill, accessible from the new Vanderbilt Road, to erect a 100-bed fireproof structure. After a second incident on March 7, 1921, Chauncey Beadle wrote to Charlotte L. Yale that on Saturday the hospital was again on fire. "It is a sad fate that institution is facing since New Years, and it must now rise or fall in its ashes. The destiny is up to its friends." (Biltmore Village Historical Museum.)

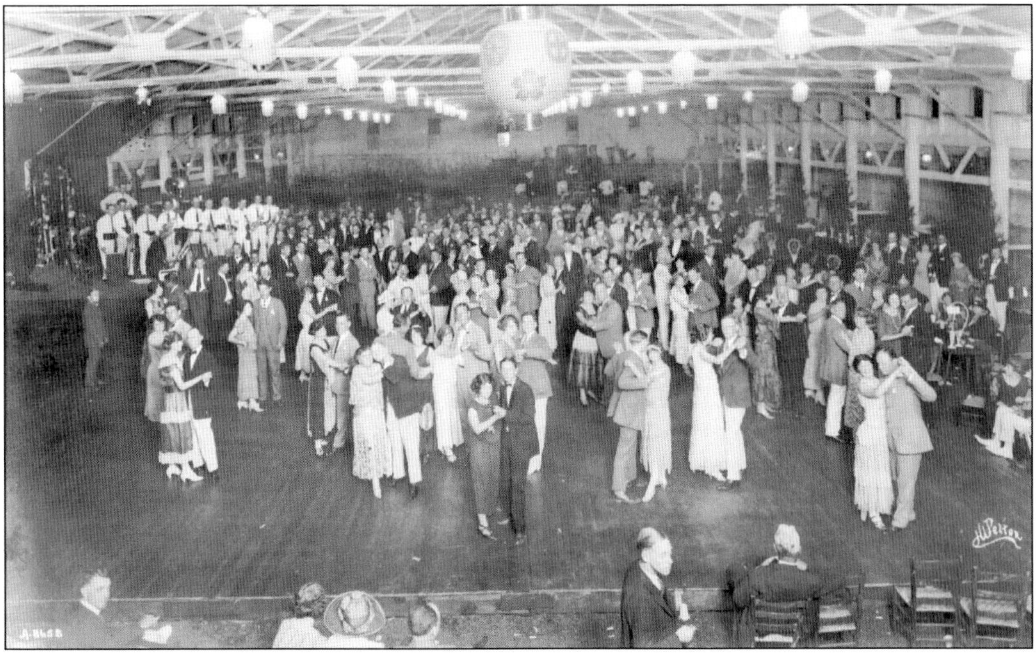

HOSPITAL BENEFIT, 1923. Cornelia Vanderbilt held a benefit cabaret in August 1923 to raise money for a new hospital. The cabaret, held at the Kenilworth Hippodrome on Swannanoa River Road, lasted six evenings, from August 6 to 11. The inside dimensions of the hippodrome were 75-by-150 feet, with about half the space being occupied by the dance floor.

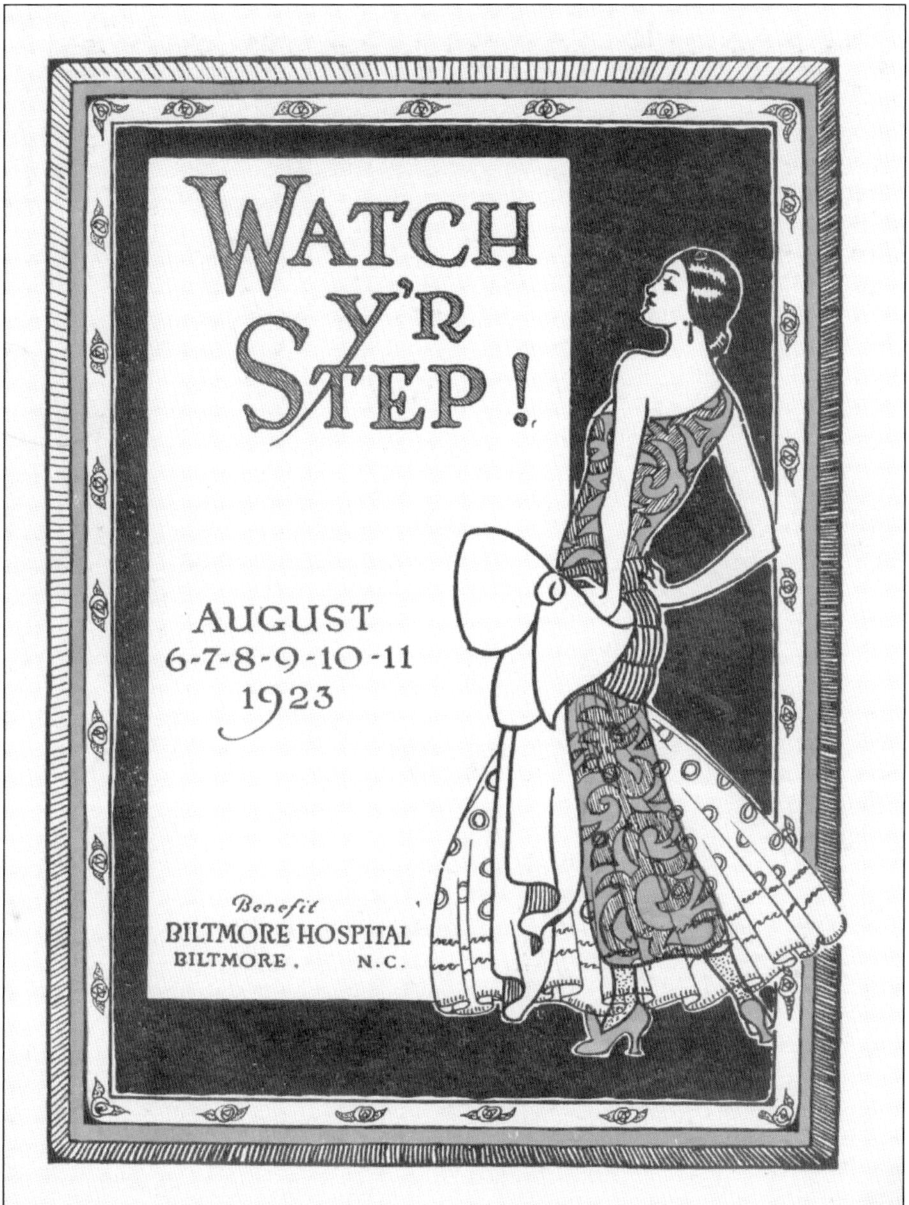

WATCH Y'R STEP, 1923. Beautiful graphics grace this flyer announcing the cabaret sponsored by Cornelia Vanderbilt as a benefit for a new Biltmore Hospital. The cabaret featured dinner, dancing, a fortune-teller, cold drinks, cigars, and a doll raffle. Mrs. H. E. Brown was the fortune-teller, and Catherine Jones was a dancer. On November 2, 1923, Edith Vanderbilt reported a profit of $6,300 from the cabaret fund-raiser given by Cornelia to Charles E. Waddell, president of the hospital. Benefits were sponsored by Cornelia Vanderbilt Cecil in successive years, including "Watch Y'r Step" cabaret dinners and dances at the Kenilworth Inn on August 6–11, 1928, and on the roof of the Arcade Building on August 14, 1929. Order forms for Biltmore Bath Salts were sold by the Watch Y'r Step Company, which became the theme of the annual charity cabarets staged to benefit the hospital. The Biltmore Hospital Benefit Society, Inc., was established with membership dues of $12.

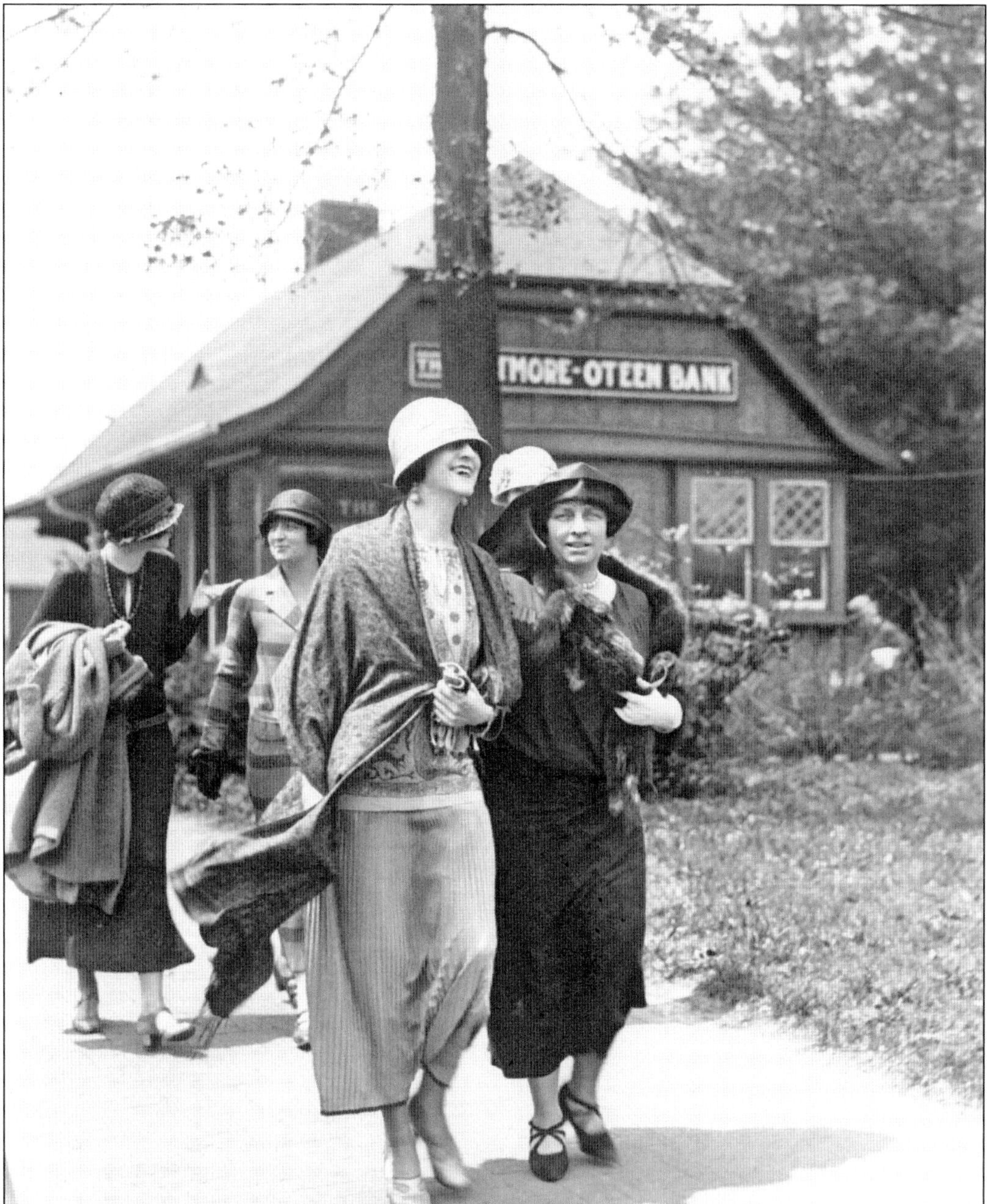

BEFORE THE WEDDING, APRIL 1924. In the days before the wedding of Cornelia Stuyvesant Vanderbilt to the Honorable John Francis Amherst Cecil, Biltmore Village bustled with activity as family members, friends, and guests from around the world arrived. Guests stayed at the Grove Park and Kenilworth Inns, Biltmore Forest Country Club, and at Biltmore House. In this photograph, Edith Vanderbilt, front left, and Cornelia, back left, are enjoying the company of unidentified guests near the Biltmore-Oteen Bank on Lodge Street as preparations are being made for the much-anticipated event.

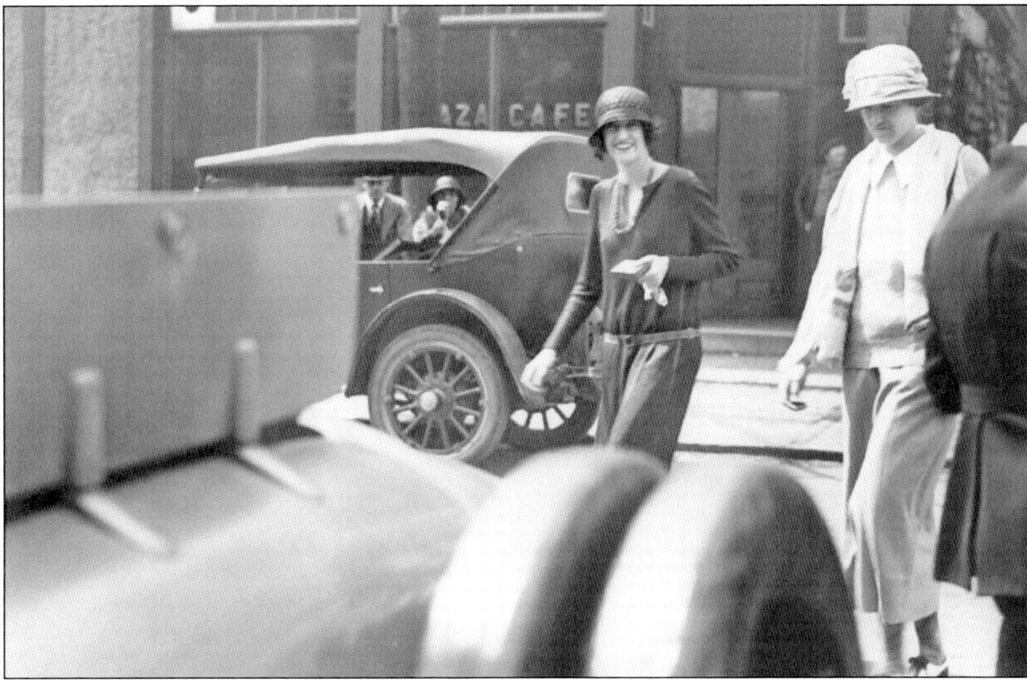

GUESTS IN TOWN, APRIL 1924. In these two photographs, Cornelia Vanderbilt is spending time with unidentified guests as she shows them around the village in the days before her wedding. In the photograph above, the Plaza Café, run by Thomas Arakas, is visible behind Cornelia and her guest. In the image below, Cornelia is behind the wheel of a 1918 Cadillac Roadster, one of several cars she owned, in addition to a 1918 Packard Landaulet, a 1917 Dodge Touring Car, and a c. 1911 Stevens-Duryea.

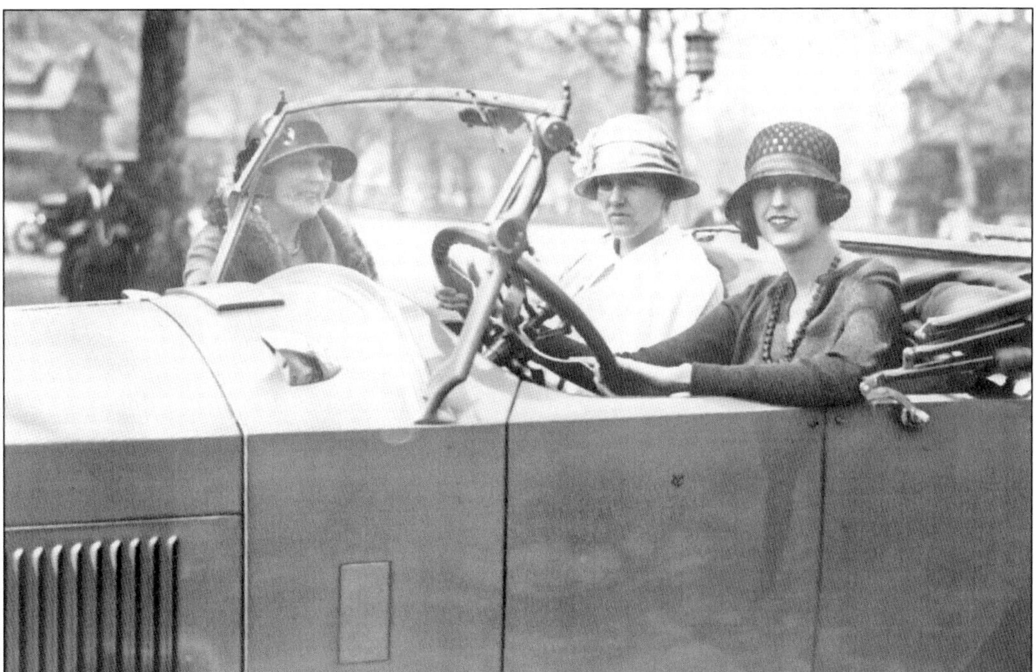

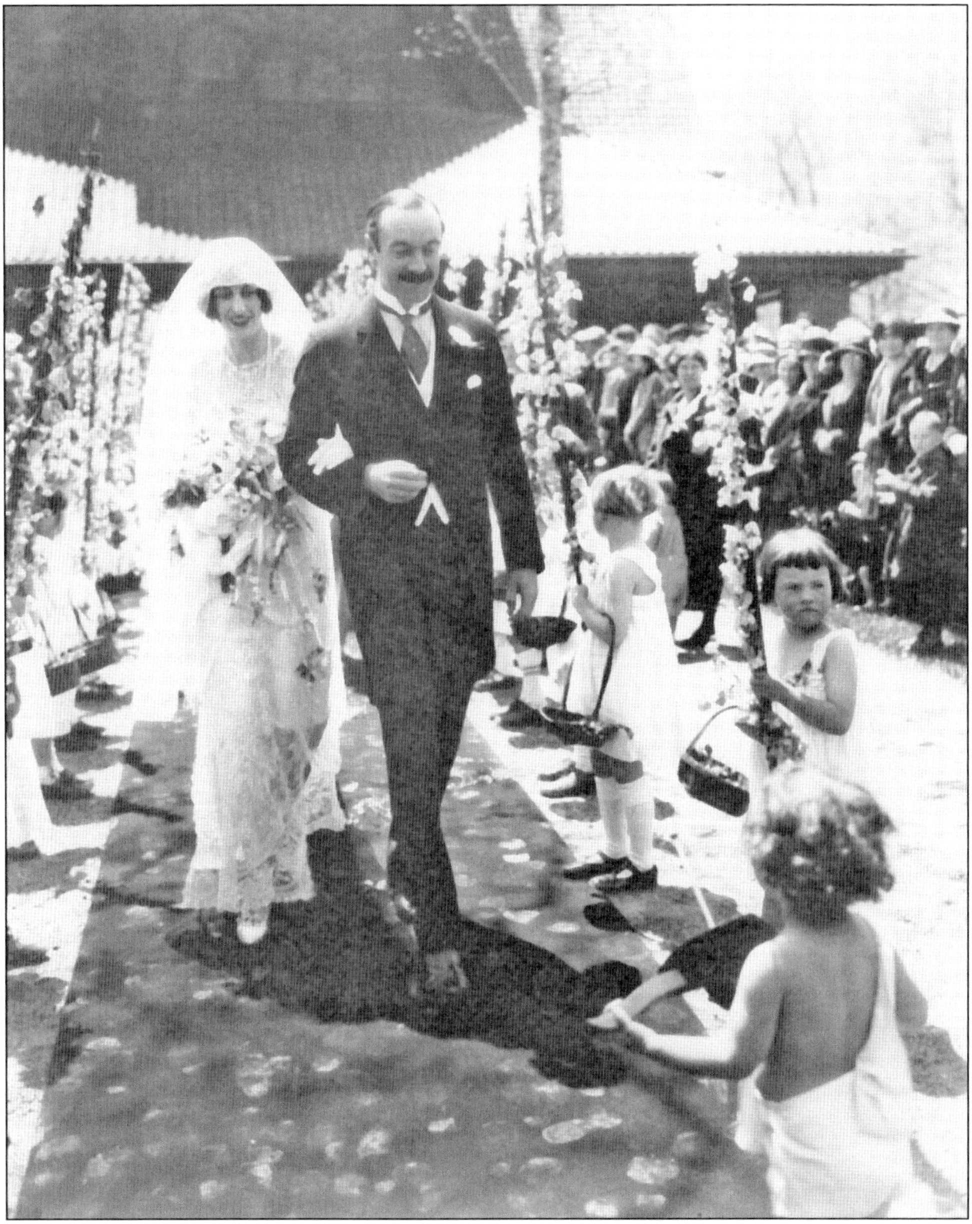

THE HONORABLE AND MRS. JOHN F. A. CECIL, APRIL 29, 1924. As the newlywed couple left the church, they were greeted by children of Biltmore Estate workers forming an aisle with branches of flowers held high. Cornelia and John Cecil's wedding was perhaps the most significant social event that occurred in Biltmore Village during the 1920s. After a honeymoon in Europe, the couple settled into life at Biltmore. John became involved as a member of the vestry at All Souls Church and joined the Asheville Rotary Club. Cornelia was a member of the Biltmore Forest Bridle and Saddle Club, played polo, and looked after her setters and other breeds at the Biltmore Kennels. Days and nights were equally filled with entertaining friends and guests, and sponsoring charitable benefits for such causes as a new hospital and the art museum. The Cecils' first son, George Henry Vanderbilt Cecil, was born on February 26, 1925, and their second son, William Francis Amherst Cecil, on August 17, 1928.

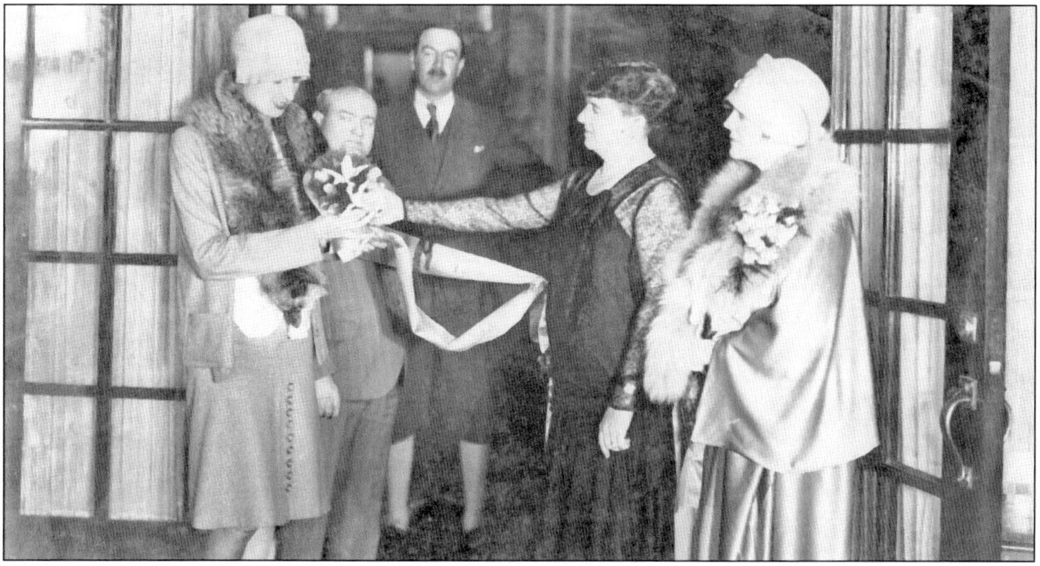

KENILWORTH ART EXHIBITION, 1928. At the opening of the first annual Kenilworth Art Exhibition, held at the Kenilworth Inn on April 23–28, 1928, Mrs. James M. (Leah) Chiles presents a corsage to Mrs. John F. A. Cecil while a Mrs. Arrington, president of the North Carolina Arts Association, looks on. Inn manager Roscoe A. Marvel, standing next to Mrs. Cecil, and John F. A. Cecil were both sponsors of the event. With help from Roscoe Marvel and the Cecils, Leah Chiles converted the ballroom and surrounding solarium into Kenilworth Galleries. Comprising 625 paintings, it was the largest show in the South at that time. More than 100 artists from 12 states and three foreign countries had paintings on display. Among them were Kiffin Rockwell, one of the seven founders of the Escadrille Américaine, and famous English landscape painter A. C. Wyatt. Kenilworth Galleries hosted other art shows through November 1928, each one larger and attracting increasingly more attention. (Both, North Carolina Collection, Pack Memorial Public Library.)

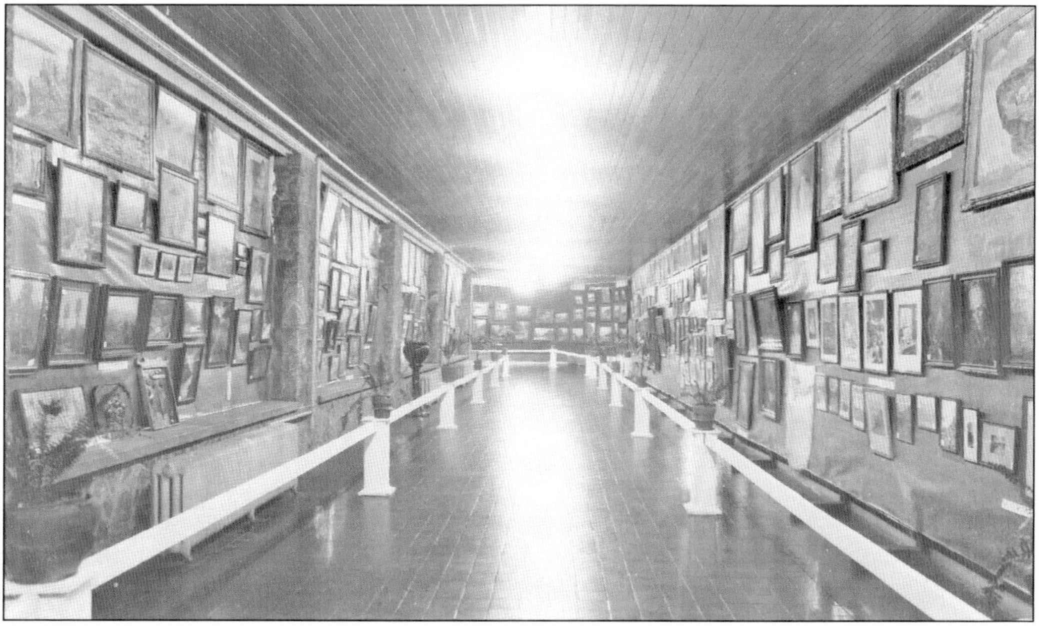

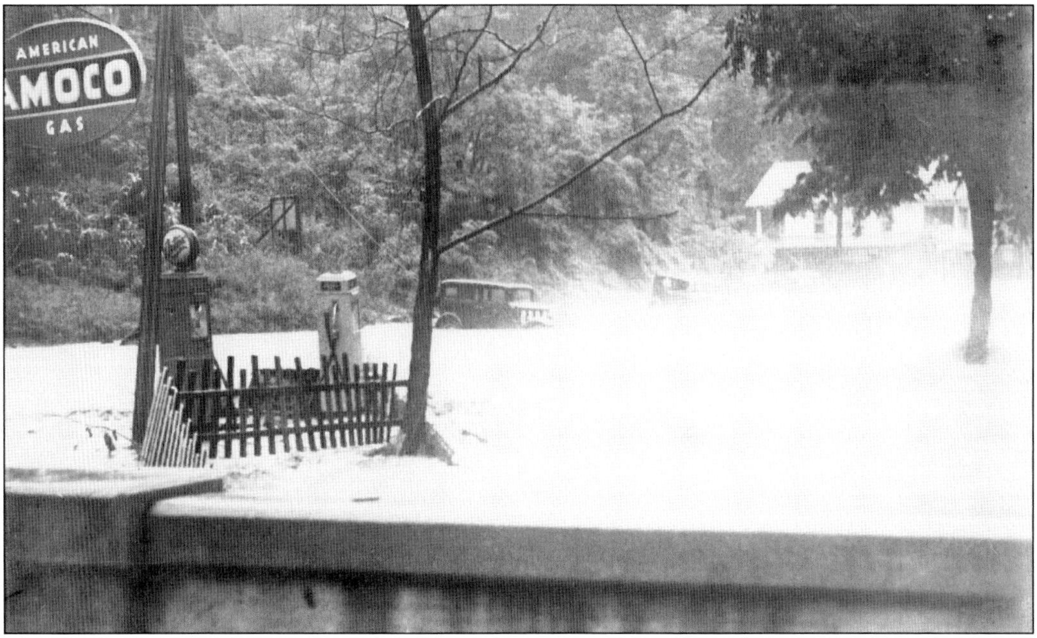

ANOTHER FLOOD, 1928. This photograph is believed to have been taken from the bridge across the Swannanoa River at the intersection of Biltmore Avenue and Swannanoa River Road during the flood of August 16, 1928. The official flood stage, measured 100 feet downstream from the bridge, peaked at 18.75 feet, as compared to 20.70 feet on July 16, 1916, and 19.00 feet on August 13, 1940. (Richard "Dick" Gray.)

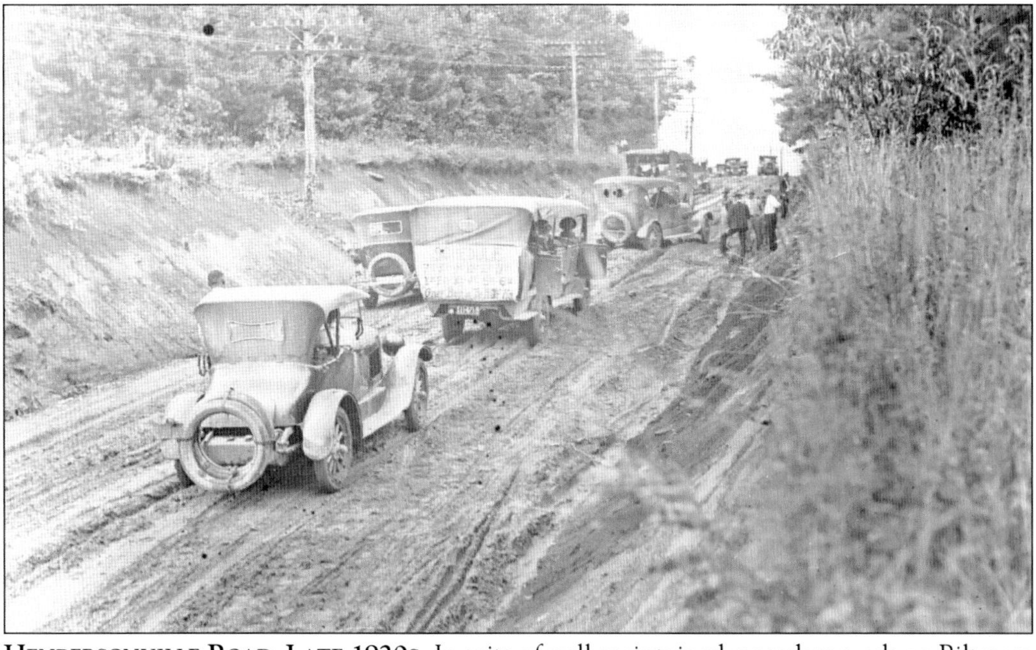

HENDERSONVILLE ROAD, LATE 1920S. In spite of well-maintained macadam roads on Biltmore Estate, in Biltmore Village and much of Asheville, this view of an unidentified section of Hendersonville Road shows that travel could still be a little tricky if one ventured far from town in the 1920s. (North Carolina Collection, Pack Memorial Public Library.)

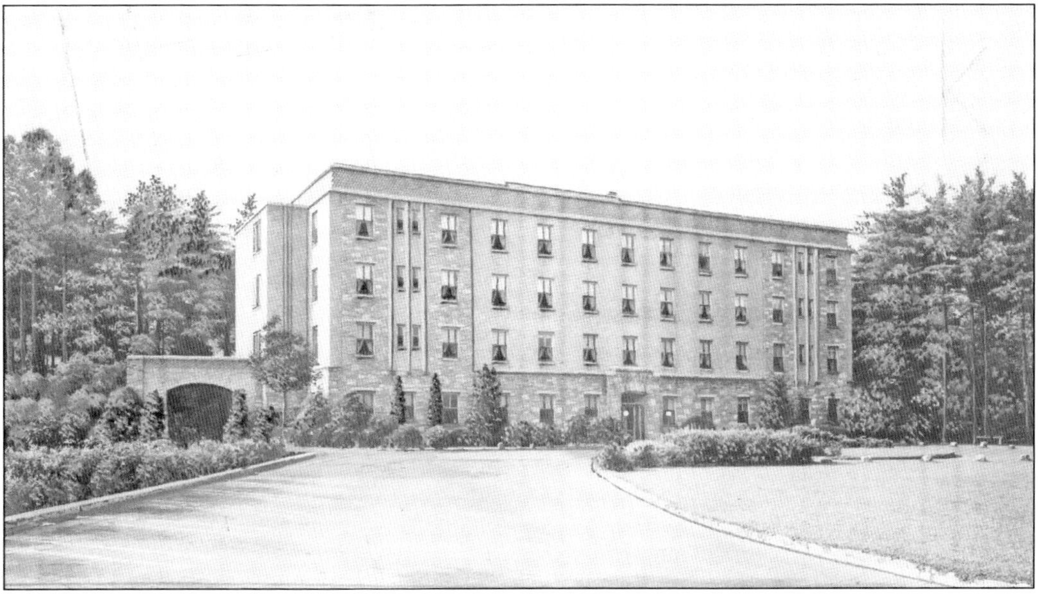

BILTMORE HOSPITAL, 1930. This new home for the Biltmore Hospital was designed by architect Douglas D. Ellington, who was noted for turning Asheville into an art deco showplace. The four-story building with 65 rooms was made of fireproof brick and was completed in 1930. It replaced the former Clarence Barker Memorial Hospital, which suffered severe fire loss in early March 1921 and had been renamed the Biltmore Hospital. (North Carolina Collection, Pack Memorial Public Library.)

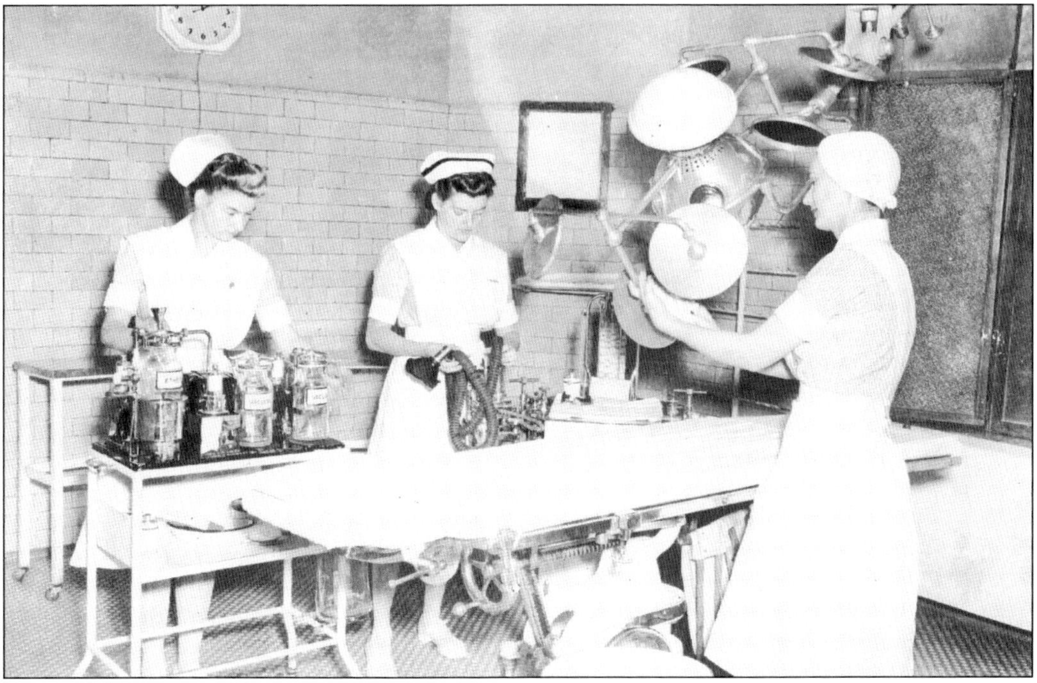

BILTMORE HOSPITAL, C. 1930. In this photograph, nurses are checking equipment in the modern and efficient-looking operating room of the new Biltmore Hospital. (Biltmore Village Historic Museum.)

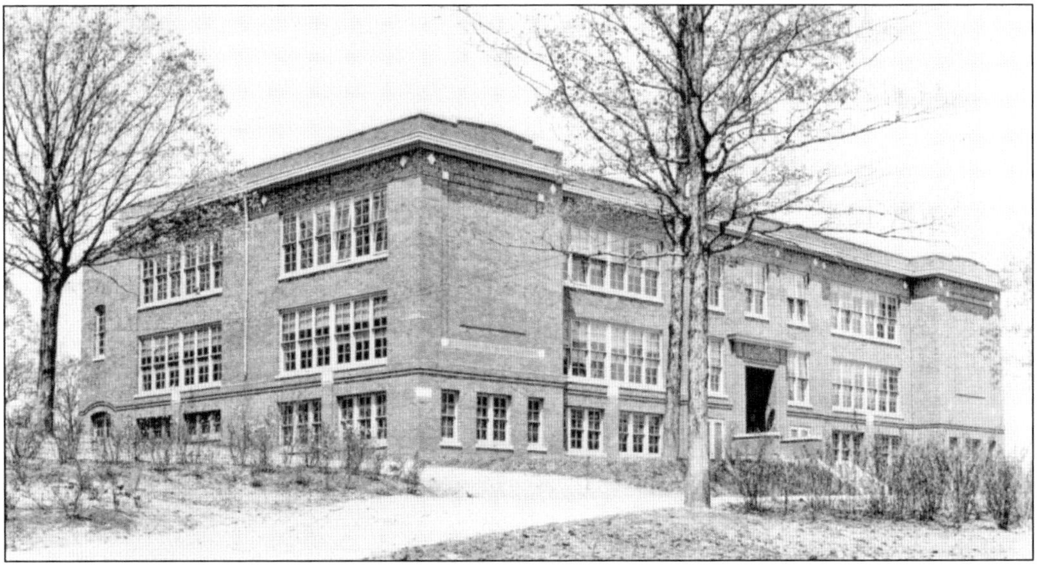

BILTMORE SCHOOL, 1920. This well-known, three-story, brick school building is a landmark on Hendersonville Road at the top of the hill south of Biltmore. Constructed around 1920, the Biltmore School was well-respected and served a wide community that included Biltmore Village and the South Biltmore areas. By 1925, the school included separate gymnasium and science buildings. (North Carolina Collection, Pack Memorial Public Library.)

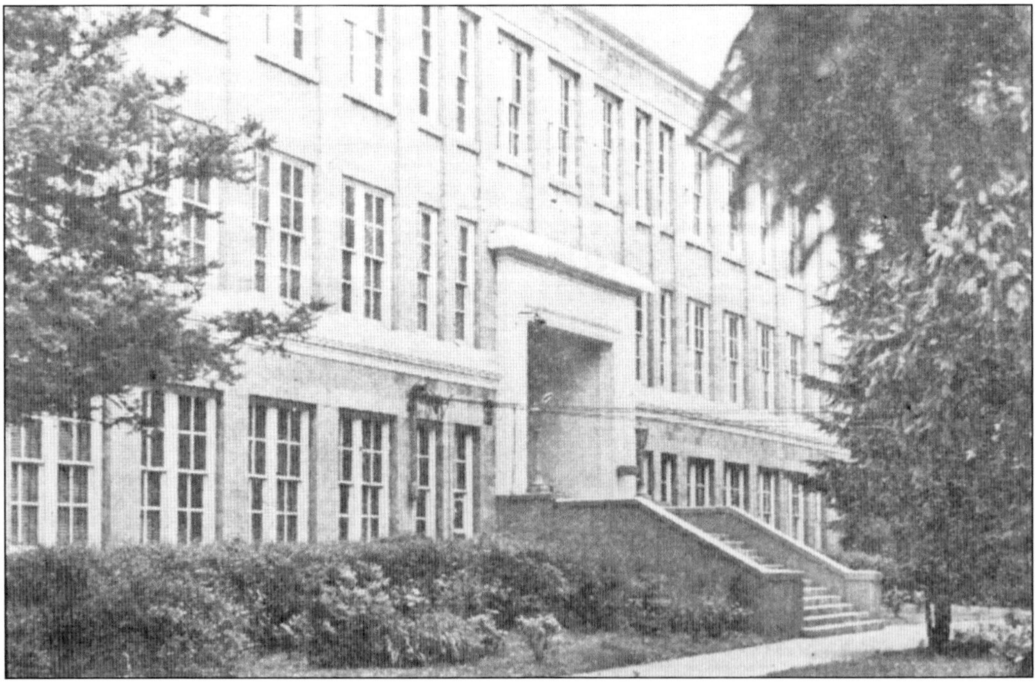

NEWTON ELEMENTARY SCHOOL. The first school west of the Blue Ridge had its origins in a log structure known as Union Hill School, established in 1793 on land provided by William Forster II. It was replaced by a brick building and renamed Newton Academy in 1809 for Rev. George Newton, the school's respected headmaster since 1797. Newton Elementary, the fourth building on the site, was constructed in 1922. (North Carolina Collection, Pack Memorial Public Library.)

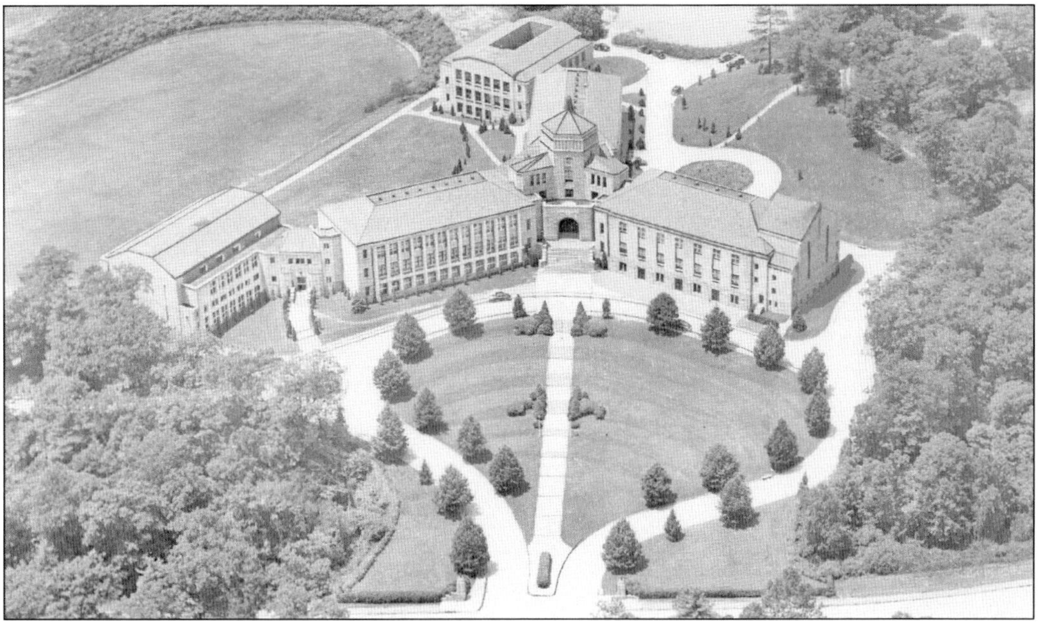

ASHEVILLE HIGH SCHOOL, C. 1930. Asheville High School was designed for a 2,000-student capacity by architect Douglas D. Ellington and was completed in 1929 at a cost of $1 million. This aerial view shows the symmetrical layout of the buildings and the spacious grounds of the campus. In 1935, it was renamed the Lee H. Edwards High School after a former principal who died that year but later assumed its original name. (North Carolina Collection, Pack Memorial Public Library.)

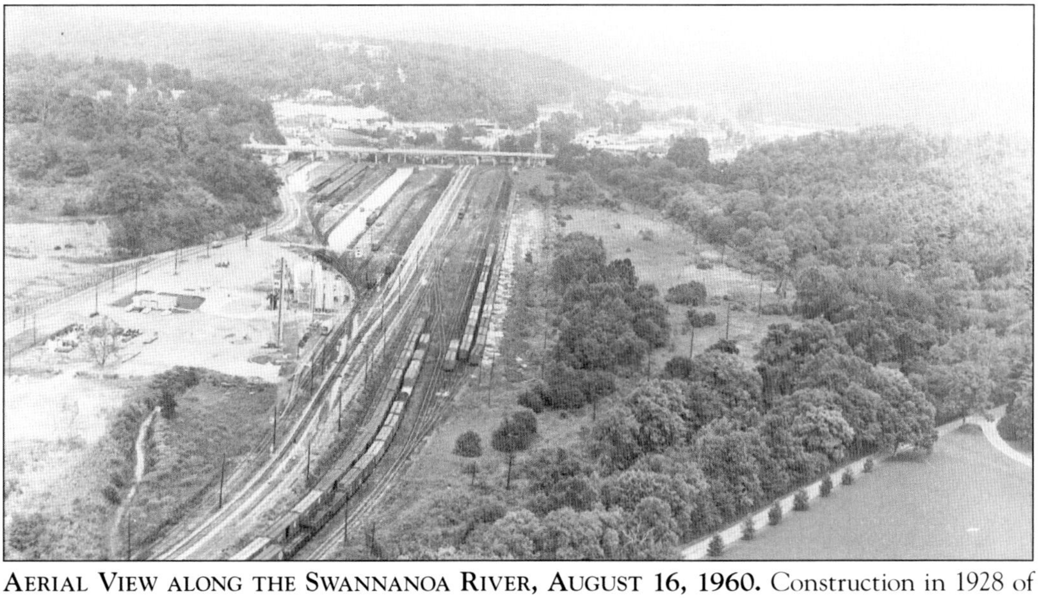

AERIAL VIEW ALONG THE SWANNANOA RIVER, AUGUST 16, 1960. Construction in 1928 of the McDowell Street Viaduct across the Southern Railway Yard, seen in this view, marked the beginning of significant change and growth in Biltmore and the surrounding areas. The mixed pastoral and forested landscape of Biltmore Estate, seen on the right, stands in stark contrast to the industrialized areas sprawling along the adjacent valley. (North Carolina Collection, Pack Memorial Public Library.)

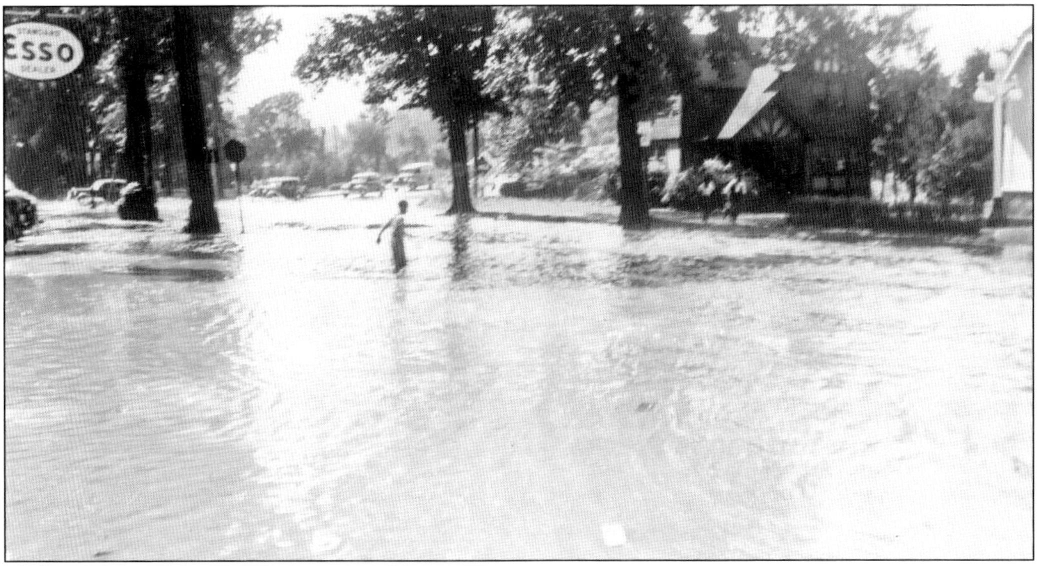

BILTMORE FLOOD, AUGUST 13, 1940. The peak flood stage at 19.00 feet in the Biltmore area during the 1940 flood was nearly two feet lower than the 20.70 feet in July 1916, but the impact was nonetheless felt. The cars in the above photograph are heading south off the viaduct and crossing the Lodge Street intersection near the entrance to Biltmore Estate. The view in the photograph below is looking east on Lodge Street across the intersection, with All Souls Crescent on the right and the viaduct on the left. Hendersonville Road is one block past the Esso station. (Both, Biltmore Village Historic Museum.)

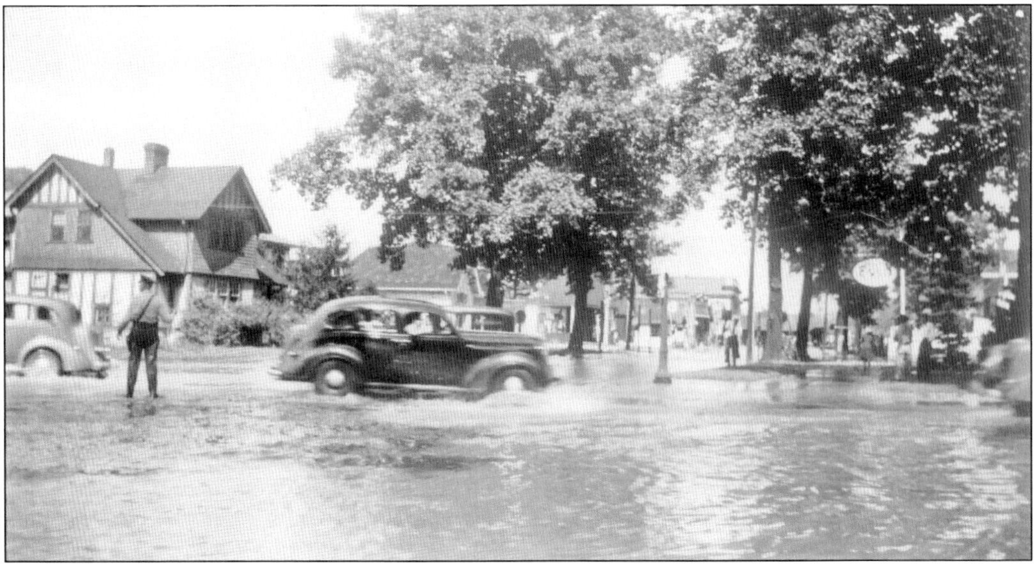

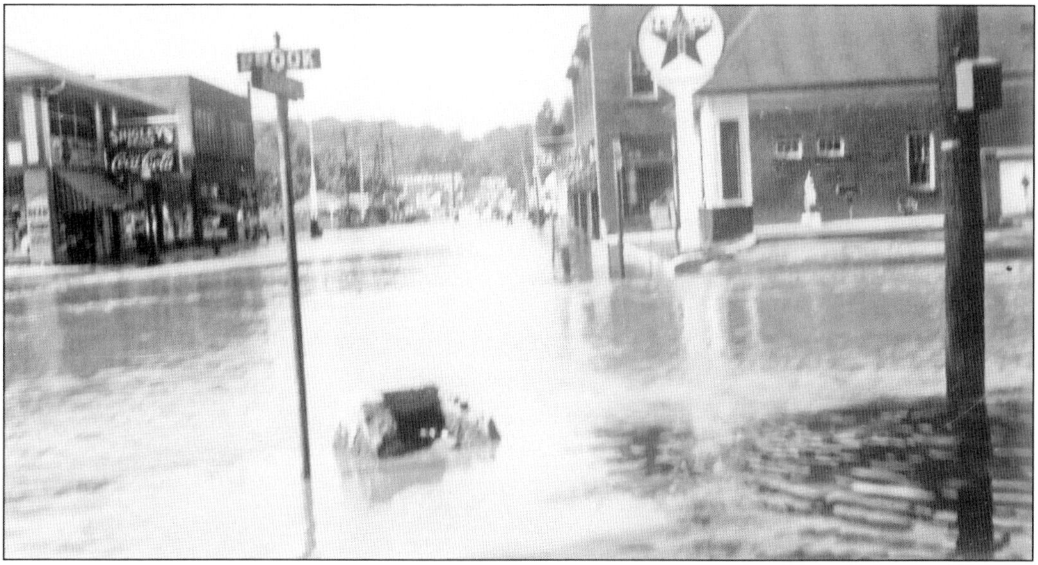

BILTMORE FLOOD, AUGUST 13, 1940. The photograph above was taken near the intersection of Hendersonville Road with Lodge and Brook Streets looking north toward the Swannanoa River. Shigley's Drug Store and Thomas and Howard Grocery Warehouse are ahead on the left, and the Biltmore Hardware Store is on the right past the Texaco sign. In the photograph below, the deserted Homespun and Shoe Shops on Brook Street are reflected in the flood waters stretching across Biltmore Plaza. (Both, Biltmore Village Historic Museum.)

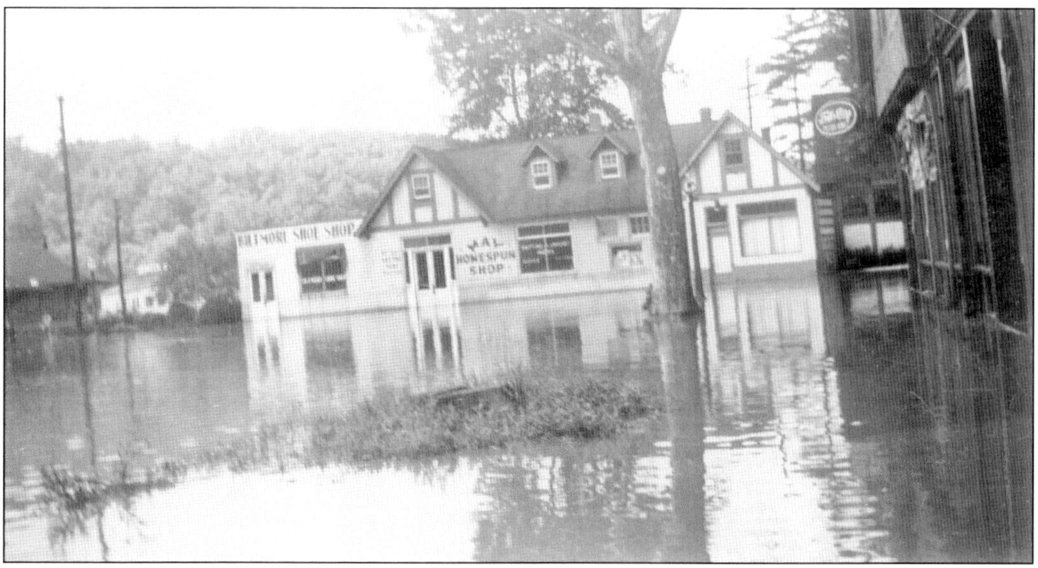

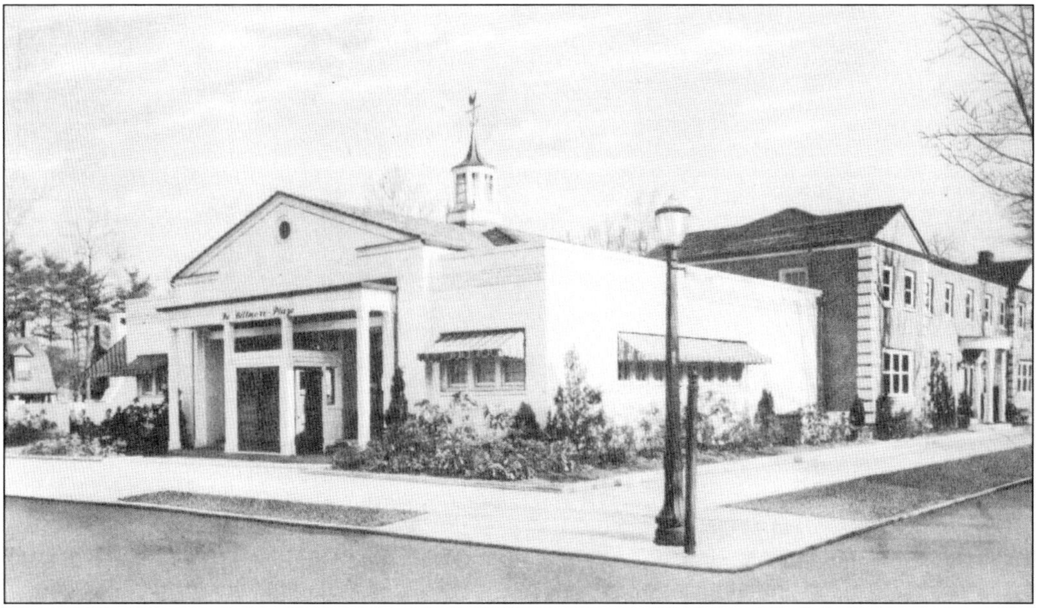

The Biltmore Plaza Recreation Center, 1942. The recreation center advertised that it was "at the crossroads of Western North Carolina in Historic Biltmore Village" and featured bowling, dining, dancing, and a fountain. The Bowling Club House had 12 Brunswick deluxe maple lanes for tenpins or duckpins and featured "all the latest improvements and are the finest in the south," as promoted on postcard advertisements. The Dining-Fountain Building boasted a "historic fresco mural painted in brilliant colors by a world famous artist on a marble base constructed in scroll effect." The name of the "world famous artist" was not disclosed in the advertisement. (Both, North Carolina Collection, Pack Memorial Public Library.)

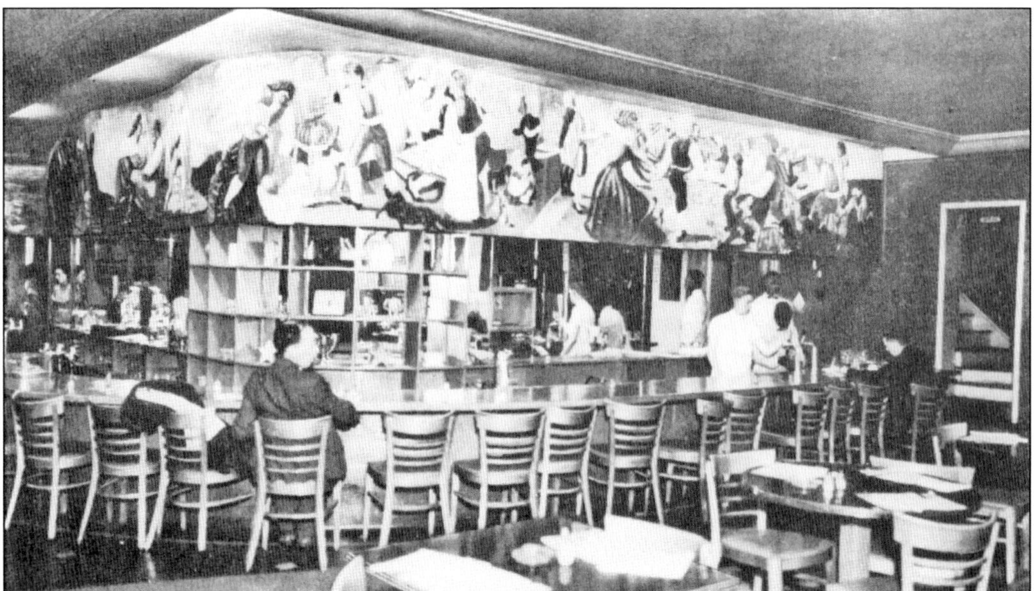

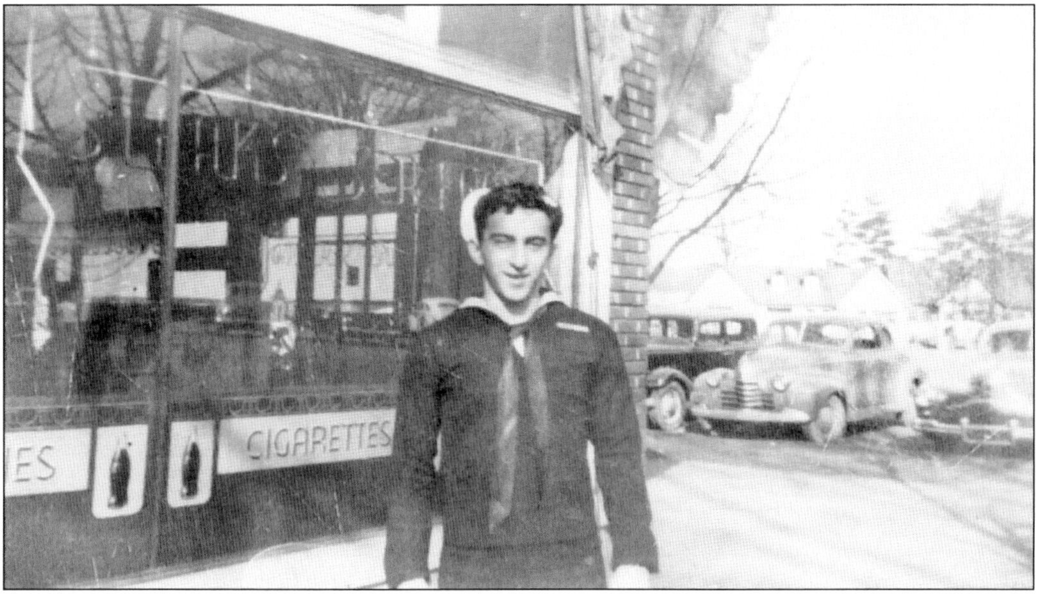

TOMMY ARAKAS AND FRIENDS, MARCH 1945. Thomas "Tommy" Arakas was born in March 1925 in his parents' apartment in the Biltmore Plaza Building, which his father, Isidoros Arakas, owned until he lost it in 1932 during the Depression. Tommy grew up helping in the Plaza Café, owned by Sam and Jim Coutlakis and run by Tommy's family. The café was in the north end of the Plaza Building until 1932, when it moved across the Plaza to the McGeachy Building on the corner at Boston Way. After serving in the navy in World War II, Tommy came home to run the Plaza Café from 1945 to 1957. A full-plate lunch with a meat, two vegetables, rolls, and a drink cost 40¢ or, with dessert, 50¢. Tommy, on furlough, is pictured above at the Plaza Café and below with friends (from left to right) Tula (Pathemos) Melehes, Kiki (Mimides) Kavonis, Tommy Arakas, Joann (Caplanides) Demopoulos, and Stamatia (Mimides) Sigmon. (Both, Mr. and Mrs. Tommy Arakas.)

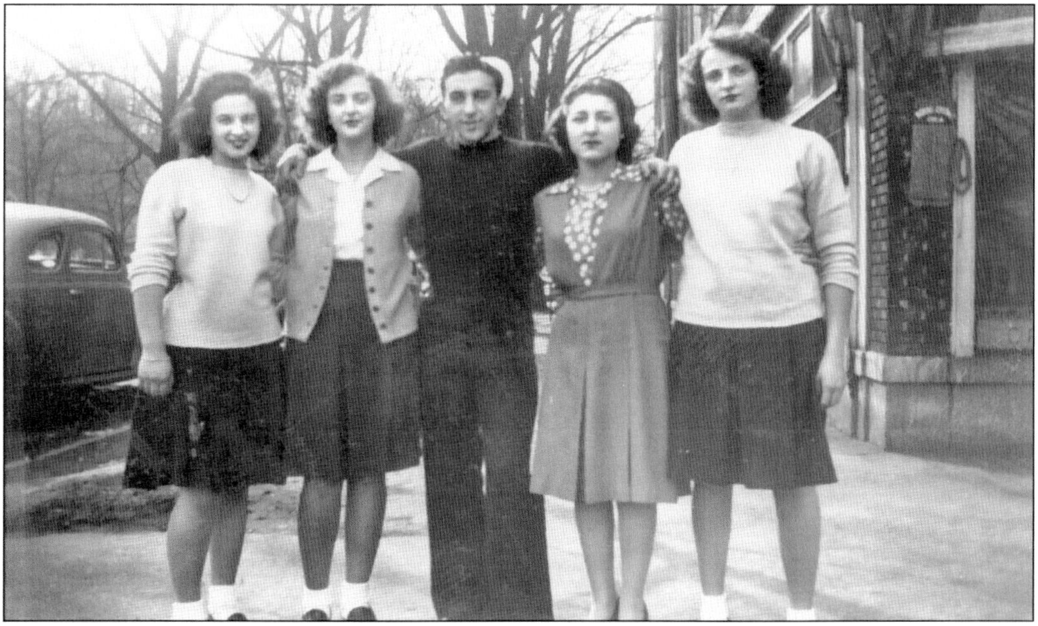

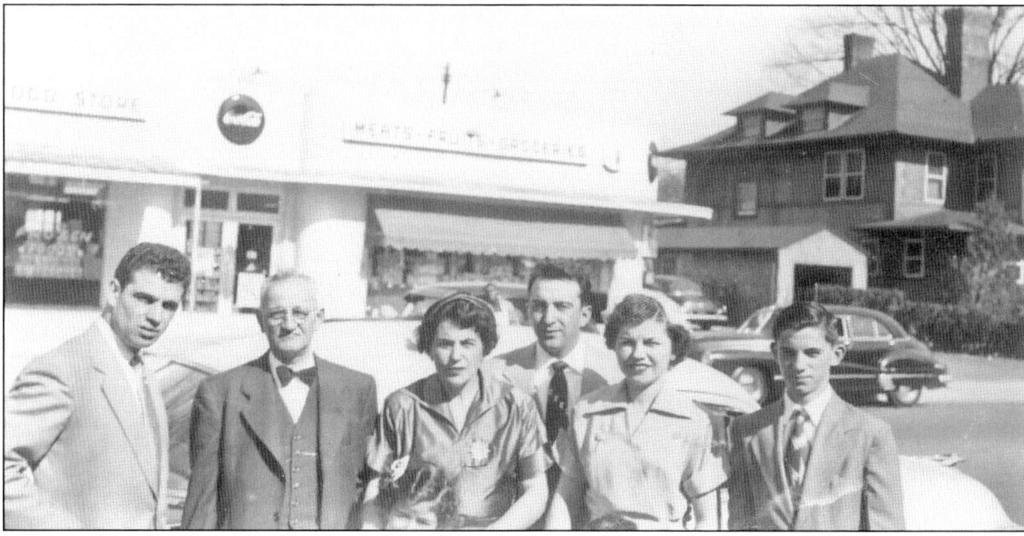

ARAKAS FAMILY, 1953. This photograph of the Arakas family was taken outside their house at 7 Boston Way. Trantham's Grocery and Food Store and the Reed House are seen across the street. Pictured from left to right are Tommy's cousin Arnold Kalogerakis; Tommy's father, Isidorus Arakas; Tommy's mother, Mary Arakas; Tommy; his wife, Catherine Arakas; and his first cousin James (Jimmy) Arakas. (Mr. and Mrs. Tommy Arakas.)

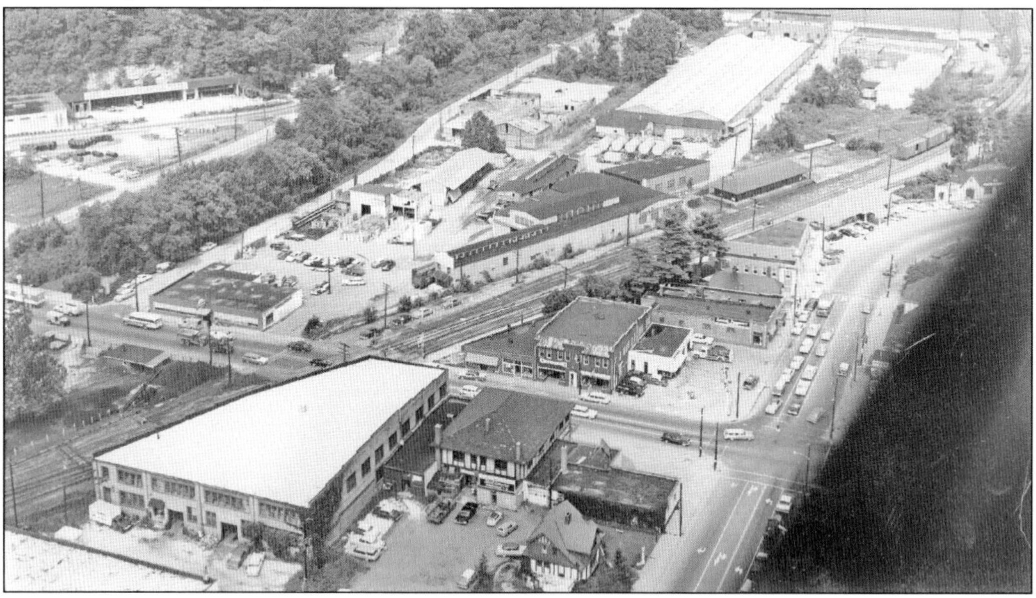

AERIAL VIEW ALONG THE SWANNANOA IN BILTMORE, AUGUST 16, 1960. The changing face of Biltmore is evident in this view looking east along the Swannanoa River, in the narrow strip of trees between Thompson Street and Swannanoa River Road at left. In the two angular blocks between Lodge Street and the railroad tracks, seen in the foreground, are the following businesses: Thomas and Howard Wholesale Grocers (the large wedge-shaped building) and Shigley's Drug Store to its right, Biltmore Hardware, Biltmore Texaco Station, Aiken's Drug Store, the Hot Shot Café, the former Biltmore-Oteen Bank Building, and the train station. The rest of Biltmore Village (not seen) is to the right. (North Carolina Collection, Pack Memorial Public Library.)

Six

Biltmore Forest

Headlines in the *Asheville Times* on June 20, 1920 proclaimed, "Biltmore Estate Land Is Sold For Residence Park. 1,500 Acres on Hendersonville Highway Purchased By Asheville Interests." The *Sunday Citizen* likewise announced, "Biltmore Estate Company Acquires Tract Two Miles Long on Hendersonville Road, for Greatest Development in the History of Western North Carolina." A holding company known as the Biltmore Estate Company, an incorporated firm, was formed to be in charge of the real estate venture. Besides Edith S. Vanderbilt of the Biltmore Estate, members of the firm included two well-known Asheville men: Thomas Wadley Raoul, former president of the Albemarle Park Company, and Judge Junius G. Adams, an attorney and the local legal advisor for the trustees of the George W. Vanderbilt estate. Burnham S. Colburn of Detroit, former vice president of the Peoples' State Bank of Detroit and retired director of the Canadian Bridge Company, and William A. Knight of St. Augustine, Florida, who also had a summer residence in Skyland, were the other members. Donald Ross, a celebrated golf course designer, was engaged to lay out the 18-hole golf course, and Edward Palmer Jr. of Baltimore was to design the clubhouse. Chauncey D. Beadle, who had been in charge of the Biltmore Nursery since 1890 and for the previous 15 years was Biltmore Estate's superintendent, was retained as a landscape architect in charge of the work of laying out the roads and drives, grounds, and other landscape operations. Plans called for an initial outlay of $500,000, which was to be increased as the development progressed. The golf course was to be among the first undertakings, and plans were made to get the course under construction as soon as it was laid out and approved by the firm. Tentative plans for a hotel were initially being considered. A well-designed system of roads and lighting were planned for the development, and the water was supplied initially by the Biltmore Estate water supply on Busbee Mountain. Restricted residential tracts were to be a minimum of 2 to 5 acres in size, with some larger ones up to 100 acres, the idea being to encourage the development of individual estates with country houses. Restrictions included no subdivision of tracts for 21 years.

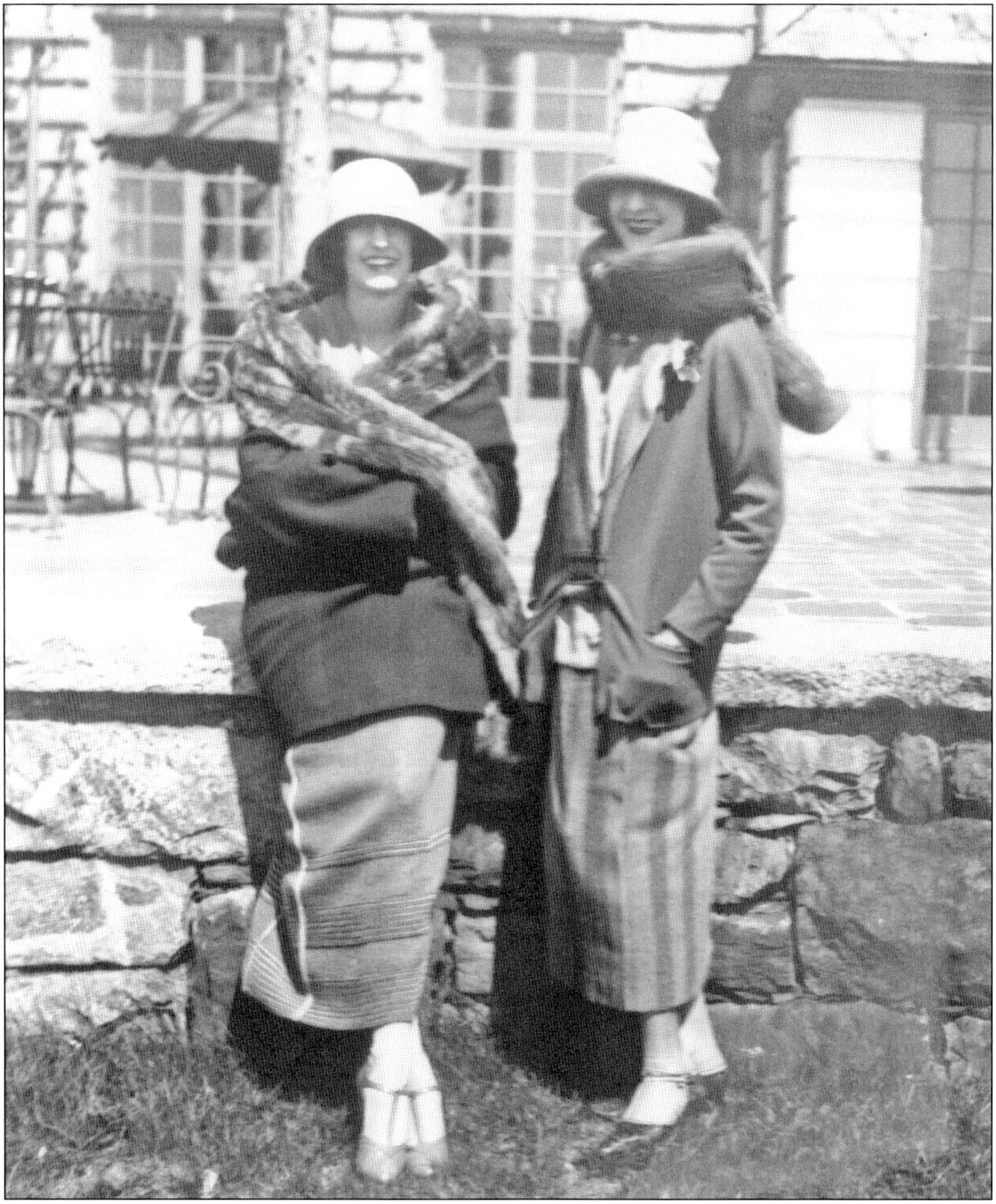

CORNELIA VANDERBILT AND EDITH VANDERBILT, APRIL 1924. In the days before Cornelia's wedding to John Cecil, she is seen here (left) enjoying time with her mother at the Biltmore Forest Country Club. Both had been active in the design and furnishings of the clubhouse during its construction in 1921 and opening on July 4, 1922. Shortly after receiving her inheritance at the age of 21 in August 1921, Cornelia's first business deal was the purchase of the 130-acre golf course in October for $30,000, which was leased back to the Biltmore Estate Company to operate for 50 years. A retaining clause in the original deed provided for the repurchase of the tract to assist in the financial development of the club. Her inheritance was the source of an additional $60,000 capital loan to the Biltmore Estate Company that helped to fund the construction of the country club and roads.

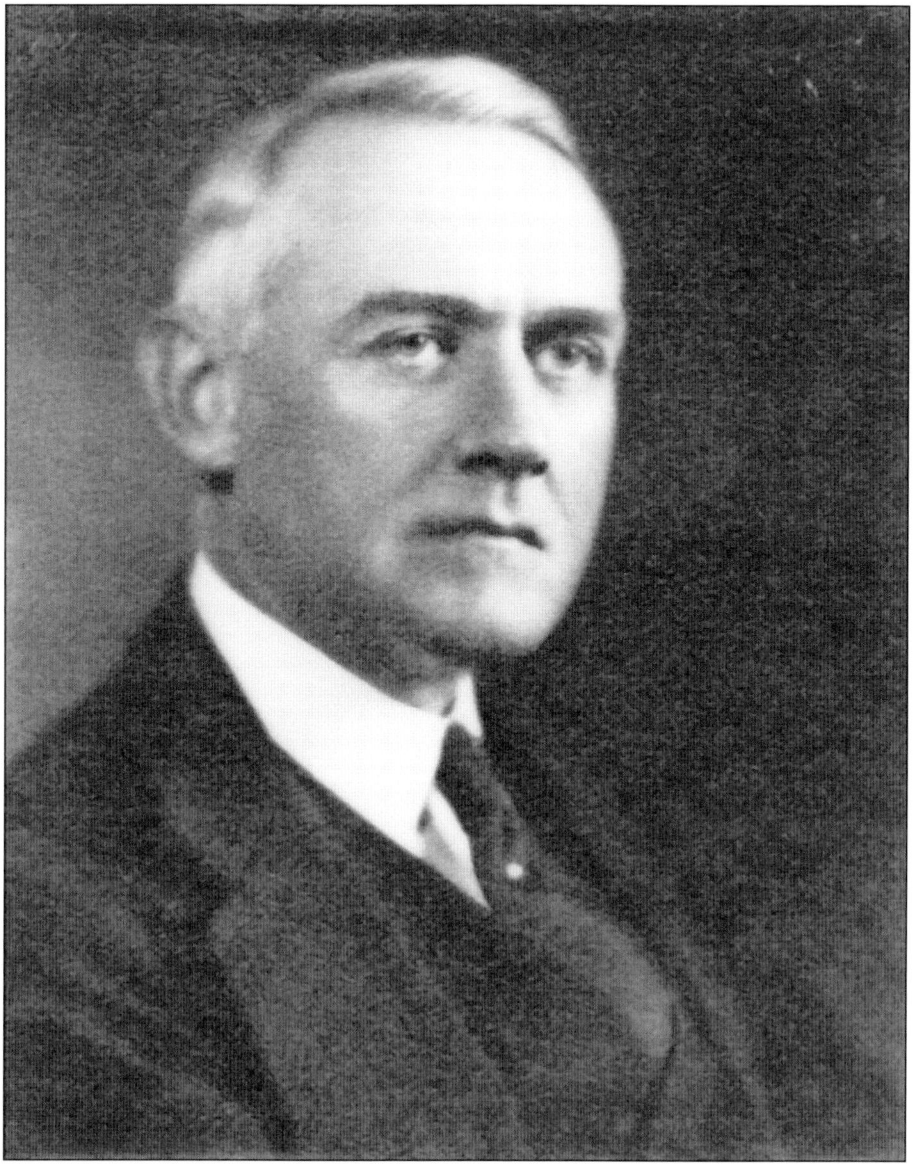

JUDGE JUNIUS G. ADAMS. Following the devastating flood of 1916 and resulting damage to both Biltmore Estate and Biltmore Village, the trustees of the George Vanderbilt estate requested Judge Adams, a respected lawyer in Asheville, to make a study of the properties and develop recommendations to reduce the cost of overall maintenance. Adams's report included, among other things, recommendations that Biltmore Village should be sold and that some 1,500 acres of Biltmore Estate bordering on Hendersonville Road be declared a restricted residential section and sold off in lots. The trustees agreed and approved the plan, but due to America's impending involvement in World War I, Adams advised that it be postponed until conditions were favorable. In August 1920, Biltmore Village was sold, and the time seemed right to move forward with developing the Hendersonville Road property. The Biltmore Estate Company was organized the same month with a paid-in capital of $100,000, and the tract of 1,451.85 acres of Biltmore Estate land at the agreed price of $355,790 (mostly in bonds) was conveyed to the development company.

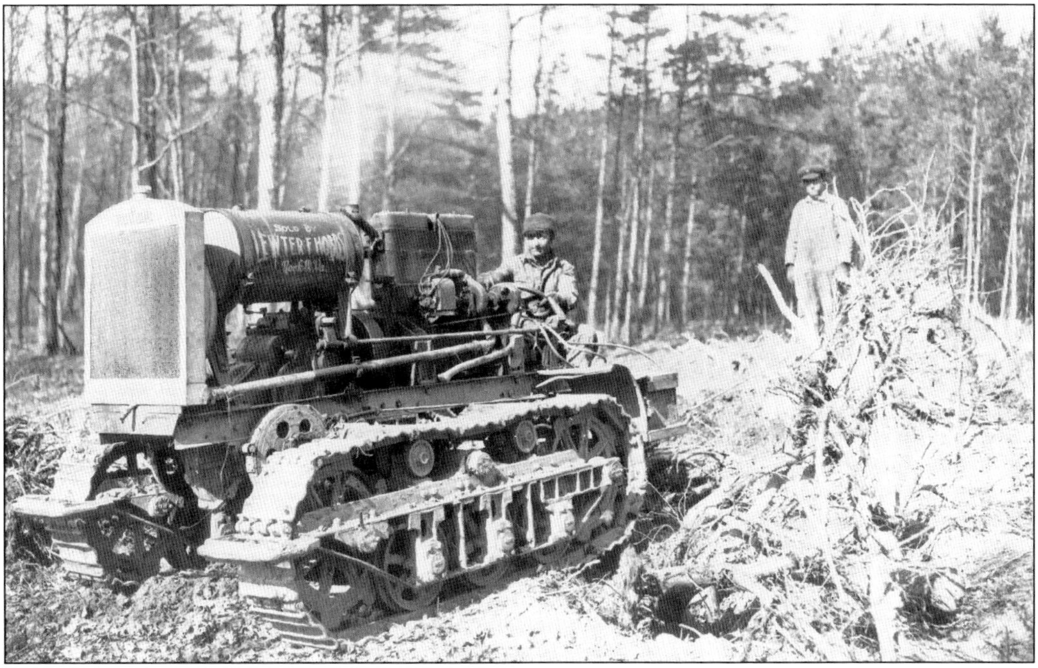

ON VANDERBILT ROAD SOUTH, FEBRUARY 19, 1921. Construction of the 2-mile-long Vanderbilt Road leading out of Biltmore Village commenced in October 1920. Chauncey D. Beadle reported that an old warehouse that had been purchased and the former Fern Hill Baptist Church at the upper end of the village were torn down "for the express purpose of making a better entrance to the new thoroughfare called Vanderbilt Road."

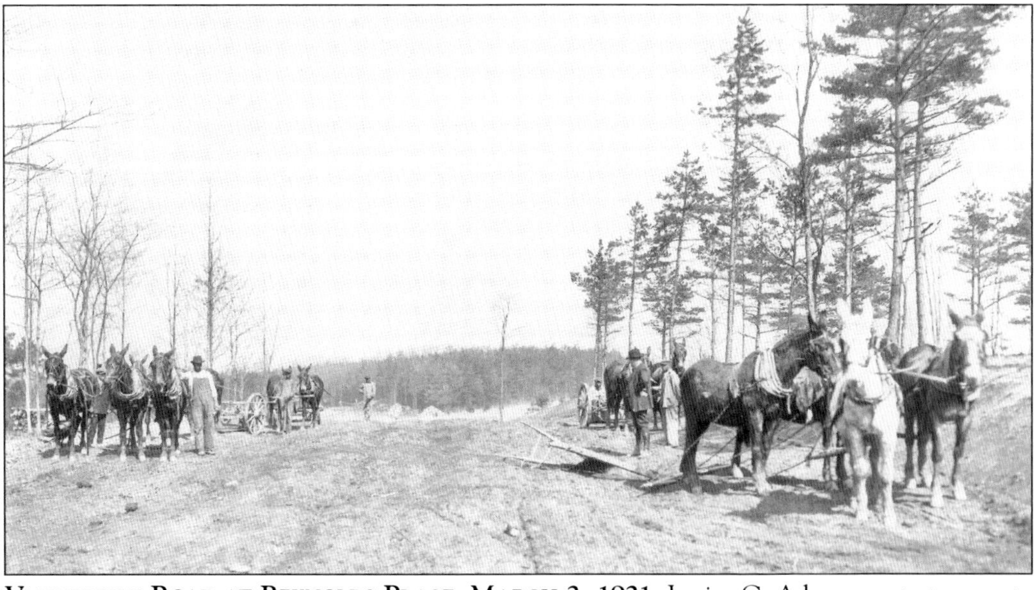

VANDERBILT ROAD AT REYNOLDS PLACE, MARCH 2, 1921. Junius G. Adams wrote to county commissioner B. A. Patton in April 1921 in gratitude that residents of Limestone Township wanted to rename Long Shoals Road between Skyland and the bridge Vanderbilt Road. He pointed out, however, that a main artery of the developing Biltmore Forest was already being called Vanderbilt Road and wondered if the other road could be named something else.

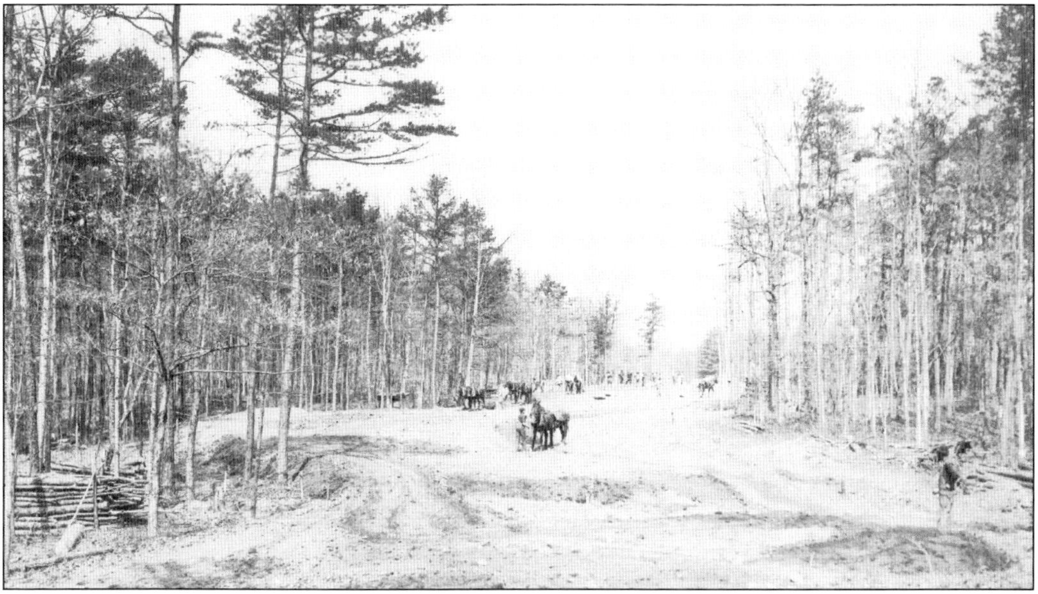

VANDERBILT ROAD AT STUYVESANT ROAD, MARCH 2, 1921. Road construction in Biltmore Forest progressed rapidly. By July 25, 1921, the construction of Vanderbilt Road between Biltmore Village and Cedarcliff Road was well underway, and in September 1922, estimates were prepared for "resurfacing Vanderbilt Road between Cedarcliff Road and Biltmore." Judge Adams reported to Edith Vanderbilt on February 6, 1923, that a new road parallel to White Oak Road called Buena Vista Road had been opened.

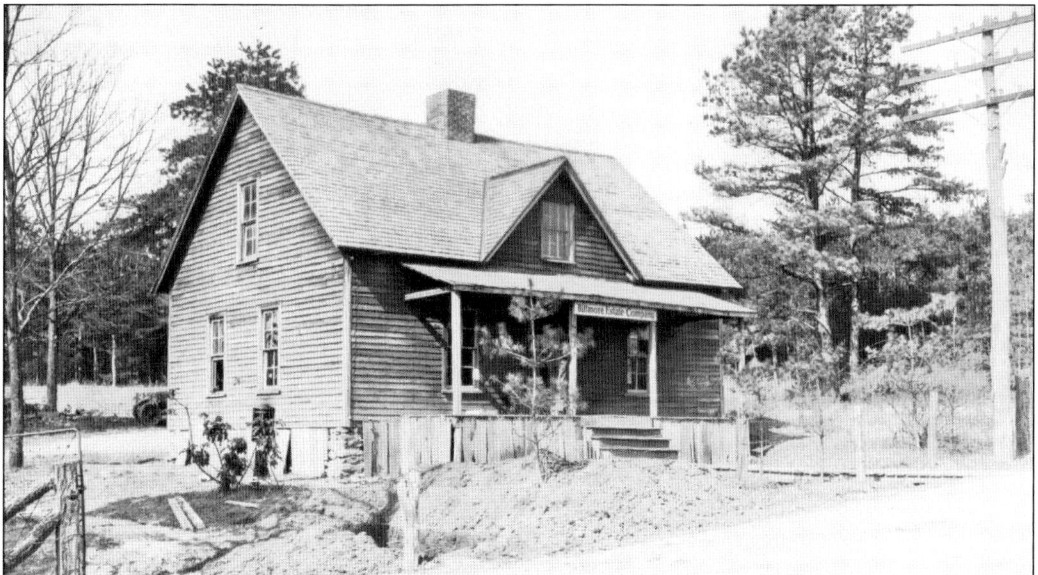

BILTMORE ESTATE COMPANY OFFICE, FEBRUARY 14, 1921. This preexisting house near Hendersonville Road at Buena Vista Road served as the general administrative office, and residential tracts were sold here until the new office was completed in early 1923. City health officer and physician Dr. C. V. Reynolds, along with the company's directors Junius G. Adams, Burnham S. Colburn, and William A. Knight, and company president Thomas Wadley Raoul, were among the first to purchase tracts for building.

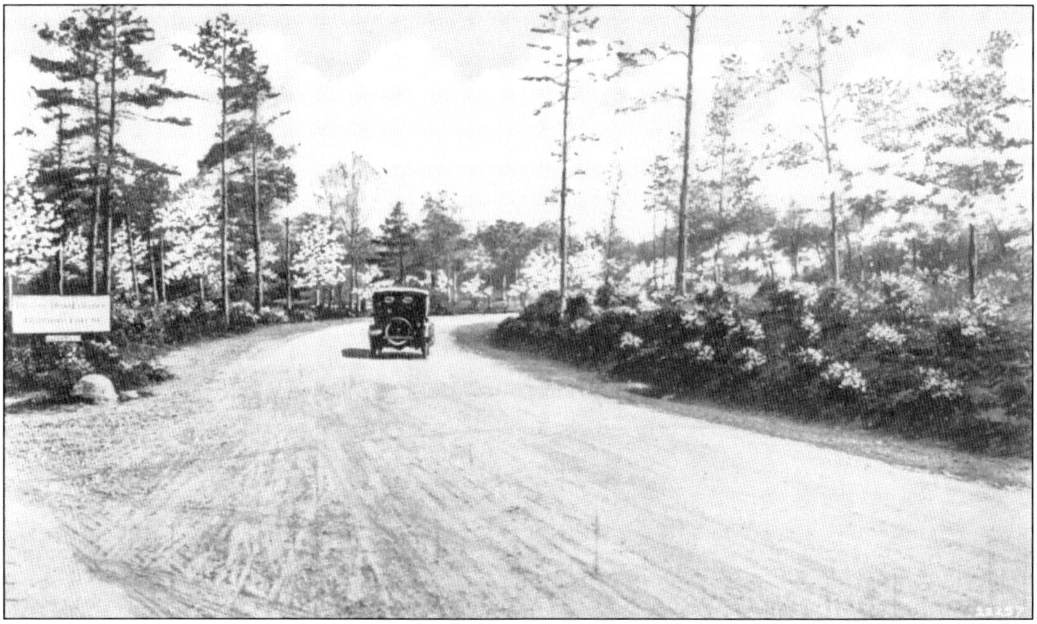

BUSBEE ROAD. Busbee Road was constructed as a primary access from Hendersonville Road to Vanderbilt Road and the nearby country club. On August 18, 1923, Judge Adams corresponded with Edith Vanderbilt regarding financial arrangements to borrow back money from Cornelia Vanderbilt's original $60,000 loan to do roadwork in Biltmore Forest, including constructing Busbee Road from a new lodge gate to Vanderbilt Place. (Hal Branch.)

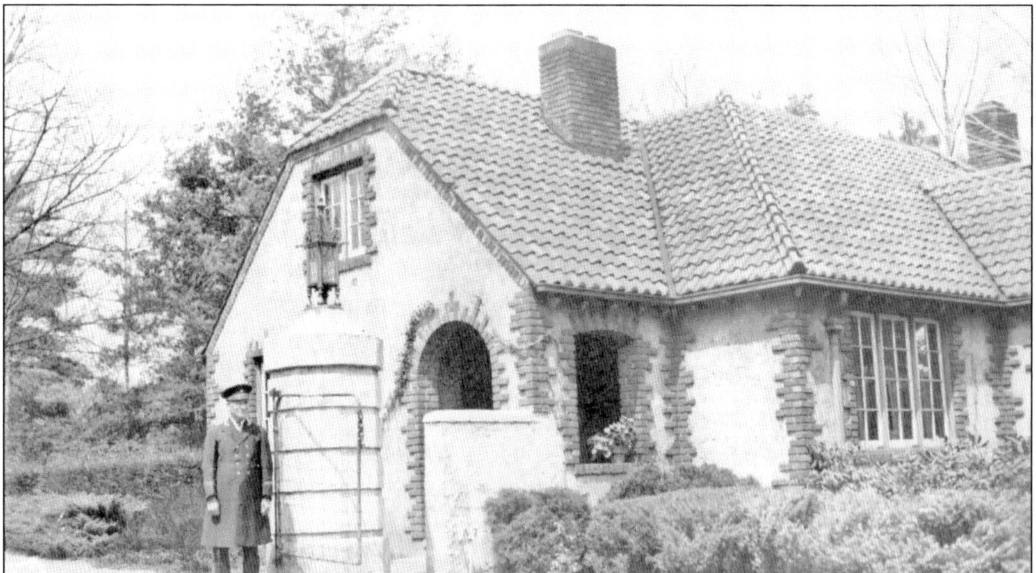

CEDARCLIFF GATE LODGE. Cedarcliff Gate, located at the intersection of Cedarcliff and Busbee Roads, controlled access to Biltmore Estate. Cedarcliff Road and the gate were completed in 1921 and the gate lodge in the fall of 1922. George Bell, employed by the estate in 1901, became the keeper of Cedarcliff Gate when it was established in 1921. He retired on October 1, 1952, when the gate was discontinued as a public entrance to Biltmore Estate. (Estate of Agnes [Bell] Barber Blake.)

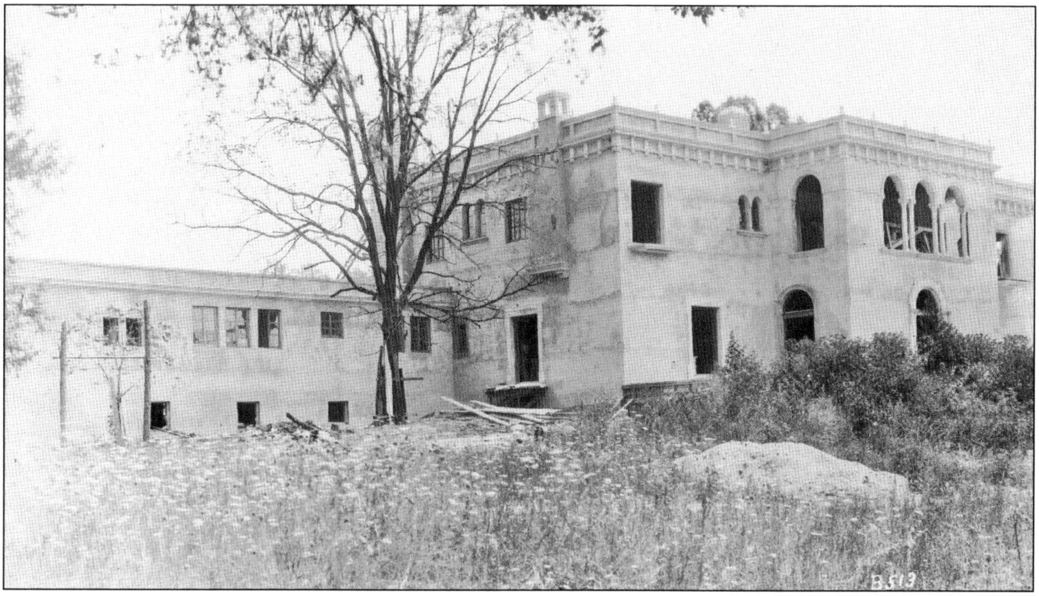

THE FRITH UNDER CONSTRUCTION, REAR VIEW, 1925. Edith Vanderbilt hired Palm Beach architect Bruce Kitchell, a protégé of Addison Mizner, to design a house for her in Biltmore Forest in early 1925. Known as the Frith, meaning "peace" or an "open space in the woods," her house was a two-story stucco construction in a restrained Spanish style with a suggestion of the classical. The house featured a glassed-in loggia on the second story of a projecting central pavilion. (Town of Biltmore Forest.)

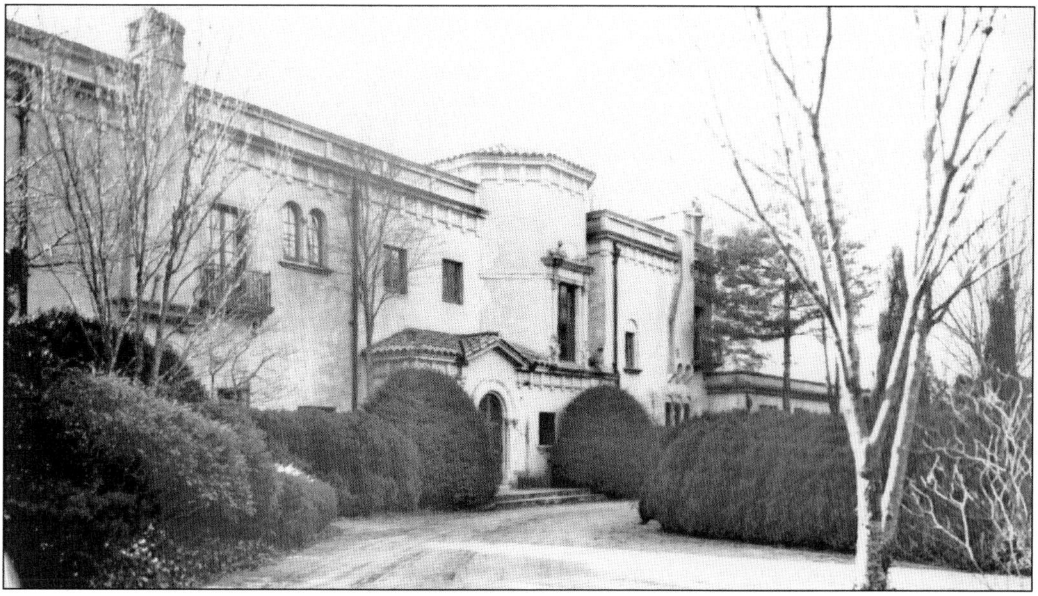

THE FRITH, FRONT VIEW, 1940S. Edith Vanderbilt remarried in 1925, some months before the completion of the Frith. Her husband, Sen. Peter G. Gerry of Rhode Island, most likely suggested that landscape architect Fletcher Steele be hired to design the gardens and grounds in early 1926. Steele was at that time working on the landscape at Ancrum House on Lake Delaware in New York for Peter Gerry's sister, Angelica Gerry. (North Carolina Collection, Pack Memorial Public Library.)

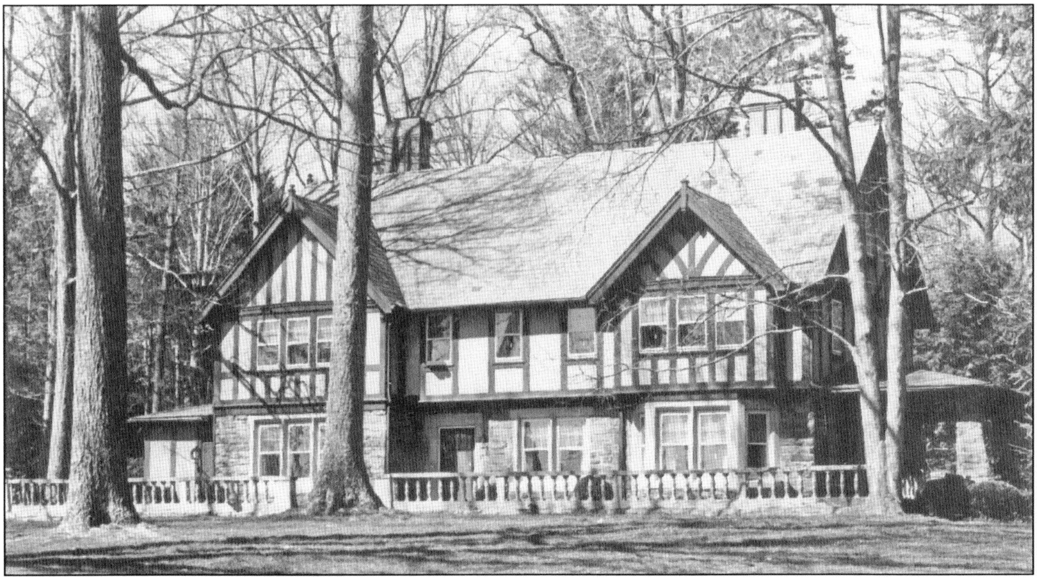

Judge Junius Adams House, c. 1978. Asheville architect Charles N. Parker designed this grand Tudor Revival–style residence for Adams's expansive five-and-a-half-acre tract, purchased in February 1921 on the edge of the golf course. The house features an ashlar ground level with contrasting stucco and applied half-timbers on the upper level and gables. (North Carolina Collection, Pack Memorial Public Library.)

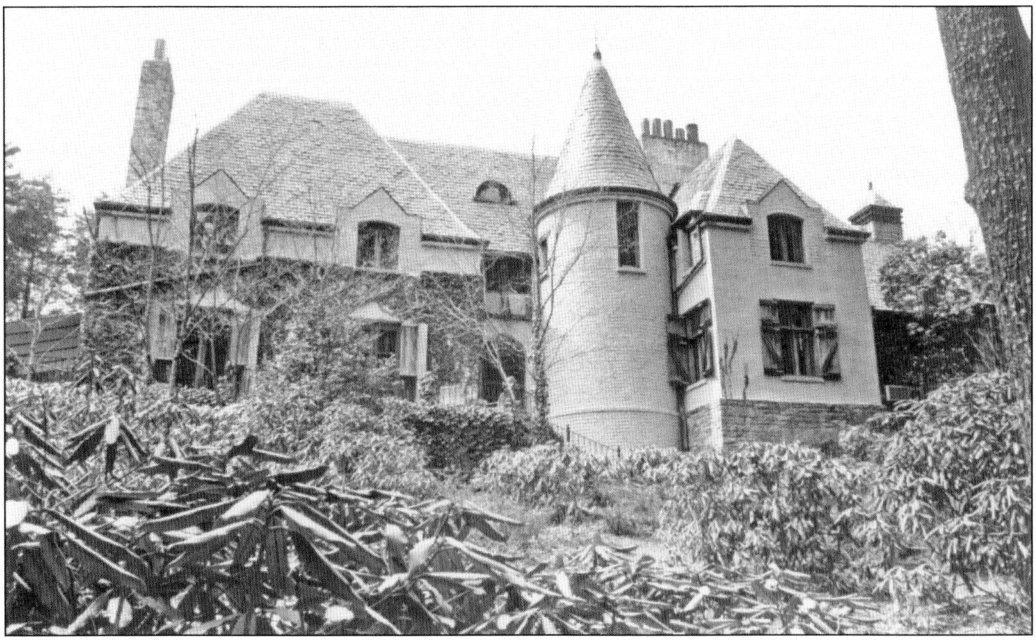

William Knight House, c. 1978. This unique chateau, designed by architect William Dodge Jr. in 1925–1927 on East Forest Road, was the home of William A. Knight, one of the members of the Biltmore Estate Company. Retired from St. Augustine, Florida, Knight also had a summer residence in Skyland. A botanist by avocation, Knight became one of the famous "Azalea Hunters," which included botanists Chauncey Beadle, Frank Crayton, and Sylvester Owens. (North Carolina Collection, Pack Memorial Public Library.)

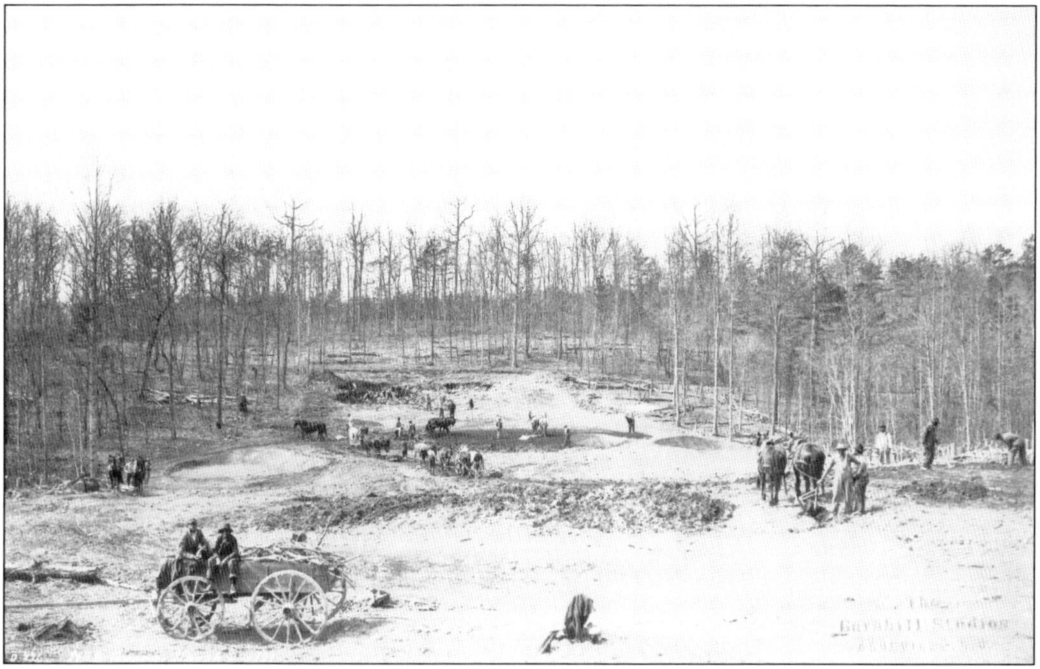

No. 8 Green, March 2, 1921. As a golf course and country club were to be part of the Biltmore Forest development and were considered to be essential to the success of the undertaking, plans were made to get the course under construction as soon as it could be laid out by noted designer Donald Ross. Junius G. Adams reported to Edith Vanderbilt on October 31, 1921, that "the golf course is complete with the exception of 'a little scratching around.' "

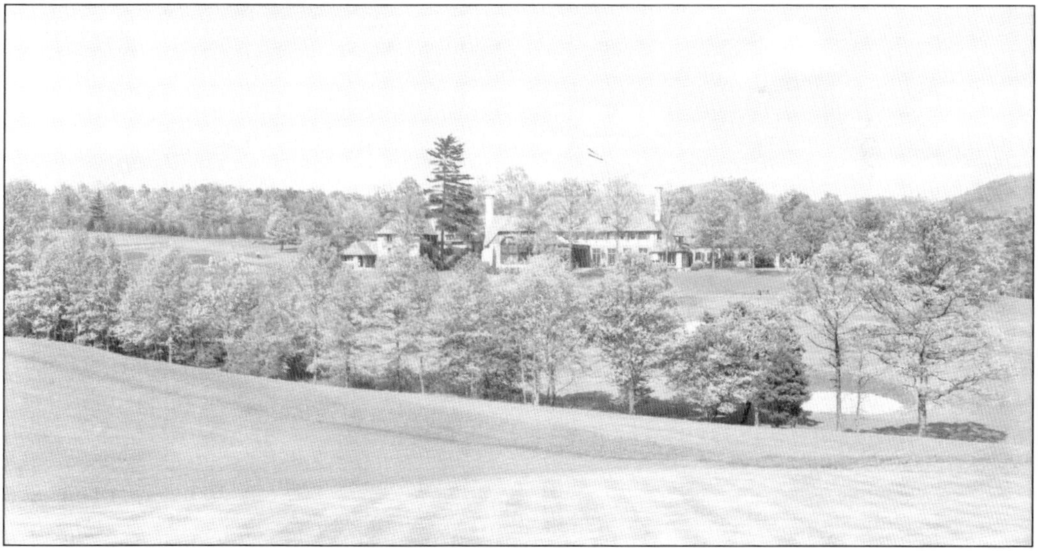

Biltmore Forest Country Club from Golf Course. The country club opened on July 4, 1922, amid considerable fanfare. Donald Ross wrote afterwards to Edith Vanderbilt on September 22 thanking her for letting him know what a success the course is: "I felt even while it was thickly wooded country that it had the possibilities for a magnificent golf course and country club." (E. M. Ball Collection, D. H. Ramsey Library, Special Collections, University of North Carolina at Asheville.)

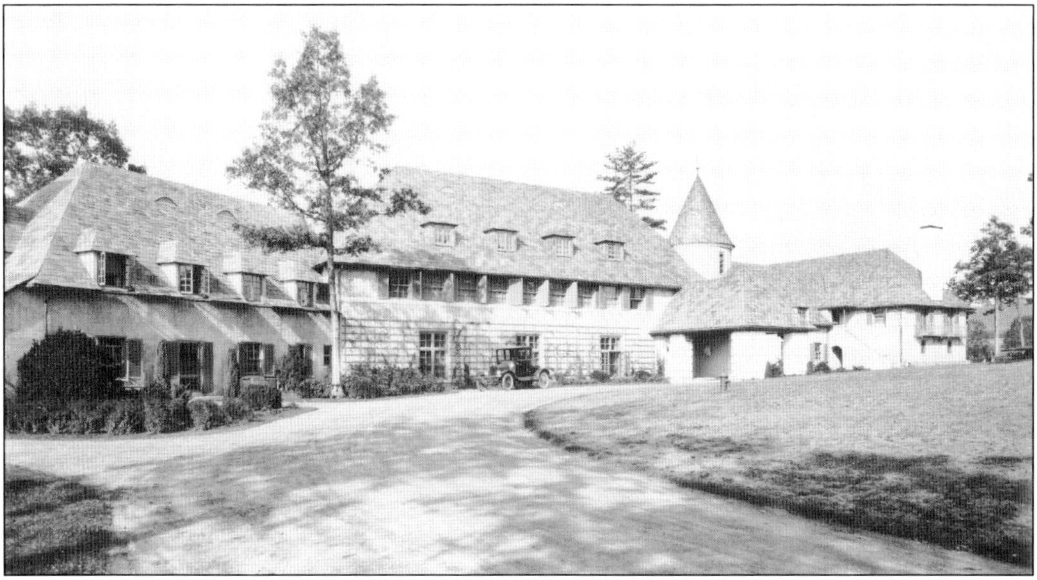

BILTMORE FOREST COUNTRY CLUB, 1920S. Two months before the grand opening, the country club had 108 acceptances to charter membership invitations. Chauncey Beadle wrote to Edith Vanderbilt on February 21, 1923, that he was meeting Donald Ross to go over the golf course and note all of his suggestions and recommendations. He added, "Affairs at the Country Club are quiet just now, especially on the outside; but considerable interest is in evidence in using the Club as a social centre. Almost daily groups of members and friends gather there." Junius Adams reported on January 30, 1923, that the "man in charge of the club has cut expenses to a minimum and they expect big spring season; course is in wonderful condition. Raoul is proceeding with building a servants house, enlarging pro shop, laying terrace slate floor and building a verandah." (Both, E. M. Ball Collection, D. H. Ramsey Library, Special Collections, University of North Carolina at Asheville.)

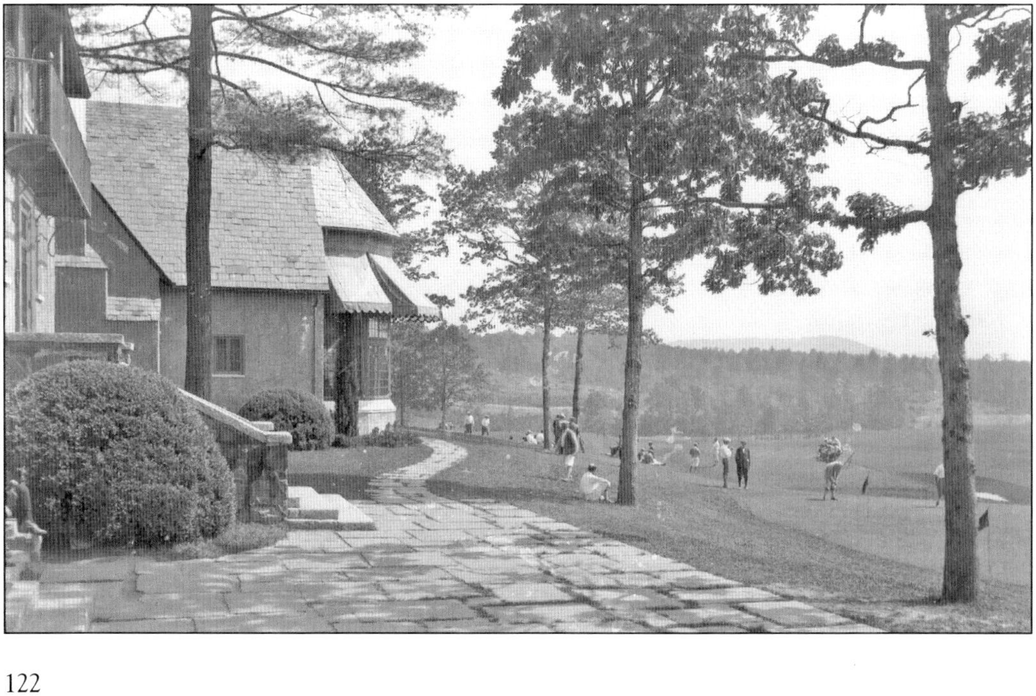

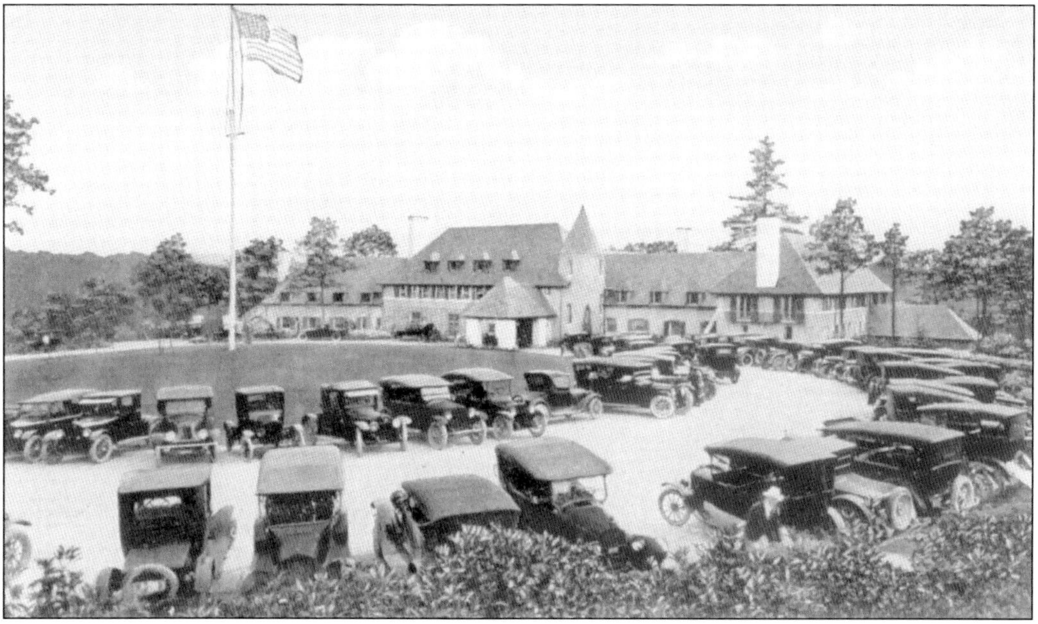

BILTMORE FOREST COUNTRY CLUB, LATE 1920S. When the country club opened on July 4, 1922, a charter membership for a family was $75 per year and $50 for individuals. The price of a daily lunch was $1. Thomas E. Byron was secretary and manager of the club for the first few years. During the Depression, bachelor rates for rooms at the club were reduced to $3. The crowd gathered around the swimming pool in the postcard below attests to the popularity of the Biltmore Forest Country Club. There was apparently a competitive event to draw such a large number of spectators. Note the canoe floating in the pool on the right. (Both, Hal Branch.)

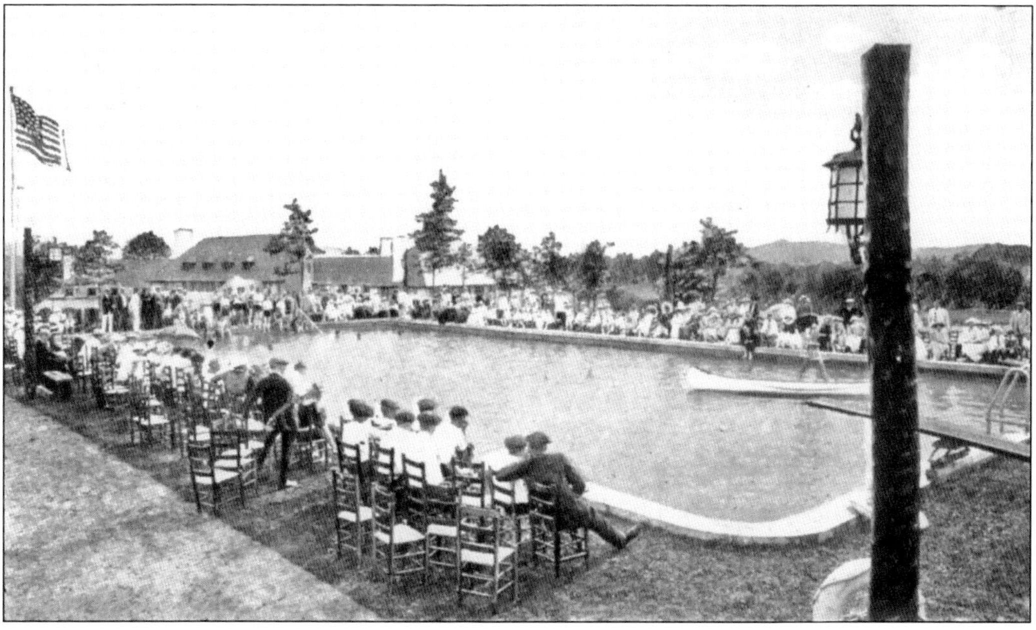

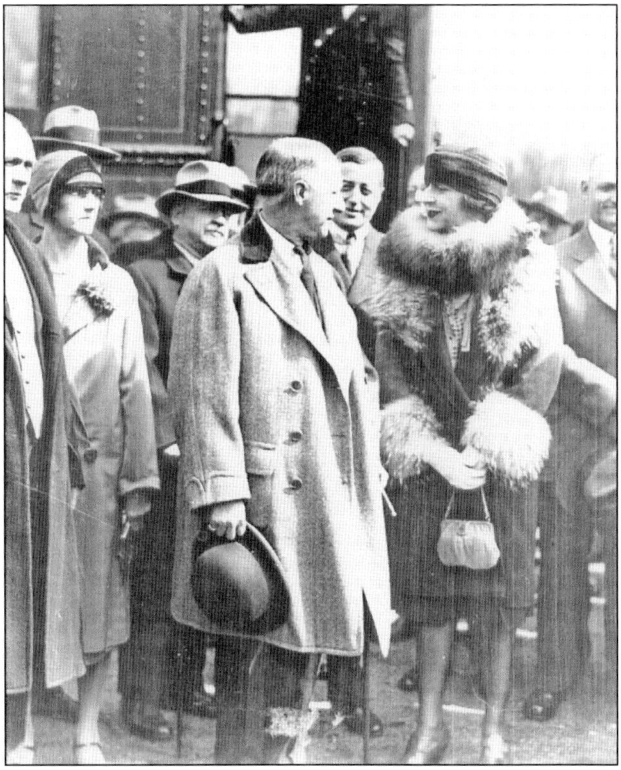

EDITH VANDERBILT AND GOV. AL SMITH, 1920S. Alfred Emanuel Smith Jr., known in private and public life simply as Al Smith, was elected governor of New York four times and was the Democratic U.S. presidential candidate in 1928. He was the first Roman Catholic and Irish American to run for president as a major party nominee but lost the election to Herbert Hoover. In the photograph at left, Edith Vanderbilt is greeting Al Smith upon his arrival at the train station. Below, Edith Vanderbilt (center), Cornelia (right), and an unidentified man watch Gov. Al Smith takes a swing during a round of golf at the Biltmore Forest Country Club. Edith and Cornelia frequently hosted and entertained friends and other guests at the country club. Golf professional J. Victor East attended the opening of the club.

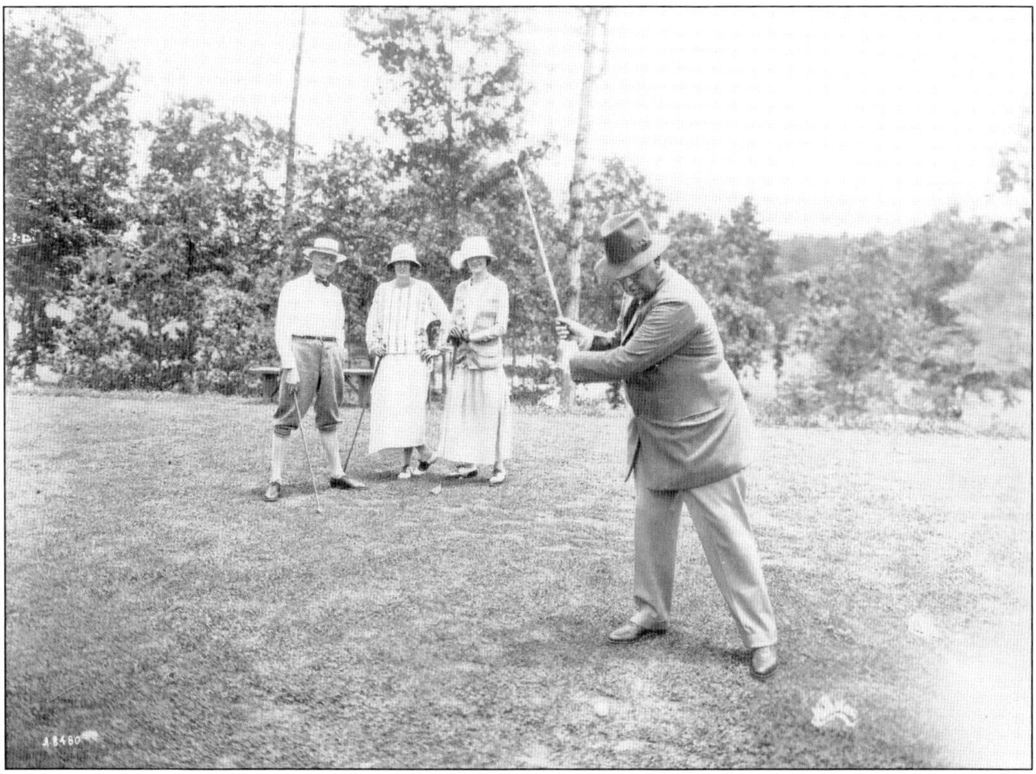

MAP OF BILTMORE FOREST, 1930S. The simple but elegant graphics on this guide map of Biltmore Estate and Biltmore Forest were designed and sketched by William Waldo Dodge Jr., an architect, artist, and silversmith. The map identifies some of the key attractions, including his own Dodge Silver Shop, "maker of hand wrought silver;" the Artisans' Shop, "makers of fine furniture and wood carvers;" and the Forest Frock Shop, all clustered near the Biltmore Forest Office. (Mitch Leonard.)

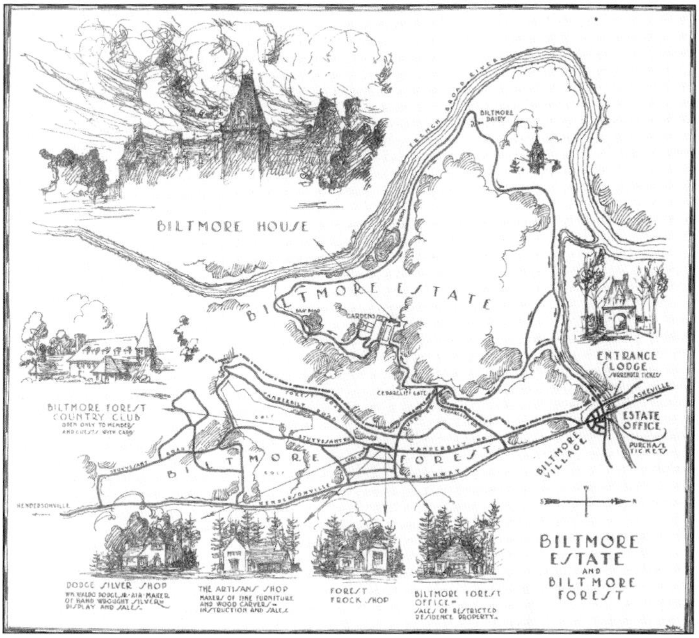

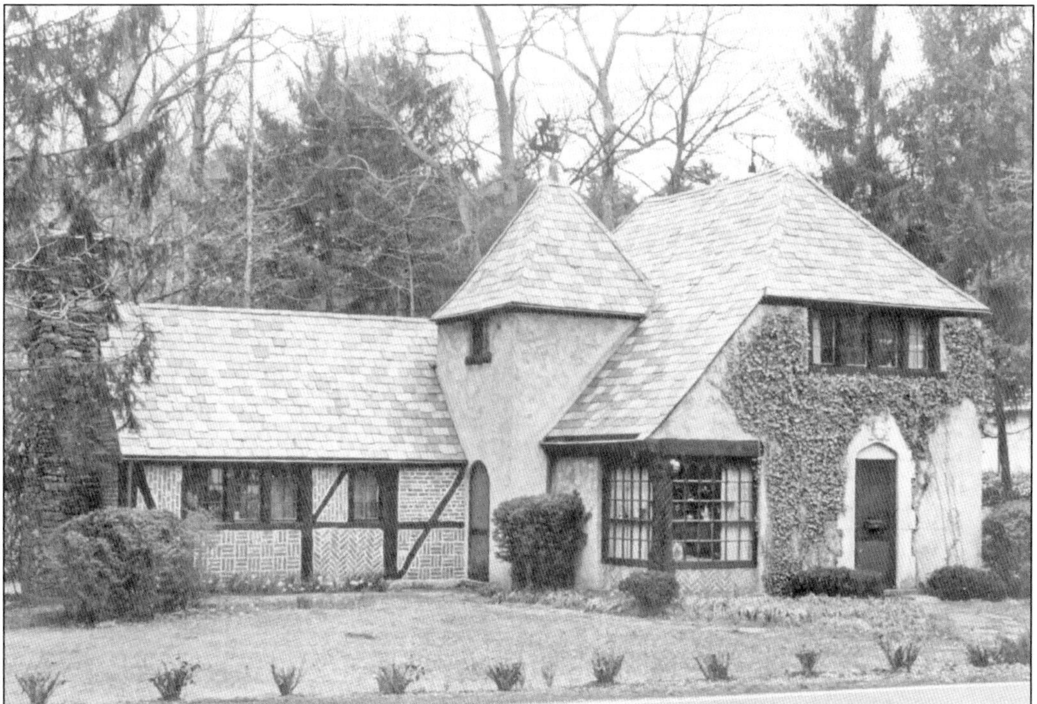

DODGE SILVER SHOP, C. 1978. The architectural details in William Dodge's silver shop, established at 365 Vanderbilt Road in 1928, reflect the same quality of craftsmanship and fine detail as in his hand-wrought silver pieces. Educated in architecture at MIT, William Dodge is said to have taken up the art of silver craft while recuperating from World War I wounds at Oteen Veterans Hospital. Assisted by three talented artisans, Dodge's silver became world renowned. (North Carolina Collection, Pack Memorial Public Library.)

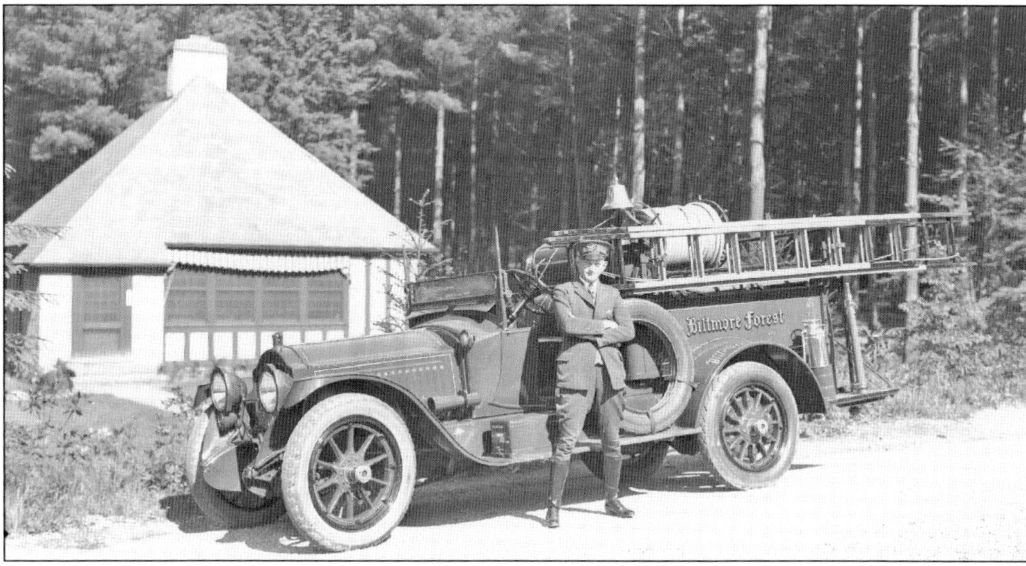

BILTMORE FOREST FIRE TRUCK, 1920S. The town of Biltmore Forest was incorporated on February 14, 1923, and the first town meeting was held at the newly completed real estate office, seen here, on March 20, 1923. Standing committees were formed for public safety, building, fire, police, sanitation, finance, streets, lights, and parks. The first fire truck, purchased in 1923, was this one, which was built on a Packard chassis. (E. M. Ball Collection, D. H. Ramsey Library, Special Collections, University of North Carolina at Asheville.)

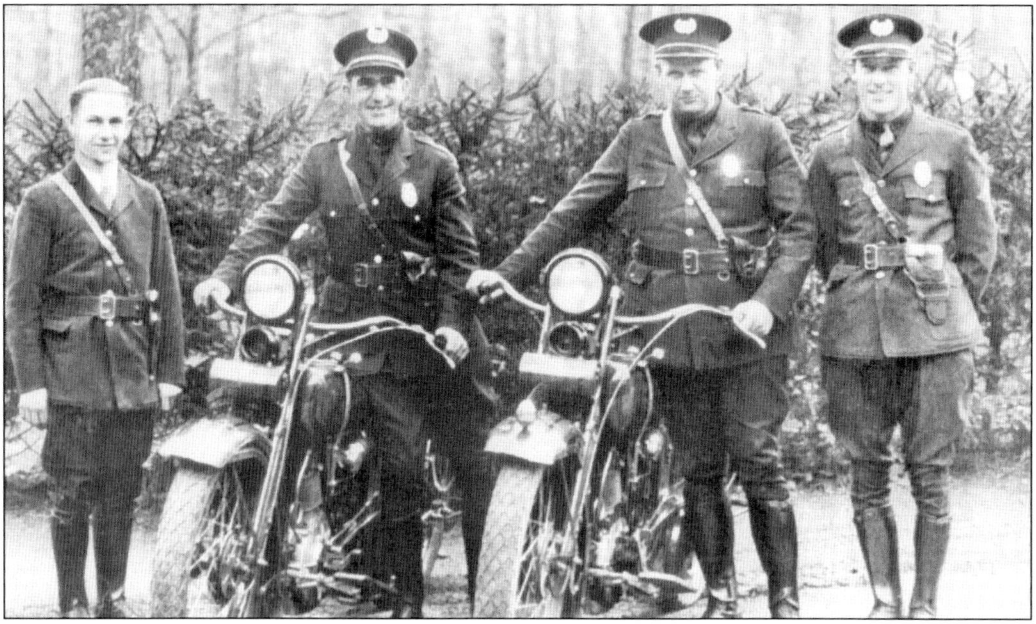

BILTMORE FOREST POLICE OFFICERS, C. 1930. When the town was established in 1923, architect Charles Parker designed the police and fire station. Compensation for the police chief was $90 per month, an apartment above the station, and two uniforms. Biltmore Village paid one third of his salary, for which he made four rounds through the village every day on his Harley Davidson motorcycle. Roy R. Creasman, second from left, was police chief from 1926 to 1953. (North Carolina Collection, Pack Memorial Public Library.)

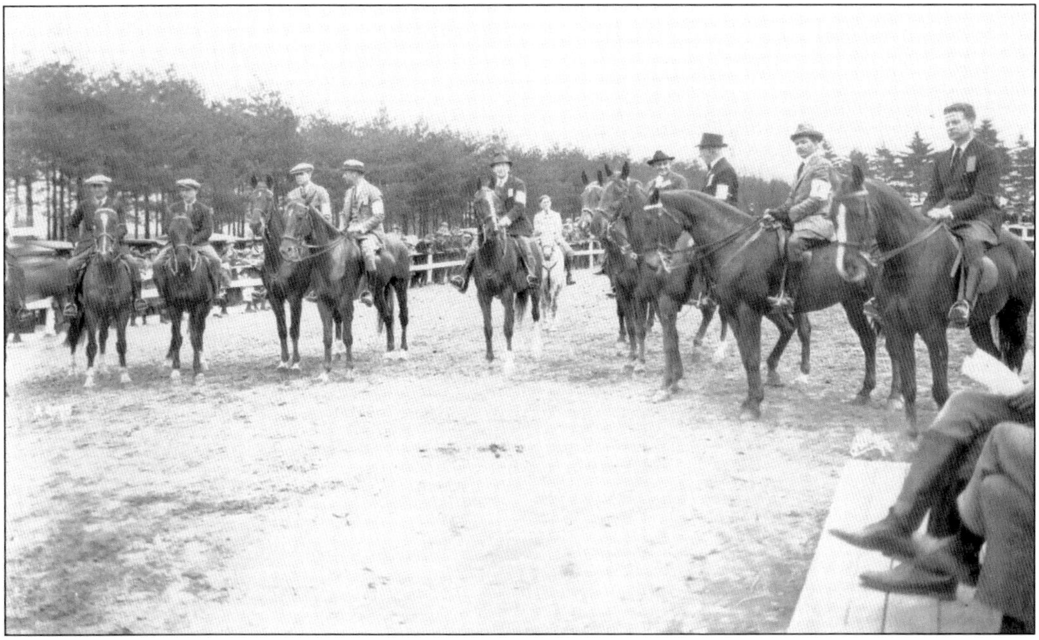

BILTMORE FOREST HORSE SHOW, 1920S. The popular riding club, under the management of Anna N. Wheeler, kept about 25 saddle horses for renting and lessons, and sponsored equestrian events. The Biltmore Forest Stable, which later became the Biltmore Forest Bridle and Saddle Club, was located near the police station, and the riding ring was on the southwest corner of Vanderbilt and Busbee Roads. Rosebank Park was used for polo games.

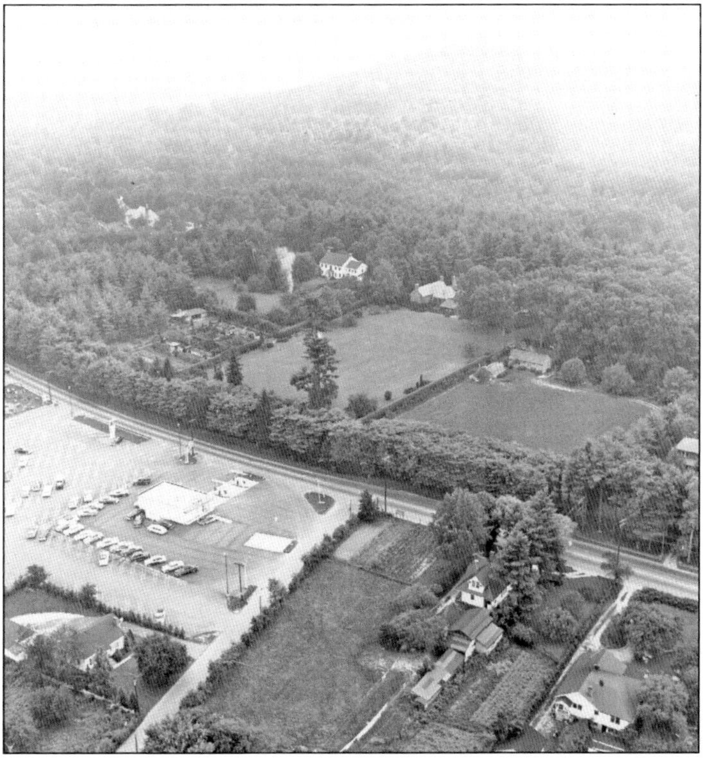

AERIAL VIEW OF HENDERSONVILLE ROAD AND ADJACENT BILTMORE FOREST, AUGUST 16, 1960. This birds-eye view shows a Pure Oil service station next to the A&P food store's parking lot on the left at the intersection of West Chapel Road. All but one of the Biltmore Forest residences on the opposite side of Hendersonville Road face Vanderbilt Road between Cedarcliff and Busbee Roads. The densely wooded landscape clearly characterizes the aptly named Biltmore Forest. (North Carolina Collection, Pack Memorial Public Library.)